*Envisioning Cyberspace*

*We put thirty spokes together and call it a wheel;*
*But it is on the space where there is nothing that the utility of*
*the wheel depends.*

*We turn clay to make a vessel;*
*But it is on the space where there is nothing that the utility of*
*the vessel depends.*

*We pierce doors and windows to make a house;*
*And it is on these spaces where there is nothing that the*
*utility of the house depends.*

*Therefore just as we take advantage of what is,*
*We should recognize the utility of what is not.*


*Lao Tsu*


*Tao Te Ching  Chapter XI*

Quotation from Arthur Waley's *The Way and Its Power*, London, 1934.

# Envisioning Cyberspace

Designing 3D Electronic Spaces

Peter Anders

*McGraw-Hill*

New York   San Francisco   Washington, D.C.   Auckland   Bogotá
Caracas   Lisbon   London   Madrid   Mexico City   Milan
Montreal   New Delhi   San Juan   Singapore
Sydney   Tokyo   Toronto

**Library of Congress Cataloging-in-Publication Data**

Anders, Peter
     Envisioning cyberspace : designing 3D electronic spaces /
Peter Anders.
        p.    cm.
     Includes bibliographical references and index.
     ISBN 0-07-001632-1
      1. Computers and civilization. 2. Cyberspace. 3. Virtual
reality. 4. Computer-aided design. I. Title.
QA76.9.C66A5  1998                98-26053
006–dc21                                CIP

## McGraw-Hill

A Division of The **McGraw·Hill** Companies

1 2 3 4 5 6 7 8 9 0   DOC/DOC  9 0 3 2 1 0 9 8

ISBN 0-07-001632-1

The sponsoring editor for this book was Wendy Lochner, the editing
supervisor was Jane Palmieri, the designer was Peter Anders, and
the production supervisor was Pamela Pelton. It was set in
Helvetica Oblique by Peter Anders.

Printed and bound by R. R. Donnelley & Sons Company.

McGraw-Hill books are available at special quantity discounts to use
as premiums and sales promotions, or for use in corporate training
programs. For more information, please write to the Director of
Special Sales, McGraw-Hill, 11 West 19th Street, New York, NY
10011. Or contact your local bookstore.

This book is dedicated to

My wife Cathy and son Konrad, and our parents Edith and
Oswald Anders and Cal and Mary Lou Goeders

In love and gratitude.

# Contents

## Acknowledgments

Of all the pages in a book, the acknowledgments are easiest to write. While this book represents my obsessions and work, I am grateful to many for their generosity, encouragement and contributions in making it possible.

First I want to thank my colleagues at the New Jersey Institute of Technology for their support and enthusiasm for my efforts. In the School of Architecture I had the help and inspiration of Glenn Goldman, Peter Papademetriou and Dean Urs Gauchat. For consultation and technical help in setting up Internet/cyberspace projects with my students I thank Tom Terry, Fadi Deek, Alan Leurck, Mike Hoon and Karthik Krishnan. I am also deeply indebted to my colleagues at the school for their encouragement, particularly Peter Lang, whose insights and friendship I value greatly.

I am grateful to others whose timely conversations and advice helped shape many of the ideas in this book. I thank William Mitchell, dean of MIT's School of Architecture, for his thoughtful foreword to this book and for taking time to review the manuscript. Thanks also to artist Jamy Sheridan and Bill Manspeaker for catalytic brainstorming and to Julio Bermudez and Dace Campbell who stoked the fires as well. The occasional jolt of intellectual adrenaline was provided by Wolfgang Baer, Marcus Fromherz, and my software collaborator Craig Caldwell, whose experience in computing far predates my own. Finally, I could not have done this without the examples set by Amy Bruckman, Marcos Novak, Kristinn Thorisson and Annika Blunck in proving that technology is a cultural and human endeavor.

One of the unexpected pleasures of writing a book on cyberspace is making new friends you may never encounter physically. I hold out hope that I will actually meet them. I appreciate my contact with Andreas Broekman and the folks at V2, as well as Roy Ascott and Kathy Rae Huffman who proved to be vital hubs in the cyberspace design community. I am very grateful also to Bruce Damer, author of the book Avatars!, for generously providing advice and images on virtual communities.

The artists, designers and technologists from around the world who contributed to this book deserve special mention, for their images make en**vision**ing cyberspace possible. I am grateful for the help and access provided by Monika Fleischmann and Wolfgang Strauss at G.M.D. Their collaborations and efforts in the cyberspace design community set an inspiring example for me.

I thank the following for their participation, enthusiasm and patience: Will Bauer, Simon Birrell, David Blair, Richard Brown, Stuart Card, Tom Corby, Char Davies, Karel Dudesek; Tracey Matthieson, Dirk Donath, Gerhard Eckel, Stephen Feiner, Monika Fleischmann, Bernhard Franken, Wladek Fuchs, Stuart Gold, Clay Graham, Knut Graf, Rory Hamilton, Lisa Haskel, Ian Horswill, Sheep Iconoclast, Sergi Jorda, Ed Keller, Lisa Kimball, Christof Huebler, Susan Kozol, Jeffrey Krause, Myron Krueger, Jaron Lanier, James Leftwich, Patrick Lichty, Dirk Lüsebrink, Richard MacKinnon, Peter Maloney, Ganapathy Mahalingam, Steve Mann, Phillip Morle, Sally Jane Norman, Eric Paulos, Stephen Perrella, Steven Pettifer, Mark Pesce, Claudio Pinhanez, Mark Palmer, Martin Rieser, Marcel.li Antunez Roca, Miroslaw Rogala, Manuel Saiz, Joachim Sauter, Thecla Schiphorst, Bill Seaman, Paul Sermon, Karl Sims, Martin Sjardijn, Mel Slater, Joel Slayton, Amanda Steggel, Stahl Steinslie, Wolfgang Strauss, Atau Tanaka, Constantine Terzides, Thomas van Putten, Victoria Vesna, Thomas Vollaro, and Nik Williams. I am pleased to represent these people in this book as I consider their work to be at the cutting edge of cyberspace design.

For their help in editing this text into legibility, I am grateful to my friend Larry Yu and to my editorial and artistic support at McGraw-Hill, Wendy Lochner, Jane Palmieri, Robin Gardner and Margaret Webster. Their insightful critiques have helped immeasurably to the benefit of the reader. I especially want to thank Chris Yessios at Auto•Des•Sys, Rodger Payne at Autodesk, and the folks at Visio Corporation for their contributions in making this book possible.

Finally, I want to thank those to whom I have dedicated this book. They are family. I am grateful to my parents, Oswald and Edith Anders, and thank also my parents-in-law, Calvin and MaryLou Goeders, for their support, enthusiasm and encouragement. I am thankful to — and for — my son Konrad, whose energy and humor are inspiring. It's to my wife Catherine, however, that I owe the greatest debt. Her attentive review of the text led to several invaluable changes that shaped it. Her support throughout this project goes beyond my ability to thank her adequately. Thanks, Cathy. And thanks again to all those who were part of this effort.

September 1998

# Foreword

## Who Put the Space in Cyberspace?

*William J. Mitchell*

*Our English language typically assimilates new technologies by tacking prefixes onto familiar nouns; thus we got the coinages "horseless carriage," "wireless telegraph," and "electronic mail." Then, over time, the terminology gradually shifts to reflect the subsequent success stories. Today, we have far more horseless carriages than either horses or carriages, and they are called automobiles. The telegraph is long gone– indeed, almost forgotten – and we listen to the radio. Electronic mail has become e-mail or email, and we are finding that we now need to distinguish the old-time post office service – snail-mail – by a newly minted prefix.*

*It is the same, of course, with electronically constructed virtual places – the subject of this useful and stimulating book. In the latter part of the twentieth century, computer and telecommunication technologies began to create an important new condition for which we had no obvious precedent and no ready name, so it seemed most natural to extend a familiar concept to cover the gap. Thus the ancient ideas of space and place – the traditional foci of architectural and urban design discourse – were reconstituted and sucked into a vortex of vigorous critical reexamination.*

*But how, exactly, is the now-commonplace cyberspace metaphor grounded? Why does it seem to work so well? What is so place-like about virtual places?*

*For a start, you can enter and exit virtual places like rooms. Back in the 1960s, in the early days of timesharing computer systems, the idea developed of logging on and logging off virtual machines; users came aboard these software-generated entities, then they left. In the 1970s, as computer networks developed, they could begin to Telnet into remote machines. Following the PC revolution of the 1980s, increasing numbers of network users began to drop into on-line chat rooms. Now, it is routine to surf from site to site on the Web.*

*Sequences of virtual entries and exits create a new kind of architectural promenade, and yield the possibility of exploring an extended territory. A vivid sense of space is produced simply by progression and branching. This is the core trope of MUDs and MOOs, and of on-line games like Doom.*

You don't have to be alone out there; multi-user operating systems and networks can support multiple occupancy of virtual places. Hence these places can function not only as settings for individual action, but also as meeting venues. And this, in turn, creates a demand for some form of electronically mediated self-representation. In response, software designers have presented such spaces as scrolling text in which users are minimally designated by their "handles," as two-dimensional graphic domains like The Palace – with simple two-dimensional pixel-puppets standing for users, and most elaborately, as three-dimensional walkthrough environments which are depicted in perspective and inhabited by three-dimensional characters known as avatars. Step-by-step, code-hackers and pixel-pushers have reinvented the agora. Or maybe – depending on the interactions that interest you – it's the pick-up bar, the seminar room, the mardi-gras, the shopping mall, the library, or the office.

However, a standard computer screen has its limitations as an instrument of interaction. It functions like the proscenium of a stage, or the frame of an aquarium; you always feel like a spectator looking in, rather than a fully immersed and engaged participant. This limitation can be overcome by deploying various combinations of head-tracking and stereo display technology to create the illusion of being truly inside virtual places. Just as removal of the proscenium was an avant-garde theatrical move to challenge the traditional distinction between performers and audience, so immersive 3D environments provocatively transgress the boundaries between real and simulated architecture.

Unlike their stone and brick counterparts, though, virtual places have no inherent persistence. They are ephemeral electronic constructions that disappear in an instant when the supporting machines are turned off. But this apparently devastating defect can be overcome simply by storing the state of a virtual place in non-volatile computer memory so that it can instantly be reconstituted – just as you left it – when you boot up again. That is the trick employed with the desktop on your laptop or PC, and it can readily be extended to complex, large-scale, three-dimensional, immersive virtual places.

Since the spatial metaphor does turn out to work so well in so many ways, it is tempting to take the idea of electronically constituted architecture literally. And, indeed, it is not hard to find hokey examples of on-line, virtual places that have carefully been crafted to look like familiar sorts of rooms, urban public spaces, and even entire villages. But it never rains in cyberspace, so you certainly have to question all those pitched roofs. There is no gravity or weight (unless you take a great deal of trouble to program it in), so elements like beams and columns serve little purpose. Nor is there any air or sunlight, so it isn't clear what windows might be for. You don't really walk, so floors and stairways seem superfluous. And you can jump instantaneously from place to place at the click of a mouse, so doors and elevators seem like dumb ideas. The closer you look, the more risible all this seems.

Here, then, is the nub of the design challenge. Virtual places have many of the functional properties of bricks-and-mortar gathering spots and information repositories, and we are increasingly finding that they can effectively serve many of the same purposes — plus some exciting new ones as well. But form and function are not coupled in the same ways in virtual space as they are in physical space, so there is no compelling reason to make virtual places look like material, gravity-bound ones that stand out there in the weather.

No doubt about it, we are opening up a new design frontier. We will have to invent whole new languages for design in cyberspace.

# Introduction

## Background

In the spring of 1994 I attended a conference, Cyberconf 3, in Austin, Texas.[1] As an architect I was interested in virtual reality and computer modeling of space. Architecture, a driving force in 3D imaging, uses virtual reality as part of its toolkit for building documentation. I thought the meeting in Austin would confirm what I already knew.

I was wrong.

1. This conference was sponsored by the School of Architecture at the University of Texas, Austin. It was organized by Professor Michael Benedikt.

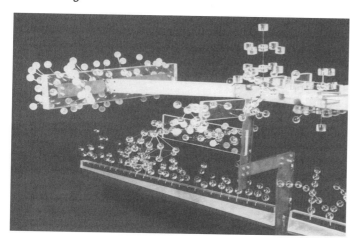

Fig.1
Logical Adjacency Model of MediaMOO's spatial configuration. MediaMOO, created by Amy Bruckman, is a multi-user domain, or MUD, an on-line social environment.
Model: Michael Lisowski and George Paschalis

I recall Bob Jacobson, a developer of virtual environments, declaring virtual reality to be passé – the Internet was what was hot. I didn't recognize half the terms he used: email, MUDs, MOOs. Feeling a little lost, I looked around the room.

The audience was made up of artists, engineers, philosophers, and academicians. Cyberspace seemed to be a hybrid subject drawing from various disciplines. Though the program was sponsored by the School of Architecture at the University of Texas, architects were in a minority. Just as I was beginning to wonder if I was in the right place, I heard something that radically changed my world view.

Amy Bruckman, then a Ph.D. student at MIT's MediaLab, presented a paper on a multi-user domain, MediaMOO, that she had created for the conference (fig.1). Multi-user domains, or MUDs, are on-line social environments in which players use text to chat and experience the MUD itself. Unlike the electronic bulletin boards they resemble, MUDs use spatial references to create a social setting. While some are situated in castles or space colonies, Ms. Bruckman's MediaMOO was set in the Wiesner Building, the site of MIT's MediaLab. The five-story building comprises labs, offices and work areas. But it lacks social spaces for the events that the domain's designer had in mind.

Up to this point I was on familiar ground. The building was an easy reference for the MUD's structure. It was no surprise that a lab building wouldn't accommodate large gatherings – there was a mismatch between the metaphor of the building and its intended use. Fortunately, Bruckman was no architect.

MUD visitors who make it to the "roof" of MediaMOO sense a space above them. This surprise sixth floor is the site of the MUD's ballroom – complete with changing rooms (with costumes!) and dance floor. The ballroom is a fiction hovering over the Wiesner Building. It is a mental space that extends the physical building beyond its original use.

MediaMOO's ballroom jolted any prejudices I had brought to Austin. It opened the door into a world where fictional spaces took the status and purpose of physical buildings. Architecture here was symbolic, yet still orienting and situating the actions of its users.

In the years since I have tried to reconcile the spatial issues surrounding cyberspace. This book is the product of research in the areas of design, psychology, anthropology and human-computer interface design as well as contributions from many fields of state-of-the-art cyberspace design. This is fitting as cyberspace is a collaborative environment – the mixed audience in Austin exemplified a cultural convergence on cyberspace. In the following pages I will present ideas culled from this on-going interdisciplinary discussion.

## What This Book Is About

This book describes the spatialization of cyberspace and its social and cultural consequences. It proposes an information environment that can be managed through relational means – native to how we think and live with space. I will illustrate its underlying principles with work done by artists, designers, scientists and technologists in visualizing these environments.

Images of cyberspace found in movies and television are as baffling as the cyber-jargon we read in magazines. They illustrate the confusion surrounding cyberspace. While the design of purposeful on-line environments is to orient rather than confuse, what we see now in popular media expresses information chaos – uncontrolled, unmanaged information.[2]

2. Mok, Clement. 1996. *Designing business*. San Jose, Cal.: Adobe Press. p.xiii.
Chaos, in this case, is the confusion resulting from unrelated phenomena. Design - and ultimately cyberspace - offers a way to relate parts, resolving ambiguities through experiential presentation.

Many of these images indulge in the excitement of a new medium. The illegible graphics that arrived with desktop publishing were expressions of short-term novelty. But cyberspace, a cognitive, social environment, can transcend fashion and become an important force in our information-based culture. **Cyberspace, as I will use the term, refers to the emulation of space in electronic environments,** particularly those of networked computing. It is present in computer graphics, online social spaces and video games. As we will see it resembles and yet differs from perceived space in many important ways.

The subject of this book is the spatialization of cyberspace, and as such addresses the nature of space itself. What is space and how do we perceive it? Is space external or internal to us? How do objects in space relate to our language and thought? What distinguishes simulation from real space? This book is intended to provoke as well as inform, and with it we begin a discussion of how we use space and its electronic equivalents.

## Overview of Book

The following pages describe themes covered in the book. I will present cyberspace in a way that is native to spatial thought. I will also present cyberspace as a cultural phenomenon, a point of convergence for many disciplines.

### Space: A Tool for Cognition

We use space as a tool for managing information, thought and memories. Without it we wouldn't be able to effect the most primitive actions. It is the medium of thought. Metaphors taken from the physical world use our shared reality of space for communication.[3] We share internal and external space much as we share our language and our common physiology.[4]

Relating objects to one another creates in our minds the space that contains them. Each of us forms internally our own idea of what that space is. The space of a child, for instance, is quite different from that of an adult. As we mature we create spaces of memory and cognition. I will later refer to the relationships between those spaces and ourselves, as they form the matrix of our awareness.

### Space: A Medium for Managing External Relationships

We surround ourselves with tools to help us think.[5] We use files, books, paper and pencils to extend our thoughts beyond our bodies. The more tools we place in our environment, the more resourceful we become in solving problems. It is as if the objects become extensions of our minds. Richard Dawkins, the

3. Lakoff, George, and Mark Johnson. 1980. *Metaphors we live by.* Chicago: University of Chicago Press. p. 232.
The negotiation of metaphors results in a shared vision. We use metaphors like "back East" and "up North" to establish common ground in conversations.

4. Lakoff and Johnson, op. cit. p. 235.
"...metaphor is a matter of imaginative rationality."
It is a conceptual structure that conveys qualitative and aesthetic ideas by referring to our shared, sensory experiences.

5. Norman, Donald A. 1993. *Things that make us smart.* Reading, Mass.: Addison-Wesley. p.44.
Norman's description of the materials we use to enhance our understanding reveals the interdependency between our minds and the physical world.

biologist, would say they are our phenotypes – *as much a part of being human as our own extremities. Arguably, computers are also phenotypical extensions of our thought processes.*

**Space is itself a tool for thought**. *Our language is rich with metaphors and spatial terminology – ideas build upon one another, this concept connects to that, we see the structure of an argument. We frame, overlay, link, and lay out ideas just as we do objects.*

*Space lets us relate to objects, translating them from abstract to physical states and back again.[6] Sometimes posing questions spatially and experientially clarifies the way to an answer. The diagrams of Richard Feynman that graphically present subatomic, almost sub-physical interactions show how space is used in problem solving. Einstein's thought experiment of travelling on a beam of light eventually led to his general and special theories of relativity.*

6. Norman, op. cit., p.55.
"Bad representations turn problems into reflective challenges. Good representations can often transform the same problems into easy experiential tasks. The answer so difficult to find using one mode can jump right out in another."

## Space Shapes Identity

*Tied with our use of space is our position within it – objects relate to us as well as to each other. Our position within the space sets our relationship to its contents. It gives us the Big Picture.[7,8] We are also surrounded by personal spaces, comfort zones and territories that are defined internally. In cyberspace these exist at the same level as physical spaces – as creations of the mind. This book will include a discussion of those spaces, their uses and cultural differences and how, ultimately, they apply to a cyberspace setting.*

7. Gelernter, David. 1991. *Mirror worlds: Or the day software puts the universe in a shoebox: how it will happen and what it will mean.* New York: Oxford University Press. p.30.
Providing a large scope of view spatial images. It gives us an overview, what Gelernter calls "topsightedness."

8. Gelernter, op.cit., p.183.
"People build microcosms to find topsight." Beyond this, space is not populated solely by objects. People are there as well. As we shall see, space plays a powerful role in our societal presence and identity. It is crucial to the ongoing negotiation of who we are and what we do.

## Cyberspace – A Cultural Phenomenon

*The conference in Texas that introduced me to cyberspace had people from a variety of professions and backgrounds. At the break-out sessions, I found artists talking with programmers, dancers with entrepreneurs, engineers with philosophers. Everyone was excited. Suddenly, it seemed, there were no barriers – you could see walls coming down. Cyberspace was a subject all could gather around, share points of view, contribute.*

*My enthusiasm for cyberspace stems from this confluence of ideas. Cyberspace already has computer scientists, performance artists, psychologists, artists, game designers – even monks – among its developers. The results are disorienting but unified by conviction and enthusiasm – a movement toward an unseen goal.*

*The development of cyberspace is, at heart, a cultural project. Though its engine, the computer, is clearly a technical triumph, the computer's work is not of a physical nature. It is a cultural*

*Envisioning Cyberspace*

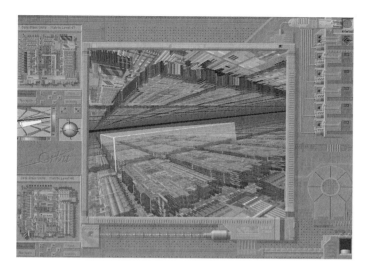

Fig.2
"Cyberport" layout for computer screen by James
Leftwich, I.D.S.A., shows several representations
of information space, including 2D and 3D graphics. Designers of interfaces must incorporate
skills from different disciplines.

machine, an extension of our being. As such, cyberspace can
become as rich a means of expression as any other art form,
as rich a subject of research as any science.

This space is a mediated extension of traditional arts, technologies and professions. As a spatial art form it is in the same
category as theater, performance arts, fine arts, sculpture and
architecture. Each creates immersive, symbolic environments
using spatial expression (fig. 2).

As yet, cyberspace has no innate principles. Current work
extends various existing disciplines. Graphic artists do home
pages, copy writers produce text. Artists and designers interpret the medium to best present their work – all in the terms of
their training. Workers in conventional media and business also
affect the content and form of cyberspace. The military uses
cyberspace for surveillance, briefing its staff, as well as training
its pilots. Games manufacturers have placed their bets on networked computing, letting remote players fight it out on the
Web. Traditional disciplines and arts will continue to form cyberspace, bringing their values to bear.

Designers of cyberspace must create a strategy of transition to
distinguish the principles of various disciplines at work. Dialog
between these fields is crucial if they are to create interdisciplinary criteria for design and evaluation. By isolating principles
of traditional media, we can recognize concepts innate to
cyberspace. [9] These design principles can then be developed
into strategies for developing cyberspace environments.

9. These principles should only be applied in the
evaluation of the work, not in its generation. If
the new work is limited to illustrating earlier concepts, it will slow the development of principles
unique to cyberspace.

These new principles may come from surprising sources. For instance, the concepts underlying the design of a space might come into play along with the principles of choreography. We could imagine spaces changing shape or position on the basis of dance. Rather than our moving from one space to another, the environment could reshape itself around us, gracefully.

Principles are almost always about relationships. They may involve proportion or aspects of composition, but they always concern the conceptual connection between objects or ideas. For example, designers and architects must constantly be aware of relationships. It is the nature of design. Whether the discussion is about forms, colors or materials, no issue is isolated. The selection of any material or form can affect all ensuing decisions.

Space, the primary medium of architecture, demands this attention – the selections are all part of the same composition. Yet space also reveals the correct decisions to best effect, for each reinforces the other within space's continuity. Space, being a medium, is about connection. Ultimately, the creation of cyberspace ties into our understanding space as a medium for thought – an extension beyond ourselves to others.

## Structure of This Book

This book is divided into three major sections. In the first I will discuss anthropological and psychological considerations for developing principles of cyberspace. Here we will look at work done by designers and artists in spatializing cyberspace environments ranging from the most abstract to the most concrete. I will refer also to conventional artifacts of daily life, discuss their cultural role [10] and compare them to those of cyberspace. This portion of the book will conclude with a more detailed look at the psychology of spatial thought, discussing cyberspace as a sensory and cognitive environment.[11]

The second section of the book is about society, and our presence (and immersion) in on-line environments. This section extends the concerns of the first section, describing avatars, representations of users in cyberspace, and agents that represent the computer itself. Finally this section will take the discussion beyond individual presence to that of a human/non-human society.

The final section of the book returns us to the physical world by presenting projects that span physical and cyberspaces. Cyberspace will have unforeseen effects on our work, social environment and physical world. William Mitchell, dean of the School of Architecture at the Massachusetts Institute of Technology, has written about the cross-pollination of building

10. Bødker, Susanne. 1990. *A human activity approach to user interface design.* Hillsdale, N.J.: Lawrence Erlbaum. p. 31.
We share cultural objects in most cases like natural objects. They are the bases for communication in a culture.

11. Bødker, op. cit., p. 23.
Our consciousness, through its supporting physiology and resulting conceptual structures, is a reflection of our social and material world.

*Envisioning Cyberspace*

types, banks' automated teller machines being installed in shopping malls and airports.[12] And this is only the beginning. Cyberspace may let us add functions to physical structures – as utilities – or supplant them entirely as organizations opt for distributed collaborative networks, office hoteling, and telecommuting. These are among the many ways we will see the integration of physical and cyberspaces into new, useful hybrid entities.

The works presented in this book come from individuals in many fields. Though the images reflect the text, they are not illustrations per se. Instead, they present an archipelago of world views – their designers speak of dream spaces and new realities. Cyberspace is linked to our understanding of the world, ourselves and our connection with others. It is a psychological, social and cultural space.

Yet cyberspace is presently inconsistent, ill-defined. To some, it is utopian, to others it is fraught with conflict and doubt. This book is a start at placing it in a broad enough cultural context so that the variety of people and talents needed will participate in its realization.

12. Mitchell, William. 1995. *City of Bits*. Cambridge, Mass.: The MIT Press. pp. 78-79. Mitchell's presentation of the effects of media on our built environment is one of the first to discuss the changes to conventional building types due to media technology.

Fig.3
Logical Adjacency Model of the MUD, Diversity
University
Model: Kevin Spink and Thomas Mesuk.

*Envisioning Cyberspace*

# Toward a Model for Anthropic Cyberspace

"...we thrive in information-thick worlds...[Images dense with information] are an appropriate and proper complement to human capabilities...High-density designs also allow viewers to select, to narrate, to recast and personalize data for their own uses..."

Tufte, Edward R. 1990. *Envisioning information*. Cheshire, Conn.: Graphics Press. p.50.

*Cyberspace presents us with beings, objects, volumes and forces. Its designers found it on human behavior and thought – reconciling our experience in the world with our mind's cognitive landscape. Their success will symbolically extend our presence in the physical world. At their best, they will develop this extension to the point that we are unaware of the interface. This can only be done by designing from our fundamental awareness of the world.*

*In this section I will describe a model for cyberspace founded on proven principles of spatialization – an anthropic cyberspace. The model proposes a multidimensional spatial environment intended for human communication. Some of the issues discussed in this section will be elaborated later in the book.*

## Anthropic Cyberspace

*We think with space. Using our mind's ability to dimensionalize information, we reduce complexity to manageable units – objects – of information. When we look up to see migrating birds we identify the flock before we focus on individual birds. The mind sometimes spatializes information to the same end. What looks like a snowflake could be a cube if some of the details are changed (fig. 4). The mind uses spatial thought to manage incoming information, reducing its complexity for our use.[1]*

*Spatialization lets us distinguish objects and establish relationships between them. In so doing it augments our qualitative judgement. Computers can help us by presenting information in ways that capitalize on this skill. Indeed, the spatial presentation of a problem can often lead to new ways of solving it.[2]*

*We also use space to communicate.[3] Our bodies participate in an on-going dialog with our social environment through gestures, facial expression and speech. In social situations our location in space, body position, and gestures are choreographed to either amplify or modulate what we say.*

*Ultimately, we use space to define ourselves. As we occupy a space, so too are we ready to defend it. Strangers can only*

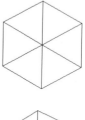

Fig. 4
The mind interprets information by favoring the simplest reading. The symmetrical diagram at the top is a stable, 2D image. But if the lines are moved slightly, the mind infers the third dimension to compensate for the distortion. We see the second diagram as a cube rather than a tangle of lines

1. Mok, op. cit., p.78.
As complexity increases, so does our tendency to increase the dimension of representation and understanding.

2. Norman, op. cit., p.27.
Reflective cognitive environments allow comparison and let users take their time to evaluate and learn. This implies a space common to the elements, hosting their comparison.

3. Mok, op. cit., p.77.
Making the invisible visible is critical for conveying information on the Web. Relationships, for instance, are usually implicit. Cyberspace allows us to symbolically represent these explicitly.

approach so far before we fend them off. On a larger scale, social groups also have zones of identity extending beyond visible borders. At its extreme, these territorial boundaries define cultures and nations by using space to reinforce identity and our position in the world.

But how can computers and new information media tap into these innate strengths? What model harnesses the computer for our ways of thinking? Space. Spatial thought forms the foundation of our awareness. Spatial, anthropic cyberspace [4] links to a pre-linguistic knowledge of the world – a knowledge crucial to our navigation, operation, and communication. We understand spatial representation regardless of its cultural origin. Spatial thought – a shared, human trait – underlies the images of objects and spaces from all cultures.

## Mythic Space

Cyberspaces offer a communal mind space – a shared, but non-physical environment. We can enter them collectively as active environments. They are a new form of mythic space. Traditional mythic spaces convey meaning on many levels. Noah's Ark is simultaneously a wooden vessel as well as a refuge for the innocent. Eden is both a garden and an origin of humanity.

Cyberspace has not yet achieved this cultural richness. Despite contributions from many fields there is no unifying view of what cyberspace can become. As a result we have hybrids, graphic images pasted into text Web sites. This approach understandably responds to the rushing advance of technology. But the effort so far has been technology-driven rather than guided by a vision based on human aspiration. We should now take the time to describe the cyberspace we want.

## The View Beyond the Machine

Some may object. Planning cyberspace seems so entwined with its technology that we can't anticipate it without knowing the tools to create it. This is true, to a point. But let's look at this another way.

Imagine standing before a window overlooking a valley. As the mist rises houses and trees come into view; people and cars move in the streets below. But the blind is half-drawn, the glass is dirty and cracked. You pull aside the curtain to wipe the window with your hand. The glass is clearer, but cleaned properly you could imagine it gone altogether. You could imagine yourself suspended over the valley.

The window is the technology that lets you see the view. The window is imperfect but improvable – its ultimate goal is to van-

**4. Anthropic Cyberspace**
An electronic environment designed to augment our innate use of space to think, communicate and navigate our world.

I have borrowed the term "anthropic" from Stephen Hawking and Brandon Carter. Their Anthropic Principle states that if certain aspects of the universe were any other way, we would not be here to question them. I use the term to stress the importance of our spatial perception and cognition in creating information space. If this space were developed any other way, we would not understand it.

*ish entirely. The essence of the window is what it is not. And so it is with the technology of cyberspace.*

*Transfer speeds and memory storage increase exponentially with the goal of infinite, unrestricted access to information – a technology-driven goal. This is not to undervalue the efforts of those engaged in technology's development. But we must remember the purpose of the window – to view the distant landscape. There are human needs for cyberspace as there are for windows. But to meet them we must also focus on the view beyond.*

## Developing Anthropic Design Principles for Cyberspace

*The spatialization of cyberspace is happening in many forms. We see it in games, scientific visualizations, and multi-user environments. Many fields contribute to its emergence. Since its final form is impossible to predict, we have to take our evidence from current trends and patterns.*

*The principles underlying existing disciplines may foreshadow those of cyberspace design. This is in part because they are already engaged in cyberspace's creation, but also because these disciplines are based on principles of human perception and expectation. Paintings, music and books all depend on continuity, composition and definition to connect with their audience. The designers of cyberspace can certainly learn from such cultural precedents.*

*I will examine the different aspects of cyberspace to propose principles for its future development. This book will present concepts of what the cyberspace can become, what its characteristics may be and what consequences it may have on the physical world.*

## Space, Experience and Understanding

*Since our experience of space is multi-modal, involving all our senses, space offers us a perfect model for creating a multi-dimensional information environment. It lets us use speech, text, visual and acoustic information in conjunction with one another (figs. 5, 6, 7). Spatialization also lets us relate subject to context – focus on details or stand back for a better view. We take this facility for granted though we use it every day.*

*Spatialization allows the translation of problems from cognitive to experiential modes. It helps us model and organize abstract concepts by presenting relationships in a palpable way. Difficult mathematical formulas, for instance, can be modeled graphically for easier comprehension. Problems stated in text or*

Figs. 5, 6, 7
In these scenes from "The Telepathic Motion Picture of 'The Lost Tribes,'" film maker and media artist David Blair has produced electronic spaces that rely on our ability to understand different media concurrently. Note the use of 2D and 3D graphics and text in the same scenes. Our ability to visualize space lets us view these without confusion. If designed properly, different means of communication can occur in the same space without conflict.

speech can, at times, be better resolved graphically or spatially. If lost in a city, for instance, I would prefer a map to a complicated set of instructions, however well-meant they may be.[5]

Spatial presentation can also show multiple resolutions to a problem. If I come upon a road-block, the map shows me alternate routes. Verbal instructions, on the other hand, would leave me stranded.[6] Our understanding of the material world depends on our spatialization. Anthropic cyberspace could allow dynamic motion through information, letting us rely on our instincts rather than memorized rituals of interaction. It could assist us in the navigation of information using our innate, spatial literacy.

Significantly, this literacy is linked to our use of language as well. A spatial cyberspace may be supported by the metaphors and symbols on which we base our language. This is not just a matter of illustration or reducing complex ideas into icons. A useable, anthropic cyberspace recognizes the subtle interplay between our perception of space and our language. When we use metaphors in speech we refer to our environment. In turn, our understanding of our environment is conditioned by our language. An object on top of another may be considered dominant, for example. But in another context it may be seen to be dependent upon the supporting object. Space not only is a tool for thought, it informs all our other tools such as text, speech and visual understanding.

Human cognition is comprised of three types of thought: an enactive mentality, an iconic mentality and a symbolic mentality. The enactive mentality involves navigation and operation in space. Iconic mentality is the ability to recognize and compare the images and things we find in that space. Finally, symbolic mentality lets us think abstractly, creating arguments and manipulating concepts.

No single mentality dominates the entire range of human thinking.[7] To a degree all of them are used in problem solving and thought. If we note that two of the mentalities are the result of spatial understanding, and that symbolic reasoning – even in language – relies on our experience in the world, then we see the importance of spatial cognition. It underlies nearly all of our thought processes.

These types of thought work together. Susanne Bødker, in her book A human activity approach to user interface design, writes that physical interfaces with tangible objects are easier to learn than graphic user interfaces, such as the Macintosh or Microsoft's Windows operating system. The graphic interfaces are, in turn, easier to learn than abstract, language-based interfaces. Our mentalities combined with our physical and spatial experience help us to understand more abstract concepts.[8]

5. Norman, op. cit., p.65.
Increasing the display dimension can often clarify information. This is why it is sometimes easier to understand information as a graph rather than as a list of data.

6. Bødker, op. cit., p.124.
Spatial metaphor allows for several ways of doing something. Conversely, dialog prompts from a computer force us to communicate with the machine on its terms.

7. Kay, Alan. 1990. "User interface: A personal view" in The art of human-computer interface design. ed. B. Laurel. Reading, Mass.: Addison-Wesley. pp.195-196.
"...if...human cognitive facilities are made up of a doing mentality, an image mentality and a symbolic mentality, then any user interface we construct should at least cater to the mechanisms that seem to be there...One approach is to realize that no single mentality offers a complete answer to the entire range of thinking and problem solving."

8. Bødker, op. cit., p.142.
"... it seems that user interfaces based on physical objects...seem easier to learn than user interfaces based on tangible graphic objects, such as the Macintosh interface. These are, in turn, easier than more abstract or language-based user interfaces, depending, of course, on the specific conditions."

*Abstraction is well suited for computing. After all, computers have been operating on this level for some time — technology has only recently allowed us to represent information spatially. Recently cyberspaces have emerged from being purely symbolic spaces into more experiential environments. Still, the development can go much further. Ideally, cyberspaces will simultaneously accommodate all modes of thought, including sensation and interaction as well as cognition.*

### The Spatial Matrix and Multiple Media

*Information space lets us use different modes simultaneously. In conversation, we use gesture in addition to voice. In moving about an environment we can smell the air, hear the traffic, feel the pavement under our feet. All these contribute to the experience of movement down a crowded street. Our mind creates a coherent environment in which the modes can co-exist without conflict. In fact, the relationship between modes is sometimes more important than the information we receive.*

*Imagine entering an art museum. At the desk you pick up a brochure and read about the installations. Since the museum is large, you also use a map to find your way. Entering the galleries you find artwork from many times and cultures. You walk past Renaissance nativities, Impressionist landscapes, Chinese scroll paintings and Beaux Arts renderings. Pausing before a Vermeer, you are taken by its meticulous execution. The light of the painting seems to enter your space. You are drawn in.*

*This example shows how space supports many modes of experience. The entry of the building, the brochure and map at the desk, the different images on the wall all were contents of the museum's space. The experience of entry was different from the experience of reading the brochure, however. One was physical while the other was symbolic. Reading the brochure's text was in turn different from reading the map of the museum. They both referred to the same exhibits using different modes of communication.[9]*

*The paintings in the galleries were experienced in yet another way. Though they all presented images taken from the world, they each used their own means of presentation. You experienced their spaces differently depending upon the style or substance of the piece. Still, you were able to appreciate each painting because you understood the conventions used to create it.*

*Space was the matrix for the experience. The building, brochures, map and paintings, each with its unique, symbolic code, co-existed without conflict, enriching the experience.*

9. Mok, op. cit., p.113.
Mok describes the cohabitation of spatial modes. A museum is in deep space, the paintings are representational of deep space.

Fig. 8
The German media group, Knowbotics Research, with Christian Huebler has created several immersive cyberspaces. Here an immersant engages a cyberspace with musical objects. The abstraction of music becomes tangible, concrete.

*Space is multi-modal by nature. While the museum visit was described visually, sound, touch and smell all played a part in the experience. All these reinforced the experience. Cyberspace, as a symbolic environment, might well be modeled on a principle of multi-modal space (fig. 8). The brochure helps us understand the paintings; the map helps us understand the museum. Each medium benefits from the presence of another.[10]*

### Microcosm and Plan Space

*In his book,* Mirror worlds, *David Gelernter proposes the development of a vast computer model of the world. In this model every object, action and transaction is documented, supported by on-going monitoring of the planet. He describes this not as an oppressive surveillance mechanism, but as a means for getting the Big Picture, what he calls "topsight." Topsight, the ability to see events in a larger context, helps people make better informed decisions. Politically speaking, a population that had access to this world model would form the basis for wise government and intelligent use of resources.[11]*

*Microcosms, in this case self-contained models of the world, have fascinated cultures for centuries precisely because they present this overview. Just as a globe shows the forms of continents we can't see from the ground, miniatures show relationships we can't easily see otherwise.*

*Cyberspace has the potential of becoming a microcosmic resource. Already it is used in surveillance and monitoring. Satellite images and live views taken from surveillance cameras are available on the Internet. However,* microcosm *is more*

10. Buxton, W. 1990. "The 'natural' language of interaction: A perspective on nonverbal dialogs." in *The art of human-computer interface design.* ed. B. Laurel. Reading, Mass.: Addison-Wesley. p.412.

11. Gelernter, op. cit., p.55.
Topsight is the view of a larger system. Subsystems are visible in fractal magnification.

*Envisioning Cyberspace*

than being able to see details – it is about seeing relationships between them, seeing systems at work. I believe that cyberspace's capacity for modeling relationships is one of its greatest virtues.

Not only does microcosm let us see what exists, it also lets us plan for what will be. Depending upon their representation, the artifacts of cyberspace can be rigorously detailed images of physical conditions or abstracted symbols. These symbols may show what presently exists or what is projected for the future. Architects and planners utilize this approach every day. They use scaled-down abstractions since full-scale representations would be unwieldy.[12]

A cyberspace can be an experiential space or, as in the architectural example, a plan space. This second space would allow exploration and manipulation. Links between its objects may represent subtle relationships or meaning. These spaces may help us plan spatial experiences much in the same way that storyboards are used to outline a film's sequence. In fact, these spaces may be all that is needed. They are simply different versions of the same information.

This plan-space concept underlies object-oriented programming (OOP). OOP lets code writers program using modular parts.[13] These parts, units of computer code, can be reassembled into larger programs. The idea of code-objects stems from physical reality and mass production. But the translation is imperfect. Only some of the current object-oriented programs use graphic code-objects that connect to produce flow charts. These diagrams may be viewed graphically or run as computer programs. The two modes are simply different ways of experiencing the code.

## Spatial Metaphors and Cultural Artifacts

In 1996, when President Clinton suggested building a bridge to the 21st Century he used an architectural metaphor to present his administration's goals. By analyzing this metaphor we understand that the bridge's embankments spring from the present and future centuries, the gap between them represents the distance between the status quo and his intentions. The bridge itself, a complex construction requiring many to build, is the means of spanning the gap. The bridge metaphor contains internal consistencies which support the larger reading.[14]

Lakoff and Johnson, the authors of Metaphors we live by, claim that "most of our fundamental concepts are organized in terms of spatialization metaphors." We use terms like "in," "out," "above" and "below" both spatially and metaphorically.[15] In fact, there is a reciprocal relationship between physical space and language. While much of our language is influenced by physi-

12. Mok, op. cit., p.99.
Mok's Information Architecture concerns the scale of composition (big categories vs. details) and its representation in "working-drawing" form, preferably 3D.

13. Software products like Visio let programmers do their work graphically rather than through a text interface.

14. Lakoff and Johnson, op. cit., p.52.
The authors discuss the larger structures of metaphors: "Because concepts are metaphorically structured in a systematic way, e.g., THEORIES ARE BUILDINGS, it is possible for us to use expressions (construct, foundation) from one domain (BUILDING) to talk about in the metaphorically defined domain (THEORY)."

15. Lakoff and Johnson, op. cit., p.17.
"Most of our fundamental concepts are organized in terms of spatialization metaphors." There is an internal consistency to these metaphors.

cal space, our understanding of that space is conditioned by our language. Space and language validate each other.

As soon as we create a spatial metaphor, i.e., the bridge, the reference becomes an artifact – made by humans. But artifacts are not the objects of our work; rather they mediate our relationship with other objects.[16] **This is the case whether an artifact is physical or not.**

Spatial, anthropic cyberspace is much more than an exercise in transferring conventional physical realities into a new medium. It must draw on deeper resources for a spatialization theory, including our affinity for people and objects. It should support a continuous on-going creativity in the ways we demand of physical space.

### The Great Work

Spatial experience is not purely physiological; our experience is culturally conditioned.[17] Anthropologist Edward Hall believes that "we experience our 'world' in such a way that our culture is already present in the very experience itself." Space, and by extension cyberspace, is a human artifact – an intensely human phenomenon.

In the following chapters we will see cyberspace through many eyes. Artists, designers, engineers and scientists around the world are bringing about a human-centered cyberspace. This anthropic cyberspace recognizes space as a human-generated means of thought and communication, as a site for cultural engagement.

The creation of this kind of cyberspace could be a Great Work, the electronic equivalent of the cathedrals in Europe.[18,19] People involved in its construction are building the extensions of our present world of space and thought. In coming years we will encounter resonances between physical and cyberspaces. This book will show how they can be integrated as products and tools of our human understanding.

16. Bødker, op. cit., p.31.
Here I use the term "artifact" in the way presented by Susanne Bødker. Artifacts are made by humans to operate on objects. Effectively artifacts are the cultural equivalent of objects in nature.

17. Hall, Edward T. 1966. *The hidden dimension.* Garden City, New York: Doubleday and Company. p. 140.
Hall describes a legibility of space. Spatial experience is not merely physiological; it is also culturally conditioned.

18. Mok, op. cit., p.100.

19. Gelernter, op. cit., p.35.
Gelernter describes his Mirror Worlds, an on-going simulation of the world, as a software equivalent to great works of engineering and architecture.

## Space as a Medium for Understanding Our Environment and Relationships

"Seeing comes before words. The child looks and recognizes before it can speak. But there is also another sense in which seeing comes before words. It is seeing which establishes our place in the surrounding world; we explain that world with words, but words can never undo the fact that we are surrounded by it."

Berger, John. 1973. *Ways of seeing*. London: British Broadcasting Corporation. p.7.

Fig. 9
Constantin Terzides, a professor of architecture, has used computer algorithms to generate spatial compositions. This image is of a model created using this method. It exists solely in the cyberspace of the computer.

*Space is a medium that lets us communicate with ourselves, our environment, and others. It is an entirely mental image created to organize and manage information (fig. 9). Without it we wouldn't be able to navigate, manipulate or communicate.*

*This section of the book presents how classic principles of spatial understanding can be a model for an anthropic cyberspace. It will describe the internal nature of spatial thought and the ways we use space cognitively and perceptually in order to relate to external objects and function as social beings.*

*This chapter discusses the roles space plays in our thought processes. It elaborates on the three mentalities that comprise most of our mental activity: enactive, iconic, and symbolic thought. Our internal image of space supports these mentalities to varying degrees. Cyberspaces modeled on space may augment these processes, extending our cognition to shared environments. The chapter concludes with a discussion of the role space plays externally in our social world.*

## Three Mentalities

*Three mentalities are integral to our day-to-day mental activity. Our enactive mentality helps us navigate, sense and react to our external environment. Our iconic mentality lets us recognize, identify and compare objects. Finally, we use our symbolic mentality to think abstractly and connect long chains of reasoning. We use these faculties in conjunction with tools to do our physical and mental work.*

*Alan Kay, computer scientist and theorist, suggests that "because none of the mentalities is supremely useful to the exclusion of the others, the best strategy in computer interface design would be to gently force synergy between them in the user interface design." A rich information environment – a cyberspace – would let us operate on all levels, capitalizing on our inherent abilities. Its graphic images would "spatially" situate us. Presenting many resources on a screen would appeal to our iconic mentality, offering alternative strategies and stimulating creativity. A variety of symbolic modes could suggest larger orders and relationships that would help us develop arguments or courses of action. [1]*

1. Kay, op. cit., pp.196-197.

*Two of the three mentalities employ spatial references and depend on our spatial understanding. Enactive mentality relates us to objects and environments; iconic mentality identifies objects and establishes relationships between them. While symbolic mentality seems related more to language than objects it depends in part on information obtained from our the other mentalities. Symbols, metaphors and allusions link language to our spatial experience. The three mentalities and our understanding of space are mutually dependent.*

### Enactive Mentality

*Experiencing space depends on many modes of perception, using all our senses and faculties. When I walk through a forest I see the trees, hear the birds and smell the damp earth. The space of the forest is created from many sources. Sights, sounds and textures combine to convey its presence. I automatically model an image that situates objects and associates sounds. My engagement with the space results from the constant negotiation and reconciliation between the senses.*

*Jean Piaget, the noted child psychologist, wrote that all spatial construction is oriented toward compensation.[2] Our mind interprets inconsistencies to favor the simplest reading. An object seen through one eye is slightly different when seen through the other – yet our mind reconciles these two images as one three-dimensional object. One ear hears something different from the other and the mind interprets this as sound coming*

2. Piaget, Jean. 1985. *The equilibration of cognitive structures*. Chicago: University of Chicago Press. pp. 92-93.

from a point in space. As complexity increases, so does our tendency to increase our dimension of understanding. [3]

Synthesizing many modes into a spatial experience is an important information tool. Information environments such as cyberspace augment this strength by appealing to our spatial understanding. Indeed, at times, increasing the display dimension can help us to clarify [4] and present information. Indeed, multivariable, complex information is often best presented using two or three dimensions. As active humans in a material and moving world, we are equipped to handle information in this form. It seems natural to us. [5]

## Iconic Mentality

"Does that shoe go on this foot?"

Tough question. My son Konrad is learning the difference between right and left shoes – not an easy one to explain to a five-year-old. I usually refer to landmarks like the little picture of Mickey Mouse on the outside upper. This time, though, his question isn't so easy. The shoe is lying on its side in the corner. Before answering, I have to mentally flip the shoe to orient myself to it. Konrad is facing me, so I have to re-assign my right side to his left. After a moment I answer him and we're off to kindergarten.

I used my iconic mentality to select the shoe from the other items in the corner. I turned the shoe around in my mind, manipulating a mental image of the shoe until it was recognizable. Finally, I compared the mental image to Konrad's foot, compensating for his orientation to me. In less than a second, I used space to locate an object, communicate with myself and finally, with my little boy. My iconic mentality helped me identify, relate and decide. Space provided the context for this thought and action.

## Symbolic Mentality

In the 1992 United States presidential election, Ross Perot, an independent candidate, used a unique tool for presenting his case on television. He came equipped with several charts to discuss government spending and the national deficit.

Perot's diagrams presented the U.S. budget so that I could see relationships between parts. His pie charts and bar graphs allowed comparison, engaging the viewers. Charts are simple devices, and in the hands of Perot, were crucial for making his case. They helped the public get a quick overview of a complex issue.

3. Arnheim, Rudolph. 1974. *Art and visual perception: a psychology of the creative eye.* Berkeley: University of California Press. p. .248. "The basic principle of depth perception derives from the law of simplicity and indicates that a pattern will appear three-dimensional when it can be seen as a projection of a three-dimensional situation that is structurally simpler than the two-dimensional one."

4. Norman, op. cit., p.65.

5. Bødker, op. cit., p.125.

Perot relied on the viewers' spatial understanding to make his case. This common, basic skill underlies much of our thought and is constantly reinforced through our daily spatial experience. Sometimes spatial imagery, like Perot's charts, is the best way to communicate a concept. [6]

I didn't vote for Perot, but I liked his approach. Space helps us think qualitatively. While iconically we identify and relate objects and artifacts, with our symbolic mentality we can interpret graphic symbols to follow an argument. Perot's charts were accessible precisely because we all think spatially. Spatial literacy is one of our first acquired skills.

Alan Kay agrees with Marshall McLuhan that "you must internalize a medium in order to subtract it when recovering a message." We have to first learn a language before having a substantial conversation in it. Space and its imagery is so internalized that it is fundamental to thought. That is why Perot's charts, as abstract as they were, seemed so accessible. Subtracting the medium of space to get at the message required hardly any effort at all. [7]

## Dimensions of Understanding

We use different qualities of space to support each of our mentalities. Our enactive thought processes thrive in rich, high-dimensional space, while iconic and symbolic mentalities are more focused and abstract, using fewer dimensions. Often, if we need to limit our options, or convey a specific message, we resort to a lower number of dimensions. I will use text rather than images to argue a point. Conversely, I will use a high-dimensional presentation to present an overview of choices. Lower dimensions offer less freedom of interpretation and association. Higher-dimensional displays leave more up to the viewer's interpretation.

One use of rich spaces is to derive lower-dimensional information. Take a map, for instance. If I plan a hike across rough terrain, I look at a map to see which route I should take. Once I select from the various options, I draw a line on it following the trail. The trail may turn and twist to its destination but it is essentially a one-dimensional route. I could easily turn it into a set of instructions – a list – to tell others how to find me.

Here I have used a derivative of the map (iconic) and drawn a line across its surface (enactive) to create propositional information (symbolic). The map, a high-dimensional display, could be used by someone else to situate a building or find a landmark. High-dimensional displays let us create low-dimensional displays to decide courses of action.

6. Lakoff and Johnson, op. cit., pp.56-57. "...the structure of our spatial concepts emerges from our constant spatial experience, that is our interaction with the physical environment."

7. Kay, op. cit., p.192.

Maps have another interesting feature. Look at a map and you see different colored lines indicating roads and highways. Other lines indicate county borders, longitude and latitude. We accept the lines both as correlational diagrams of roadbeds, or as abstract data on the same map. While we understand the lines to be linked to the landscape, the names and letters on the map are not. Looking down from an airplane, I'd be surprised to see the names of cities scrawled across the ground.

Different modes of representation reside in the same display without confusion. If we are familiar with its coding, we can compensate for the map's inconsistencies. This is similar to the art museum example I cited earlier. Paintings, maps, sculptures and architecture all co-existed in harmony. This is because the components of the museum experience are distinct, operating on different levels of meaning.

We aren't overwhelmed by the map or the museum because our minds constantly shift between enactive, iconic and symbolic mentalities. The museum building and the folded paper of the map engage our enactive mentality which lets us move through galleries or spread out the map. The iconic mentality lets us recognize and relate objects. With it we distinguish a map from a painting, a painting from a sculpture. Our symbolic mentality lets us understand the elements of a medieval triptych or the difference between road lines and the text of a map.

## Social Space

We use our environment to help us think. [8] We have notes, files and books to hold information otherwise difficult to manage. Designers make sketches or models to record their thoughts. At a larger scale libraries and museums institutionalize these external memory systems. Monuments are built solely to maintain memories. In all these cases our consciousness extends outside our bodies into the environment. Space and its objects mediate our externalized thought to ourselves and others.

Our external memories are part of a shared experience. The realm of these information artifacts is a social space – the foundation of culture. Our literature, arts and buildings are all thought manifested in this collective, perceived space. Designers of cyberspaces can learn from this human use of space. It not only gives a perspective on the process of managing information but also on the larger goal of reinforcing social interaction (fig. 10). The success of the World Wide Web has proven computers to be a viable medium in text and graphics. Though truly rich graphic, social cyberspaces are still a novelty. However, work is proceeding rapidly and the goal appears to be an unprecedented, spatial medium – a communal place of mind.

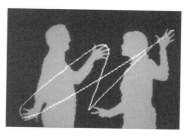

Fig. 10
Media artist Myron Krueger has experimented with computer/video interfaces and audience participation. Shown here are the silhouettes of two participants and a virtual cat's cradle that follows their gestural dialog.

8. Norman, op. cit., p.50.

Already we are seeing the birth of entities and organizations that would not exist without the Internet. Designers of cyberspace are devising new ways to represent them (fig. 11). These embodiments presage larger structures that will intersect our physical and social worlds. William Gibson, inventor of the term cyberspace, described an austere cyberspace, alien and inimical to humans. Surprisingly, the current cyberspace of the Web is alive with human activity. Chat rooms and on-line social spaces operated long before the geometries of virtually real cyberspaces were suggested. Anthropic cyberspace will better serve our need to connect. Its space is a site of culture.

Fig. 11
"Torus," a virtual environment by Marcos Novak, is part of his on-going study of algorithmically designed architectures. Novak's work has been investigating notions of space drawn from science and mathematics: higher dimensional, curved spaces.

*Envisioning Cyberspace*

# Spatial Models That Help Us Think

"All these facts show that the localization of objects of thought is not inborn. It is through a progressive differentiation that the internal world comes into being and is contrasted with the external. Neither of these two terms is given at the start. The initial realism is not due simply to ignorance of the internal world, it is due to confusion and absence of objectivity."

Piaget, Jean. 1960. *The child's conception of physical causality.* Paterson, NJ: Littlefield, Adams & Co., p.243.

*In this chapter we will explore ways we use our mental and physical spaces to help us think. We will see how we imbue our physical environment with meaning, externalizing our thoughts. Also, we will examine how we organize our thoughts through reference to physical space (figs. 12, 13). This will include a brief discussion of historical methods of spatializing memory, the memory palaces. Finally we will see the ways that combined imagined and perceived spaces play in our development and identity. These issues of space form the foundation for the design of anthropic cyberspaces.*

*Not long ago I went to the post office to pick up my mail. The clerk was loading the day's mail into the boxes as I arrived and we chatted as she worked. Suddenly she put a bundle in my hands – my mail. I was surprised. We'd met nearly half a year earlier and hadn't really spoken since. Somehow, she still managed to recall my name.*

*When I asked her about it, she said she recognized me from our earlier conversation. She then remembered the location of my box, which was in the lower left corner of the post box array and, without looking, was able to assign my name to it. It was then just a matter of leafing through her pile to get my mail.*

*The clerk was using her environment to help her think. Constant, daily repetition of her duties allowed her to create a mental model of the post office lobby and its hundreds of mailboxes. My mailbox was a component of this model. Fortunately, it was in a landmark location – the lower corner of a wall cabinet.*

Figs. 12, 13
Clayton Graham, an architecturally trained computer programmer and game designer has developed proposals for data-objects that combine to form work environments. The 3D image/object is a mnemonic device for the user as well as an interface for the computer. Though not physical, the objects use spatial reference to support thought and memory.

*A less experienced clerk would have had to ask or physically look at the box label to get my name. My clerk could always have glanced at the cabinet – it was there as a permanent reference for her mental model. The model and the mail cabinet were both tools for thought. Though one was cognitive and the other physical, both formed her perceived reality of the post office.*

## Mental Models

Our mental model of the environment has clear advantages. With a "small-scale" mental model of ourselves and our external world we can test hypotheses, try different strategies and evaluate their likely outcomes. We project into the future and use knowledge acquired in the past. We can react more competently and anticipate more fully the emergencies that may confront us.[1]

We have seen earlier that human thought is comprised of enactive, iconic and symbolic mentalities. We use our perceived and cognitive spaces to support them. My postal clerk recognized my face from our previous encounter (iconic). She mentally located my mailbox (enactive) and linked together my face to the box location and my name (symbolic). Of these, the symbolic mentality was least dependent on spatial location. But even it benefited from modeling since all mentalities depend, to a degree, upon one another.[2]

The mental model is not a stable representation of the exterior world. Unlike our sensory environment, it is constantly corrected, adjusted and updated. Differences between the mental model and the physical world create stress and stimulate learning. Reciprocally, we arrange our physical space to organize our thoughts. We make lists, create files and arrange artifacts to help our memory. Their spatial relationship is as much a part of the record as the contents themselves. [3]

Our artifacts mediate this dialog between internal and external spaces. Just as the illusion of space is a product of our minds, our artifacts are the contents of this illusion. The reciprocity between physical and mental space argues for an ecological model of thought – that is, an interdependence between the mind and its environment. Our minds use the perceived environment not only to gather information, but also to project our thoughts. We will later see how important this is to both the development of identity and our social behavior. [4]

But first let's look at how our physical environment supports our thought processes. Visual perception resembles visual thinking in many ways. Not only are they processed similarly in the brain, but we view this information in the same way. When I look at an object, my eyes flick from place to place, taking in the details through a fairly narrow field called a frame of attention. My mind compiles the information and renders the scene before me. My frame of visual attention is where my eyes are focused and is usually a foveal angle of a few degrees. The rest of my field of view is out of focus until I shift my attention elsewhere.

Visual thought uses many of the same parts of the brain that visual perception does. It also uses an attention window, simi-

1. Johnson-Laird, P.N. 1981. "Mental models in cognitive science," in *Perspectives on cognitive science*. ed. D.A. Norman. Hillsdale, N.J.: Lawrence Erlbaum Associates. p.149.

2. Kay, op. cit., p.196.

3. Norman, op.cit., p.26.

4. Altman, Irwin. 1981. *The environment and social behavior*. New York: Irvington Publishers Inc. pp.203-205.
In a discussion on different anthropological models for human behavior, Altman describes an Ecological Model of Man. This model is characterized by an inextricable relationship between the behavior of humans and their environment. This relationship is best viewed as an ecological system with mutual impact.

lar to our frame of attention. In imagining the shape of a Doberman's ears, we first have to "create" the image of a Doberman before we can determine whether its ears droop or not. It is similar to having the dog physically in front of you and shifting your attention window to the top of the dog's head. [5]

Yet it is quite different. Our ability to "see" the dog is the result of organizing our memory images into a propositional structure. We can recall the dog's ears, not because they were attached to a specific animal, but because they were generic for Dobermans and were "catalogued" as being at the top of a Doberman-shaped object. Visual thought is driven by this organizing, conceptual knowledge. Of course, we don't experience it that way – our thoughts and dreams can still be quite holistic and compelling. [6]

Whereas we can re-examine an actual Doberman for more information, the mental image of the dog is only a rough framework for more detailed image memories. And, as we know, memories can be deceiving. I may recall that the ears were short and round, for instance. Without a physical artifact present, I can't verify my memory. I might produce a surrogate dog by sketching it on a piece of paper, for instance. Actually seeing the Doberman with teddy-bear ears could convince me – or my friends – of the error. This verifiability is a major reason we externalize thought, using feedback from our physical environment to help us think.

## Translating Cognition to Perception

Experiencing information in more than one mode also helps us better understand its context and content. Donald Norman has written extensively on cognitive and experiential thought in problem solving. Experiential thought "extends our sensory capabilities providing us with entertainment, action and 'fed' experience. Reflective cognition allows us to ponder and make associations..." [7] We could say that one is represented as our perceived space, the other as our internal, cognitive space.

Sketching, modeling or writing are some of the ways we express internal information in physical objects. Sometimes, as in the sketch, the image is not a statement. It's a question – a trial balloon. Instead of the question being "What shape is a Doberman's ear?" with the sketch it becomes, "Is this the shape of a Doberman's ear?"

Herbert Simon, a prominent philosopher of information technology, writes that, "Solving a problem simply means representing it so as to make the solution transparent." [8] Our ability to transfer cognitive artifacts into an experiential mode is a powerful tool for thought. Once expressed, they can be evaluated and

5. Pinker, Steven. 1997. *How the mind works.* New York: W.W.Norton & Company. p.294.
When we conjure a mental image it is fragmentary, not whole. The sub-images have different points of view and focus. Holism, Pinker claims, is a virtue of expression or record, not internal imaging.
I am indebted to Kosslyn and Koenig's *Wet mind* for the Doberman example.

6. Pinker, op.cit., p.295.
"Memory images must be labeled and organized within a propositional superstructure, perhaps a bit like hypermedia where graphics files are linked to attachment points within a large text or database."

7. Norman, op. cit., pp. 16 and 27.

8. Simon, Herbert. 1981. *The sciences of the artificial.* Cambridge, Mass. The MIT Press. p 153.

critiqued. This process treats the artifacts as sensory stimuli which are then re-internalized and reflected upon cognitively. Further thought may require further evaluation, and we may cycle between cognitive and experiential modes as expressions and reflections lead to a resolution.

## Objects as Information Structures

Most of our artifacts hover between the status of concrete and abstract. This may be a by-product of a cyclical process of generation. Many of our artifacts are the result of cognition and expression and, despite their ultimate physicality, at one time were symbols in the course of their creation (fig. 14). This reinforces the interrelationship between our physical environment and thought.

Fig. 14
Canadian artist/engineer Will Bauer and composer Steve Gibson collaborated on this installation entitled "Objects of Ritual." The piece included images and objects that had symbolic as well as physical presence. The chalice in the middle of the image is a projection.

Cognitive artifacts are influenced by physical objects as well. Returning for a moment to our mental image of the Doberman's ears we find that the dog itself is not so much a photograph as it is an armature for details. When we shift our attention along the dog's body, other details come into "view." In this case the dog's body is part of a reference system we use to recall details we are asked to review. Similarly, if we were to memorize a list, we would recite the list in a vertical order similar to that on the page. We don't memorize the page, only its information format.

Both the page and the dog image have a verifiable referent geometry. The dog image is abstract enough that it could act as a prototype for a Doberman, or more generically, a dog. We are able to generalize this image so that details we recall can fit without disruption. As a result, the generic image may be used to remember the characteristics of other dogs as well.

Its most important feature is its conceptual stability – its virtue as a mnemonic device. Likewise regardless of our list's contents, its organization is sequential. When we recall it we ask ourselves what was next on the list in the order it was given. We may even try to visualize it.

Such prototypes – the geometries we derive from experience – help us remember specific details. These details, in turn, can become frameworks for other memories. We will return to this shortly, but before doing so we might look at how our physical world influences language and, in turn, our thought.

## Space and Language

Expressing our thoughts lets us appreciate what we are thinking in both experiential and cognitive modes. I think something first and then I say it, for instance. When I hear myself speaking, I can evaluate my message after re-internalizing it. This cycle of experience and cognition helps me clarify my motives and intentions.

An artist may render physical an image she only has in her mind. Here the parallel between mental and physical spaces is self-evident. And clearly the dialog between the artist and her work is enhanced by her critical evaluation through the re-internalization of the work. But what of speech and more abstract thought? How are these related to our use of space?

Our embodiment in physical space influences nearly everything we do. We have already seen the ways space and objects are used to help us think. In the case of language, we use nouns as objects and verbs to act upon them. At another level we use metaphors to link our abstract thoughts to the physical world. A well chosen metaphor will represent issues in ways that let us grasp and manipulate them. Good metaphors also present entailments that lead to further courses of action. For example, understanding a monopoly as an octopus suggests that we might attack the head rather than individual tentacles. [9,10,11]

9. Kay, op. cit., pp.198,200.

10. Pinker, op. cit., p.357.

11. Gelernter, op. cit., p.28.

But we use metaphors in subtler, more pervasive ways. Words like up, down, in, out, right, under, through are all used to describe abstract as well as physical states. Cultural understanding of space is reflected in language. And if we accept that much of our perception of the world is culturally influenced, we can appreciate the complex relationship between our experienced and cognitive worlds. [12]

12. Lakoff and Johnson, op. cit., p.18.

Imagine two vertically displaced objects. Since western culture places a positive value on elevation – as in the words up and high – we are likely to value the upper object more than the lower. Were we to express what we saw, our comments, influenced by metaphor, would likely favor the upper object as well: "This object is higher than the other." The link between language, space and culture is strong. Our statement concerning the object not only conveys our perception but places cultural values on it which themselves were derived from spatial experience. [13]

13. Maunsell, John, H.R. 1995. "The brain's visual world: Representation of visual targets in cerebral cortex." Science, 3 November, p.764.

## Objects of Memory

We use objects as mnemonic devices. We control our interaction with them by shifting our attention and focus. At the largest scale of attention we can see overall configurations. Scrutinizing an object reveals increasing detail. In this way a physical object potentially holds an infinite amount of information.

Another way we use objects for thought is by association. A physical object can symbolize something else similar to the way a metaphor can represent a concept. They exist both as objects and as information media. By looking at a carton of chocolate milk, I not only recall a pleasant childhood drink, but numerous associated memories as well. Marcel Proust's memory was similarly prompted by a madelaine in his book, Remembrance of things past. While the pastry was not intended as a tool for thought, it inspired Proust's meditations nonetheless.

Personal experience and culture influence our perception of the world. We encode the objects around us, often applying meaning without being aware of doing so. We filter out and fill in details to create an edited image of the world. At times the process simply lets us distinguish a chair from a table. Sometimes objects can become symbolic of a moment or a situation, embodying higher levels of meaning. [14]

14. Maunsell, op. cit., p.770.

Our capacity for connecting observations is not limited to spatialization. Sometimes issues cannot be easily mapped as objects in space. However, spatialization does offer ways to grasp complex issues, letting us alternate between cognitive and experiential modes. We need look only as far as charts, diagrams and computer models to see the benefits of such a process. [15]

15. Norman, op. cit., p.16.

## Mnemonic Structures

We use mental artifacts as reference frameworks for detailed observation. In the earlier example of the Doberman's ears, the generic shape of the dog set the context for examining the ears. The dog's shape set relationships between details we recalled later. The location of the ears on the generic shape acted as a placeholder or signifier for the precise memory of the ears.

Perceived objects are immediate. Regarding them at closer range reveals greater detail. Imagined objects are similar with the important exception that closer inspection reveals more placeholders as well as details. Imagine the Doberman, then imagine the shape of its ears. Now visualize the base of the ears, where they meet the head. At each scale, we have what seems to be a complete image of the imagined object. Yet this, in turn, reveals itself to be another reference framework. While physical reality provides this framework through spatial disposition, we subconsciously maintain a spatial system to maintain both memory and imagination. Nearly everything we recollect as a spatial image is simultaneously a framework for further inspection. [16]

16. Norman, op. cit., p.16.

Not all memory manifests itself spatially. We are able to remember facts and names propositionally or categorically without resorting to mental models. Yet we have seen that spatial reference pervades our language and culture. It also fosters shifts between cognitive and perceptual modes of thought. There may be advantages to intentionally using spatial frameworks as mnemonic devices. In the same way that our generic dog image helped us recall the shape of the Doberman's ears, other imagined spatial systems may assist in both our memory and cognition (fig. 15).

The mental image of the dog's ears on the generic body is analogous to our perception of the physical animal. We expect the ears to be at the top of its head regardless of whether the image is imagined or perceived. But what if the framework were not associated with the specific memory? Suppose that we could mentally construct a museum in which various memories could be housed. All of the memories would, so far as possible, be represented by some visualized symbol. While we would not have to

immediately recall individual memories to imagine this museum, our movement from place to place within the museum would prompt their recollection. The imagined space becomes a mnemonic structure that overarches the artifacts of memory.

To a degree, we can use similar structures in recalling past events. When I imagine the home of my childhood, I am able to "move" around in it, going from room to room. In each space I can visualize furnishings, materials and views from windows. I can also, with a little effort, remember important moments in each room. I remember sneaking out my bedroom window, or falling off my skateboard in the basement. The house is a mental image, a reference structure for these memories. Because it is spatial, I can move around in it at will. Different routes taken through the structure result in unique orders of recollection and narrative. Compared to reciting from a memorized list, with a mnemonic structure I can bypass forgotten portions or infer them from cues within the structure. [17]

However, memories organized by mnemonic structure may not be as clear as something memorized verbatim. We can clearly remember a statement because the sequential order of its presentation translates directly to a cognitive organization. Since the mental model of my house contains visual images arranged

Fig. 15
Electronic media artist Nik Williams developed the project "ChronoMnemos" as a physical and virtual display of time systems. In it participants can experience and control circadian time, solar time, and various dilations and contractions of time. "ChronoMnemos" would be a distributed, virtual memory structure as well as a physical structure placed in New York's Gothic cathedral of St. John the Divine.

Image by Funhouse Inc., New York.

17. Piaget, Jean, B. Inhelder, and A. Szeminska. 1960. *The child's conception of geometry*. New York: Basic Books. p.12.

spatially, verbatim recitation is moot since images can be described in many ways and in any order. A variety of routes leads to different recollections. [18]

18. Johnson-Laird, op. cit., p.182.

But these memory structures have some important qualities. Navigating their spaces and images lets us also make comparisons between their contents. The structure and the space between memory images lets us draw inferences. This is quite different from the memorization of lists, for instance. Secondly, the very act of building a mental model relates cognitive to experiential thinking. What was formerly a concept is now embodied as a mental image which we can regard and set in

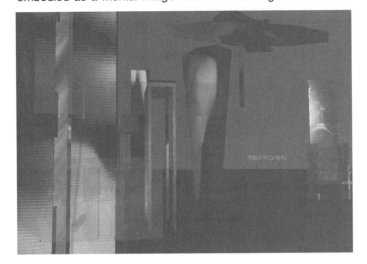

Fig. 16
Artist William Seaman's virtual environment "World Generator: The Engine of Desire" is based on principles of memory palaces. The visual elements of "World Generator" are fixed in their constructed environment, evoking memory trajectories and particular associations. Despite their abstraction or transparency the artifacts are recognizable and "solid." This facilitates naming and recalling them at a later time.

context. While not as tangible as a drawing or note, this image is a cognitive artifact for manipulation and inspection. [19]

19. Norman, op. cit., p.47.

Since this image and its space had to be consciously constructed we have a deeper understanding of the memory. Further, we can build on this artifact, extending it or influencing other memories. Beyond being a device for memory, this structure can be a useful tool for active, projective thought.

Piaget, the noted child psychologist, believed that the growth of knowledge was more than the mere accumulation of facts. Knowledge is due equally to our capacity to decenter relations from our own experience, and to place them within a framework distinct from the self. The relations then may be incorporated as elements within an independent system. Mnemonic structures objectify memory in a literal way, providing a framework similar to that suggested by Piaget.

*Envisioning Cyberspace*

# Memory Palaces

Mnemonic structures have a tradition that reaches back to antiquity. In classical Greek culture there were five art forms: sculpture, poetry, music, architecture and rhetoric. One of the disciplines underlying the art of rhetoric was the ability to recite great quantities of information. Oratory relied on a facile memory. In a culture based on oral traditions, this spontaneous access to facts was highly prized. A well-trained memory could overcome problems of information storage. The Greeks used ephemeral wax tablets, imported – and expensive – papyrus, animal skins and stone to record information. Memory provided economy, flexibility and portability to a degree that other media could not.

Orators and rhetoriticians, struggling to manage this information, created complex and highly evolved mnemonic structures called memory palaces. These mental spaces were sometimes drawn from experience, such as the layout of an existing building or city. But they appear largely to have been fabrications suited to each individual. The benefit of using an existing model was that it let the user of a memory palace refer to a physical space. Conversely, an unreferenced structure offered flexibility for personalization.

The memory palace was a non-linear storage system. Using computer terminology, it was a random access memory responsive to the user's situation in imagined space (figs. 16, 17, 18). It was ideal for spontaneous rhetoric since the speaker's narrative was mapped as a path through space. Alternate paths through the palace would produce a different recitation.

Those who practiced this art were capable of astounding feats. Cicero, the famous orator, was capable of presenting speeches lasting many hours and rich with detail. Simonides, to whom the invention of this technique is credited, was able to identify dozens of unrecognizable bodies found in the rubble of a collapsed hall using his mental reconstruction of the banquet's seating order. Later practitioners like Francesco Panigarola and Giordano Bruno were said to have many thousands of mental images at their command, all organized by the overarching geometries of memory palaces.

The organizing structure of a memory palace could be derived from any source. While buildings and cities were common references, other structures were used as well. Ludolphus of Saxony, a Carthusian monk, took the body of Christ as a map for memory. The 5490 alleged wounds sustained in the crucifixion were stations for contemplating the Passion. The 16th century Jesuit monk, Matteo Ricci, believed that there were three options in developing a memory palace. The first was an

Figs. 17, 18
Views of William Seaman's "World Generator: The Engine of Desire."

actual physical reference taken from experience. The second entailed the creation of novel and fictitious spaces. The third, a combination of the two, involved imaginative modifications of an existing space. A building one knew well might have an imaginary annex, an existing room could have an imagined door that led to another space or, perhaps, a staircase that connected to a fictive level above.

In her remarkable study of memory palace traditions [20]– ironically a forgotten art – Frances Yates stresses that the images housed by the mnemonic structure as well as the spaces themselves should be identifiable and distinct. A repetitive, grid-like organization would not be suitable for a large memory palace since the palace's effectiveness depends on landmarks, orientation and recognizable spaces. In other words, the definition of places within the larger structure define subsets, each containing a smaller number of images. Memory is scaled down to a level that can be readily grasped. This recalls our generic Doberman and his ears. If the Doberman body were a palace, one of its ears would be the equivalent of a room. The base of the ear would, in turn, be like an image contained within the imaginary room. Each icon – dog and ear – simultaneously resembles its subject and acts as a reference system for other mental artifacts.

Operation of such a palace involved a combination of cognitive and perceptual modes. The imagined sensory experience of the space helped the user recall and relate thoughts and memories. It's likely that the virtual movement of the users through imaginary spaces reinforced the memories through the repetitive reconstruction of the spaces and their contents. Just as the creation and situation of memory images requires effort, so too, to a lesser degree, does the fleeting reconstruction of spaces as one moves from one imaginary space to another. [21]

While the creation of memory palaces was primarily a mental discipline, it is likely that the practice influenced the creation of physical objects and spaces. The rich use of symbolic imagery in the artwork of the Middle Ages and the Renaissance may have been inspired by the writings of authors like Cicero and, later, Cypriano Soarez. As these texts and practices were integral to the intellectual and monastic life of the Roman Catholic Church, we can look to religious iconography in art and to the architecture of cathedrals as possible incarnations of memory palaces. Just as physical spaces influenced the creation of mnemonic structures, so too may spaces of the mind have been externalized by the hands of artists and master builders. It is as likely that the great cathedrals were inspired as much by the memory arts as by the need to teach illiterate congregations. This potent combination of mental and physical spaces has few parallels today.

20. Yates, Frances. 1966. *The art of memory.* Chicago: The University of Chicago Press.
Yates' study of memory traditions covers the practice from the time of the ancient Greeks until the Enlightenment. It is a fascinating account of memory disciplines and the social and philosophical issues attending their use.

21. Johnson-Laird, op. cit., p. 181.

*Envisioning Cyberspace*

Yet memory palaces – for all their virtues – had problems. While it was comparatively easy to remember visual images of events or objects, it was much more difficult to remember words or names. Practitioners used tricks to overcome this including the creation of elaborate punning images that would imply the name. Imagine here a bird's beak projecting from the door of a garden wall to recall Bill Gates' name. However, these led to a proliferation of images that burdened the memory or misled the user. For instance, the beak could equally recall a bird or the gate connote a pathway, neither assisting our recall of Gates' name.

Other problems with the palaces actually led to the downfall of their use. The first was that the memory palace is not information neutral. In later practice of the memory arts, the images of the palaces and their contents were biased by extrinsic faith or beliefs. After the Greeks and Romans, the tradition was adopted by the monastic communities of the Catholic Church. The use of Christian symbols to mark new memories reinforced the teachings of the Church at the same time that it influenced the new information. The problem could be illustrated by imagining a Jesuit's use of Catholic iconography to contemplate Gallileo's writings on the new – and heretical – heliocentric astronomy.

Practitioners of the memory arts were also derided by Francis Bacon, among others, as being obsessed with tricks of memory rather than the pursuit of true knowledge. Possibly Bacon saw that scientific progress would be impaired by archaic methods encumbered by faith and ritual. As the later practice increasingly referred to Hermetic traditions, the art came to be associated with witchcraft. Many were persecuted for practicing memory arts and some, notably Giordano Bruno, were put to death for it.

Meanwhile other methods for storing information had been developed. The prevalent use of symbols in art and architecture may have been an attempt to externalize the practice, manifesting it in material form. Also, as western culture depended less on oral traditions and more on inexpensive media like paper, ink and publication by the printing press, the need for memory palaces diminished. These media didn't require the discipline of maintaining a memory palace and soon superseded their construction.

An added benefit of these external media was their non-proprietary nature. As mnemonic methods were almost entirely internal, memory palaces could not easily be passed from one person to another. When a person died, his palace went with him. As a result, the practice diminished and effectively died out in the 18th century. Thanks to the pioneering research of Frances Yates there is a renewed interest in the topic, although the actual practice has not been revived.

The memory palaces historically demonstrate the power of spatial thought beyond mere recollection of existing spaces. They were cognitive spaces developed to enhance memory. While the needs they met are now filled by other media we can learn from them. For the spatial rendering of thought has been proven to be a powerful tool.

## Cyberspace and Mnemonic Structures

While earlier information demands could be met with pen and ink, today's needs require higher levels of technology and automation. The memory palace could resurface as a model for future collective memory allowing users to navigate stored information in an intuitive, spatial manner. Though we may not restore the memory arts per se, we should recognize the power of spatial reasoning and the linkage between it, our language and culture. As we develop computing environments, we should remember that our reasoning is to a large degree based on spatial thought.

Fig. 19
Knowbotic Research's musical computer agents represented as objects. These objects are both symbols and instruments. See also figure 8 on page 14.

Computers already use symbols and spatial means for user interaction (fig. 19). As this practice develops, cyberspace will evolve to be an important extension of our mental processes. We can imagine that its designers might create interactive mnemonic structures to be shared and passed from one generation to the next. Cyberspace could open these structures to public view.

Another advantage cyberspace offers is flexibility and verifiability. The structure of a memory palace, its frame of reference, needed to be stable. Its primary purpose was to situate memories within its matrix for future recollection. However, if the matrix changes spontaneously, the benefits of the structure disappear. Points of reference are lost and relationships dissolve. Such fluctuations would have been hard to manage without reference to physical artifacts like drawings or models.

Cyberspatial models of memory, however, would be visually verifiable. As a result, the architecture of the matrix could be more responsive to change than a truly cognitive structure. Users could keep track of changed locations without losing memories.

The mnemonic structure of a cyberspace might also be instantly reconfigured for specific uses. Imagine a museum-like space that re-organized itself to let viewers see artifacts in order of date, artist, style or nationality. The sorting functions that underlie much of computing software already serve similar purposes. However, here the results would be a multidimensional display of space, symbols and relationships.

Continuities between our internal and external worlds make the illusion of cyberspace an important medium. Its space and artifacts can be verified by experience and, as we will see, justified by our culture and language. Like memory palaces, cyberspace is symbolic, but in a way that can be shared by others, extending our internal cognition to the social realm.

The sharing of these internal models is perhaps the most important feature of cyberspaces. Though internal, memory palaces were originally developed to sustain the oral traditions of their cultures. With cyberspace we have an important extension of this precedent, not only through its support of thought but in its transmission to others. Only through such communication can relationships be built that transcend our personal isolation and enhance our society. Even the strongest critics of visual computing must concede this promise of cyberspace.

## Space as a Component of Identity

Our minds constantly interact with our internal and external worlds. As we have seen, much of this activity involves spatial modeling for perception and cognition. The memory palaces are an example of how this modeling can help with cognition. But, more important, they illustrate connections between mental spaces and those we perceive.

This is crucial since these relationships underlie our sense of identity and presence in the world. For instance, our mental use of space to situate objects and ourselves informs objective reasoning. Learning distinctions between perception and cognition, reality and imagination, is a large part of our maturation from children into adults.

From the time they are born until they grow to adulthood, children develop their sense of reality and objectivity in several stages. Their first five years, particularly the first two, are spent developing sensory-motor skills. From the ages of roughly 5 to 11 they develop concepts of representational space based on a topological understanding of objects and the space that separates and contains them. [22]

22. Piaget et al., 1960, op. cit., pp. 11-12.

Children's first stage is spent developing sensory-motor and perceptual space (almost entirely body-related). In the next phase they begin to develop a representational space based on a topological understanding of objects within the space. Since they have no proper distinction between their internal space and the objects outside, this understanding focuses on relationships between objects and doesn't include the child as participant.

Young children have a hard time relating more than two objects at a time. Their relationship to their environment is simple.

They are not conscious of themselves, only of immediate and palpable objects. Children at this stage are still getting used to their bodies and learning to relate to their surrounding space. There is a strong identification between the body and space because young children make no distinction between the world outside themselves and their own mental and physical processes. It is only later, when they begin to separate the two, that they can distinguish external reality from themselves. [23]

The next stage of development involves the creation of representative space in which objects are recognizable and placed in context. In order to minimize confusion and overburdening the memory, children remember relationships of objects rather than individual instances. As a result their world is based on landmarks and relationships as well as self-reference. [24]

Successful creation of this space lets the child recall absent objects and relate them to perceived objects. Children at this age are capable of mental constructions involving images, states and simple transformations. They are at the same time developing language skills that let them name and manipulate objects mentally. [25]

Children at this age can understand objects that have substance and duration. These objects are coherent – integrated into a whole – and distinct from one another. This lets children identify, name and work with them. They then can separate things according to characteristics or number. This is a foundation for further intellectual growth since mathematics and a Euclidean concept of space rely on these abilities. Indeed, by the age of seven, most children are able to use objects symbolically and show early signs of abstract thought.[26,27]

Prior to the age of seven or eight, children put a lot of effort into accounting for objects' transformations due to changes in perspective. [28] To a child, approaching a building seems to make the building grow larger. This illusion can't be overcome until they separate their point of view – and themselves – from the objects they regard. To do so, they need to create an independent spatial system in which they place themselves and the objects they see. The transformations are then understood as products of relationships within this Euclidean space.

This is a milestone in childhood development and bears directly on our use of space to help us think. By creating the spatial matrix which is independent of physical reality, the child uses it for situating images of both perceived and imagined objects. Not only are the images placed within this space, but **so is the image of the child itself.** Here we see the birth of the child's self-awareness and identity. [29]

23. Laurendeau, Monique, and Adrien Pinard. 1970. *The development of the concept of space in the child.* New York: International Universities Press. p.11.

24. Harris, Paul. 1977. "The child's representation of space," in *The child's representation of reality.* ed. G. Butterworth. New York: Plenum Press, p.84.
Children rely on a landmark (relational) coding of space as well as self-related space coding.

25. Piaget, Jean. 1985. The equilibration of cognitive structures. Chicago: University of Chicago Press. p. 85.

26. Piaget, 1985, op.cit., p.86.

27. Laurendeau and Pinard, op. cit., p.15.

28. Piaget, 1985, op. cit., p.90.

29. Piaget, 1960, op. cit., p.248.

The child's creation of the Euclidean matrix is the basis for abstract and objective thought. The use of this framework for both imagined and perceived objects has important consequences. As the child evolves this matrix of perceived and cognitive space, he or she is also developing related language skills.

Language, influenced by metaphor, helps the child bridge the gap between cognition and experience. An object viewed perceptually can become a metaphor for something more abstract. Reciprocally, an abstract thought can be expressed with metaphors taken from the perceived world. Language and metaphor ferry meaning between imagined and physical realms.[30] If this process is interrupted – as it is with autism – words become literal references to images and objects. Consequently, abstract thought is impaired as the metaphors cannot negotiate between cognition and perception. [31]

30. Lakoff, George, and Mark Johnson. 1981. "The metaphorical structure of the human conceptual system," in *Perspectives on cognitive science*. ed. D.A.Norman. Hillsdale, N.J.: Lawrence Erlbaum Associates. p. 202.
"A metaphor can serve as a vehicle for understanding a concept only by virtue of its experiential basis."

31. Grandin, Temple. 1995. *Thinking in pictures and other reports from my life with autism*. New York: Vintage Books. p.33.

At the age of roughly 11 or 12 a child can understand abstractions that are entirely mental or internal concepts. Up until that point children have a lingering connection between internal and external worlds. The Euclidean matrix they have formed to deal with the outside world is still internal and although they are able to separate themselves from other objects, there is still a tenuous, if diminishing, relationship between the self and the perceived world.

This offers children some security. They understand that even if the external world doesn't correspond to their internal world, they can still rely on a relationship between the two. Indeed the unifying nature of the spatial matrix may foster this notion. Children believe to varying degrees that the world is animate and subject to them. A typical example would be the illusion that the moon follows them from place to place. Children also believe that their thoughts and moods can affect the physical world through magic, animacy and superstition. [32]

32. Piaget, 1960, op. cit., p.253.
"Reality [for the child] is still overgrown with subjective adherences: it is alive and artificial; words, dreams, and thought reside in external objects; the world is filled with forces."

Using the spatial matrix, children establish relationships between objects and themselves – but they do it subjectively and egocentrically. Children can't separate internal from external states until they build an intellectual construct that breaks the world into subjective and objective universes. Until then imagination and reality permeate one another in a fantastic and sometimes terrifying mix. [33, 34]

33. Sugarman, Susan. 1987. *Piaget's construction of the child's reality*. New York: Cambridge University Press. p.10.

34. Piaget, 1960, op. cit., p.254.

As adults, we never completely lose this subjectivity – nor fully attain objectivity – just as we cannot fully distinguish our cognitive from our perceived worlds. In this sense the division between real and virtual becomes moot. More useful for our purposes are cognition and perception since both comprise our sense of reality. The spatial matrix we inherited from our youth is still at work, moderating between the two. So too is our *metaphorical use of language. To this extent we bring our child-hood along with us. And this is probably for the best.*

*The lingering connection between the self and the outer world saves us from alienation. It keeps us engaged, as though attention were our investment in our surroundings. A sympathy between ourselves and our environment stems the degradation of both. A tempered illusion of animacy could restore a respect and rapport with our world.*

## The Spatial Matrix

*Perhaps just as importantly the linkage between the self and the outer world lets us imagine, plan and resolve problems. The world of fantasy itself is critical to our development into adults. Bruno Bettelheim in his book,* The uses of enchantment, *makes the case that fairy tales situated in the imagination (long ago and far away) offer children resolutions to the inner conflicts of growth. Places and events set in this cognitive environment can be safely contemplated in the knowledge of their fictional nature. As adults we use this visual imagination similarly to appreciate stories and read books. Bettelheim argues that the externalization of children's internal forces through fairy tales comes at a crucial stage of their lives. And that the dreams of adults deprived of fairy tales in childhood might not be as rich, nor serve them as well in restoring a mastery of life.* [35]

*The rich world of childhood fantasy eventually gives way to a more pragmatic and useful distinction between cognition and perception. As adults we use our imagination to envision alternatives, to speculate on past and future events. A normal adult can usually separate internally generated phenomena from those taken through the senses. This keeps reality from becoming a muddle of imagination and actuality. We use our cognitive space as a kind of sketch pad for the imagination and easily distinguish it from the world around us. But despite this distinction, the worlds of subjectivity and objectivity are never far apart (fig. 20).*

*At the beginning of this chapter, Piaget tellingly describes the first years of our lives as being marked by a realism that is lost as we mature. All our imagery, whether derived from perception or imagination, is the product of internal processes. We now know that the generation of these images involves similar activities of the brain. And Piaget's "realism" reveals why – although we can distinguish fantasy from fact – we never quite lose our subjectivity. Despite our intellectual maturity, the world is still emotionally and perceptually centered on the self.*

*Piaget's realism fosters our use of space in cognition. Emotionally placing ourselves at the center of the universe is a*

35. Bettelheim, Bruno. 1977. *The uses of enchantment: The meaning and importance of fairy tales.* New York: Vintage Books. p.63.
"If the dreams of a child were as complex as those of normal, intelligent adults, where the latent content is much elaborated, then the child's need of fairy tales would not be so great."

product of our earliest years, our self-interest and defense. Although more pronounced in children, it underlies our everyday experience as we negotiate our world physically and socially. This is the basis for our on-going investment in the world, for we place ourselves at its center. Finally, the self forms the critical point of reference within the space. By default, we find ourselves at its point of origin.

Our language metaphors use place references to orient us. We have seen that words like in, out, over and under operate conceptually as well as descriptively. Beyond this, in conversation we often relocate our listeners by having them imagine themselves elsewhere or in other situations. "Put yourself in my place," for instance.

In response, our listeners re-center their reference system to where we place them. Engagement with a presentation depends on this. We lose our interest – and investment – in a presentation if we can't "see ourselves" in a situation. Once we doubt, we can no longer suspend disbelief. Brenda Laurel, author of Computers as theater, [36] stresses the importance of this investment in fostering smooth human-computer interaction. While her discussion focuses on the role of software actors and agency at the service of computing, we can see that placement and space serve similar, at times identical, ends.

36. Laurel, Brenda. 1991. *Computers as theater.* Reading, Mass.: Addison-Wesley. pp. 66-71.

Of course, when I speak of relocating the self, it is in no way a literal or simple matter. Neither location nor entity are easy to define in this context. In the early stages of our lives we create the spatial matrix that situates objects in our environment relative to one another. Although this matrix centers on ourselves, young children are not self-aware. They cannot view themselves objectively within the matrix.

Eventually, at a later stage of development, we are able to place representations of ourselves in the matrix much as we might a common object. The product is a new reference system characterized by the relativity of all contained images with respect to each other and ourselves. Our image is one among many.

Fig. 20
These spherical cyberspaces hovering above the city of Weimar, Germany, are components of a "cybercity" proposal developed by German architect Dirk Donath and his colleagues at the Bauhaus-Universität in Weimar. Although these spaces have addresses referring to the city streets, they have no physical presence – acting as a fantasy infrastructure for communication and social activity.

Yet, despite this seeming objectivity, the question of the self and its situation is elusive. We are emotionally predisposed to an egocentric point of view. This is at odds with our capacity to see ourselves objectively within a larger order – spatial or otherwise. And even the objective point of view begs the question. If we can visualize our self image in the matrix, where is our point of view in that representation? Does it lie outside it? How does the reference system of that vantage relate to the previous matrix?

Since we are able to create images of ourselves within our spatial matrix, we can theoretically have as many self images as we have frames of reference. While to this point the discussion has focused on space, it illustrates issues raised by the philosopher Jacques Lacan and others concerning social identity. My roles as a husband, father, pet-owner, architect and fly-fisherman all entail separate frames of reference, each with its own code of behavior and expectations. Much as we can re-situate – and replicate – our self image in other frames of reference, so too do we assume various concurrent roles throughout our lives.

I can only offer readers a brief summary of these issues as they lie outside the scope of this book. I present it only to show the role space plays in establishing our identity. Since much of this chapter has been devoted to our use of space for thought, we should not lose sight of the fact that space, as a tool for thought, is itself an internal phenomenon. [37]

## Culture and Space

All evidence to the contrary, there **is** an outside world. Anyone who has stumbled on a rock knows the sensual stimuli are real enough. And we ignore them at great risk. However, the stimuli – photons of light, airborne chemicals and sound waves – are presented to us as coherent objects within a continuous, immersive environment. This presentation is, as we have seen, an impressively sophisticated display of information. While it is ultimately an illusion, it is one that we use for nearly every activity. It is an illusion upon which we build our language, society and culture. We must remember this in coming chapters. Yet, while I acknowledge this illusion, our belief in the existence of an outside world is critical to us.

We take many things on faith, mainly because we have to. The world that does not appear to our senses is not perceived, so we compensate for it with faith. I have never been to China, but I believe it exists from literature and images that corroborate its existence. Our world is comprised of interpreted, sensory information and what we are able to recall or imagine.

Until a stimulus enters our senses and is registered in our memory, we are unaware of it. Let's imagine we are looking at a bicycle. The sunlight reflected from it enters our eyes and is detected by our retina. From there the signal passes to parts of the brain that register the existence of the object – its color and texture – and, separately, its location in space. As my eyes flicker over the bicycle, I gather more information that also follows this path. At a later stage of processing, I combine images and location in associative memory where I can relate the object image to others, identify it as a bicycle and reflect on it. At that point, it has my attention. I am aware of it as a coherent object. [38]

37. Laurendeau and Pinard, op. cit., p.9.
Objects are understood by their mental construction via figurative (image, states) and operative (transformations) aspects. Operative thought relies on intelligence, figurative on perception.

38. Hall, op. cit., p.39.
We can never be aware of the world as such, instead we can only know of the forces that impinge on our senses.

Prior to being even conscious of the bicycle, I already evaluated the image. Linguistic and cultural influences affect this evaluation as we have seen in the use of language and metaphor in thought. My culture can determine what I notice or ignore.

If I were caught in a Yukon snowstorm, I'd be in big, cold trouble. Though I would be able to see the snow, I couldn't distinguish one type from another – perhaps a matter of life or death. The native Eskimo and Inuit have highly specialized vocabularies for this, but it's more than a matter of verbalization. Their vocabulary shows appreciation of different snow consistencies. Having a word for a type of snow means having an awareness of it as well as the ability to express it verbally. An Inuit disoriented in a storm might find his way with knowledge simply unavailable to me. Details that are invisible to me could be vital to my survival. Culture and language are important influences on our perception of our environment. *39*

39. Hall, op. cit., p.85.
We understand our world through our language.

But let's return to a warmer climate for a moment and look at my bicycle. In my mind it is situated relative to other objects in my spatial matrix. However, I am not conscious of the matrix as an object. It is actually a process that produces the illusion of a space, one we perceive as external reality. If I regard the bicycle consciously, I can place it in my permanent memory. At each stage our mental image is subject to further processing influenced by cultural or personal proclivities.

If I close my eyes, I can recall enough detail to reconstruct the bicycle and its surroundings. As with our earlier Doberman example, I create a generalized scheme in my cognitive space and fill in details as necessary. Unlike my perceived space, the cognitive space is volatile and subjective. It is the space of thought, unconstrained by physical reality and even more subject to liguistic/cultural interpretation than perceived space. It, like my image of the perceived world, is inaccessible to anyone besides myself.*40*

40. Hall, op. cit., p. 39.
"...each animal...inhabits a private subjective world that is not accessible to direct observation. This world is made up of information communicated to the creature from the outside in the form of messages picked up by its sense organs."

This cognitive model may be manipulated and controlled independent of any external conditions. I gain a better understanding of the object as I create this model and manipulate it. And my ability to draw inferences depends to a great degree upon modeling my environment and thoughts. My illusion of a cognitive space appears coherent and consistent although separate parts of the brain and distinct mental processes let me fabricate and manipulate these mental images. *41, 42*

41. Johnson-Laird, op. cit., pp. 180, 184.
"In translating from text, first comes a propositional model, but a more profound understanding comes from building a mental model...The capacity to draw inferences rests fundamentally on the ability to construct and to manipulate mental models."

42. Grandin, op. cit., p.39.
"Visual imagery and verbal thought may depend on distinct neurological systems."

I can augment my thinking by expressing internal thoughts into my physical environment. In order to express these thoughts, I have to formulate them verbally, gesturally or through sensible media. The expression will again be processed linguistically and projected into my perceived space using skills of speech, *drawing or any of the media we use every day. At large, the information becomes experiential and can now be taken in by myself or others for further cognition.*

## Caveat

*So far, I have described the mental world as binary. For reasons of clarity, I have polarized it into two types of spatial illusions: perceived and cognitive space. With respect to our earlier discussion on childhood development, this expresses an ideal of objectivity. Theoretically, using this model, I can clearly distinguish internal from external phenomena. The connection between my perceived world and my cognitive world would be closely controlled, keeping my internal impulses from influencing my perceptions.*

*But it's clearly not so simple. Look at the number of mitigating issues involved in creating these spaces. First, **both** perceived and cognitive spaces are mental illusions. As I and my brain are part of my physical environment, there is a complicity between internal and external states before I even take in any information. I am not only subject to the physical reality of my environment but previous exposure to that enviroment affects my current experience as well. [43]*

43. Altman, op. cit., p.205.

*Secondly, as we have seen, linguistic and cultural influences affect my experience as well. While neither of these may have direct bearing on my sensory input, they can strongly influence my mental images of the environment. Just as I may be snow-blind in the Arctic, so too would I be unable to distinguish odors or sounds crucial to other cultures. Conversely, while I can laugh at the cheesy effects of an old science fiction film, someone from another culture might be impressed – even terrified.*

*Finally, once an object has our attention, we activate memories that themselves are the product of experience and cognition. What to another is a simple bicycle, to me is a cherished object from my childhood. The dent in the fender is a reminder of a birthday party, a tree, a bump in the sidewalk. My experience of looking at the bicycle, while incorporating the same senses and organs as anyone else, is unique to myself. The bicycle image I have created is unique, different from anyone else's.*

*I am more likely to see something objectively if I've never seen anything like it before. I have no handle on it, no words or experiences to define it. I am dependent solely on my sensory input and whatever understanding I have for color, texture and shape. This novel object exists almost solely in my perceived space. Even then, I am likely to make comparisons between what I have experienced and what it is I see. Children look at clouds and see animals just as we see images in inkblot tests.*

Conversely, a novel space imagined when I close my eyes may be as close to purely cognitive as I can get. It is mutable and instantaneously responsive to changes in my internal state. While I may try to envision something entirely new, it too will be influenced by remembered perceptions, the implicit presence of my body and the simulation of sensory input. Whatever I fabricate will, to a degree, be affected by my perceptions of the physical world.

This is why we are able to recount our dreams to others when we wake. No matter how bizarre they seem, we are able to describe vivid images and situations. Regardless of whether we actually experienced them spatially when they occurred, we interpret them with reference to remembered experiences and objects. The hallucinations suffered by those who have had prolonged exposure to sensory deprivation tanks can be described because we use remembered perceptions to model something new.

If I had diagrammed the relationship between cognitive and perceived space before, they would have been two distinct spaces. Now, as we acknowledge the relationship between the two, they seem to overlap. Perception and cognition pass back and forth between our spatial representations. And this is consistent with, and part of, our daily experience.

In the next chapter we will see that nearly all artifacts have abstract, symbolic qualities. This is by virtue of the fact that we mentally model them, and so place them in both our perceived and cognitive spaces. Rather than distinguish physical from conceptual artifacts, we operate on a continuous scale between extremes.

Since a large part of daily experience involves familiar objects, and since our waking hours involve continuous input from the senses, we live in a space that is a rich blend of sensory and cognitive information. The distinction between the two is made possible only by pointing to extremes. In daily practice, we imbue objects with meaning, and our thoughts with attributes taken from the physical world.

Our spatial matrix, created in the first decade of life, is itself an artifact that mediates between the concrete and conceptual. And perhaps this is its most important role. It is the reference frame that allows us to relate our internal, cognitive space to our perceived environment. It situates us in the world and establishes our connection with it. A critical moment in childhood is when we first are able to create our image within this space. It establishes us as entities separate from and yet complicit with our world. In closing this chapter, let's return to this aspect of childhood and its implications on the design of cyberspace.

# The Return of Enchantment

As children grow to be adults, they are increasingly able to distinguish between physical and imagined entities. The world becomes polarized, internal distinguished from external. They learn that will alone cannot make the wind blow and that their toys no longer talk back to them.

The world of magic and animacy is relegated to dreams, cultural traditions and turns of phrase. Symbolic meaning becomes an intellectual construct rather than part of the subtle life of childhood imagination. The increasingly abstract levels of thought we attain as adults no longer easily model themselves as physical objects, attenuating the separation of internal and external worlds.

And yet, a part of our childhood stays with us. We never quite lose the "realism" of our sympathy with the outside world. We demonstrate this in emotional egocentricity and in varying degrees of magical and animistic beliefs. Though we know the outside world is separate from us, we often act and feel to the contrary. [44]

As we have seen, our artifacts participate in a dual life, symbolic and real. While some resist change owing to their physicality, others live in the mind, their manifestations subtle and shifting. The artifacts and spaces of cyberspace appear to hover between these worlds of perception and cognition. Perhaps we can look to their development as a return to the symbolically rich worlds we experienced as children – places where a sympathy between reality and imagination encouraged speculation and hope.

Whether or not we believe in it, we understand the idea of magic. It is a way of understanding the world that we have all experienced regardless of age or culture (figs. 21, 22, 23). As we mature we realize the physical world was not designed around us. Our faith in magic is constantly shaken by a world that won't play by its rules. As a result we build perceived and cognitive spaces to accommodate us.

A major distinction between cyberspace and the physical world is that the physical world is a found environment. In contrast, the networked environment of cyberspace is designed for our use. Its express purpose is for convenient communication and manipulation of data. Given its anthropocentric nature, cyberspace presents us with a technological extension of the "realistic" world of our childhood. It approximates this world of coincidence and mystical relationships – symbols imbued with meaning.

Figs. 21, 22, 23
Shown above are scenes from "Posada Space" a virtual environment by artist Michael Mosher in collaboration with Timothy McFadden. The visual references to Mexican folklore and traditions create a fantasy space for the user's exploration.

44. Piaget, 1960, op. cit., p.244-245.
"At first we are one with the world then once distinct the world is conscious and parallel to us as children. To a degree, we never quite leave this state..."
There are a number of adherences to the original state of oneness with the exterior world: magical beliefs, animism, artificialism, finalism.

Piaget's concept of the child's world view can model how we might connect cognitively – and perhaps emotionally – with the virtual artifacts of cyberspace. Whether these artifacts are agents, images or text, their symbolism is intentional, not inferred. The consciousness of the child hovers between a literal, materialistic world and a symbolic, abstract understanding of principles. It is this consciousness that never entirely leaves us, and one that we may draw upon in the creation of cyberspace.

Computerized animacy, agency, and magically responsive spaces are sympathetic to the intermediate level of childhood development. They capitalize on the fact that everyone, in all parts of the world, is familiar with its premises. It is part of our growing up.

I don't use the term "magic" to imply anything mystical. Instead it describes a relationship between our world and our intentions. A "magical" world, one that appears in fairy tales and myth, is a useful model for cyberspace because of its universal, metaphorical nature.

Brenda Laurel's concept of the computer as a site of theater relates to this. Both theater and the space of fairy tale magic are narrative spaces in which the details of their environments have symbolic, emotive meaning. This close relationship between content (events) and surrounding (setting) is artificial yet crucial to the narrative. Magic is another instance in which the two interact, where characters can influence their surroundings without physical intervention. The surroundings are in sympathy with the action.

If computers are to extend our mental capabilities, their design must involve more than rote ergonomics. This is more than an issue of empirical human factors. Instead, their design must incorporate the humanistic values more often associated with art and theater, namely, activities that draw on our human understanding, emotions and aspirations. Cyberspace should be more aligned with the "realism" described by Piaget than the higher level abstractions attained in adulthood. It draws on our synthetic abilities, our earliest experiences and our ability to imagine. [45]

In this chapter I have shown how we use our spatial environment to help us think. In the examples of the memory palaces we have also seen how the spatialization of memory can be a powerful tool. Finally, we see the combination of imagined and perceived space plays a vital role in our childhood development and continues to aid us as adults. This complicity between perception and imagination is crucial in developing an anthropic cyberspace.

45. Rheingold, Howard. 1990. "What's the big deal about cyberspace?" in *The art of human-computer interface design*. ed. B. Laurel. Reading, Mass.: Addison-Wesley. p.450.
"...We habitually think of the world we see as 'out there,' but what we are seeing is really a mental model, a perceptual simulation that exists only in our brains. That simulation capability is where human minds and digital computers share a potential for synergy."

# The Scale of Abstraction

"Cyberspace is a human-computer interface, but it is also a mind-space, the way mathematics and music and myth are mind-spaces, mind-space you can walk around in and grab by the handles."

Rheingold, Howard. 1990. "What's the big deal about cyberspace?" in *The art of human-computer interface design.* ed. B. Laurel. Reading, Mass.: Addison-Wesley. p.449.

*This chapter concerns human artifacts [1] as tools for thought. It defines a scale of abstraction so that we can see how nearly all objects are symbolic, i.e., have a capacity for bearing information beyond their obvious, concrete presence. This scale will apply both to conventional and electronic artifacts. We will see that the distinctions between real and virtual are not as useful as perception/cognition or concrete/abstract. Within the mind, both symbols and objects have the same status of reality.*

*In cyberspace all artifacts are symbolic. Yet to varying degrees, they refer to the physical world through allusion or metaphor. This connection is necessary for the user to orient himself within the symbolic space. Our scale of abstraction helps us understand these connections to our physical world, showing ways to classify the artifacts of cyberspace.*

**1. Artifact**
In this and ensuing chapters I will be using the term "artifact" to denote anything made by human effort. This use of the term differs from an object-based definition since it is used here to describe both physical and abstract entities. This will help us situate the non-physical, yet allusive symbols of cyberspace. Cyberspace artifacts may refer to the physical world without being physical themselves.

## Concrete and Abstract Artifacts

*I recently visited Fort Ancient in Ohio. One of several sites in Ohio featuring the mound structures of the Hopewell tribe, it sits high atop a hill in the rolling landscape north of Cincinnati. Although the local museum was closed, the path that led to the mounds was open and I walked a mile or so before I came to the site.*

*Although other mounds were used for burials, "fort" mounds are walls that outline the summit of a hill. Although their uses are unknown, few archeologists believe they had the military use their names imply. Most likely they were sacred sites meant for tribal gatherings. While the tomb mounds at Chillicothe and Peebles, Ohio, are distinct from the landscape, Fort Ancient is subtle to the point of transparency. I wasn't sure what I was looking for – every bump on the ground was a potential "mound."*

*It wasn't until I found a park map that I was able to tell the difference. Now I could distinguish the landscape from the artifacts. Some bumps took on a new significance, now representing ancient activities of assembly.*

*The mounds of Ohio are silent. They so closely match the terrain that only the trained eye can spot them. And, even so, they tell us little. They are different than, say, Egyptian tombs that commemorate specific persons and events. The mounds exist* at an extreme of artifacts, approaching the state of mute, almost natural objects.

At the other extreme we have the non-material artifacts of language, i.e., words and abstract thought. While we experience them verbally and graphically, they also function as disembodied mental tools. On a scale of abstraction that ranges from the most abstract to the most concrete, we can imagine a word at one end and, say, a brick at the other.

Of course it's not that simple. An archaeologist would protest that he could find significance in a brick – or our mounds for that matter. Likewise, a cognitive scientist could claim that thought is a product of concrete, physical processes. Consequently, our scale of abstraction can only serve as a rough guide for distinguishing artifacts. Despite its limitations, the scale illustrates how nearly **all artifacts have a dual nature comprised of form and meaning.** We will use this scale to evaluate the artifacts of physical and cyberspaces – and show how they both rely on spatial presence and thought to be understood.

## The Scale

What are the extremes of our scale? While I mentioned a concrete/abstract polarity, others – such as perception/cognition – apply as well. However, the concrete/abstract polarity organizes artifacts that range from those with physical presence to those that exist only in the mind (fig. 24).

Many artifacts depend upon both physicality and thought. Abstract metaphors connect thought to our physical environment. Conversely, even the humblest artifact has some abstract value. The lawnmower in my garage is a fairly sophisticated tool for physical work. While it might tell us something about a culture that values uniform lengths of grass, this must be inferred. The lawnmower, like our Indian mounds, is relatively silent. It tells us little beyond what we perceive directly.

Though a typewriter is also a concrete tool, it serves an abstract goal: making other artifacts, letters and reports, to help us think. While the typewriter is not as information-laden as the pages it produces, its use is directed at more abstract ends than the lawnmower.

Typewriters, like paintbrushes or cameras, record information for us to share. Their products refer to materiality through symbols. A photograph by Ansel Adams, for instance, thrusts us into the vastness of Yosemite valley. The symbolic, spatial illusion of the photo is stronger than its concrete presence. Photographs and realistic paintings, like portaits, rely on direct, physical counterparts. While they are physical objects, their reference to other objects mitigates their concrete presence. We participate in the material space they occupy as well as the cognitive space of their illusion. They operate symbolically, using physical space for both presence and subject.

However, painting is less dependent on a physical counterpart than photography. An artist can evoke a space without reference to a specific place or object. Physical reality outside the space of the painting is less critical than with portraiture or photography. Such conjectural painting uses the language of spatial imagery without literally depicting its objects. We would consequently place such paintings further toward the abstract end of our scale than our photograph.

Architectural processes illustrate these uses of space. Prior to the design of a building, an architect records the site's existing conditions. A kind of portrait is made of the terrain, nearby objects and buildings. This scaled mapping is as accurate as possible to ensure the fit of any proposed work. Surveys, drawings – indeed photographs – are used to represent the site.

Design, however, is the projection of something that is **not** there. A proposed building exists only in the mind and products of the architect. It's only later that it exists in the physical world. That said, while there is still a connection with the reality of the site, the design is not as dependent on it as, say, a terrain model of the existing conditions.

On our scale of abstraction, the building's design is less concrete than the terrain model. Its ties to physical space are more attenuated despite its simulation of concrete space and objects. But since the design proposes physical construction, it is still linked – projectively – to concrete reality.

But what if that connection were broken? What if diagrams had no relationship to a specific space? We see these almost every day. Pie charts, organizational diagrams and graphs present a space with no physical counterpart. They exist in a space of symbols, signs and the artifacts of language.

## Perceptual vs. Cognitive Artifacts

Another way to polarize our scale is through perception/cognition. This is useful since some artifacts have no link to the physical world. As we approach the upper end of our scale, artifacts grow increasingly abstract. Many exist solely to mediate information. Though some – like graphic diagrams – use spatial language, they refer to perceived space only to aid their informational role. For example, the rectangles of an organizational chart have nothing to do with the people they describe. Yet, the symbols can quickly be relocated to show a promotion or reas-

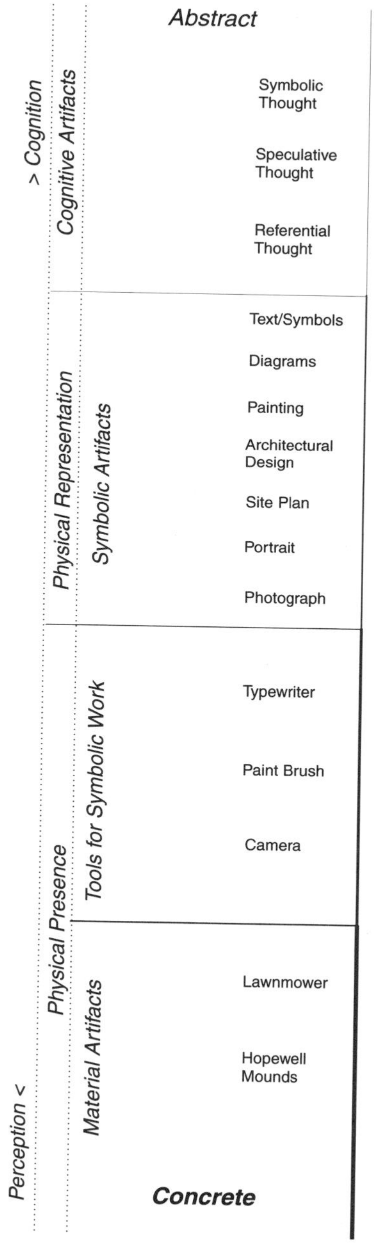

Fig. 24 **Scale of Abstraction**
This diagram shows relative locations of the artifacts discussed to this point.

signment. Such spatial presentation lets us visualize complex issues.

Finally, we reach non-visual language near the extreme of abstraction. Here the connection to the physical world is at its most tenuous. While I can spatially visualize "Sally threw Spot the ball," I can't do so for "Sally reflected on the quality of their relationship." One is linked to space and objects of the concrete world. The other describes abstract concepts – states of mind.

But language is rich with spatial reference – metaphors and symbols reflect our physical presence in the world. Not just because they represent real objects but also because they are mental objects we manipulate to think. Nouns in language are the mental equivalent to objects. Verbs are the equal of actions. Note that our scale of abstraction was described in text, not images. We imagined the lawnmower, the typewriter and the portrait in a fashion similar to visual perception. In fact, the processes that let us visualize thought depend on many of those used for visual perception. And these images are them-selves artifacts that we use to think. We can imagine turning our typewriter upside down and looking at the underside, for instance. To do so we imagine a "cognitive space" containing our typewriter. And some thoughts are best understood by cre-ating such a space. While we can categorically answer the question "Do typewriters have keys?," we have to visualize the answer to "Where is the 'T' key on a typewriter?" Typically, we first conjure the generic image of machine then focus our atten-tion to the keyboard, much as we would view a physical type-writer. [2]

The image of the typewriter refers to the physical artifact in the way the portrait resembled its subject. There is a strong link between this image and the perceived world. Unlike portraits, plans and diagrams, this image is entirely cognitive – its con-nection to the perceived world is by reference only. This makes it hard for others to experience unless we express the image verbally or graphically. But the good news is that we can access and manipulate them in otherwise impossible ways. As pure symbols, they may be modified or reassigned at will. Cyberspace is interactive in this way and – importantly – may be experienced by others as well.

In summary, we now have a scale of abstraction to evaluate artifacts for their reliance on the concrete world. Lying between our scale's extremes, most physical artifacts had abstract qual-ities, while most abstract artifacts had some physical reference. Even abstract thought itself is conditioned by our experience in the physical world.

2. Kosslyn, S. and O. Koenig, 1995. *Wet mind.* New York: The Free Press. pp.130-131.
*Wet mind* provides an excellent summary of the mechanisms underlying cognition and percep-tion.

While cyberspace implies electronic media and interactivity, there is a range of opinion on the degree to which cyberspace depends on or refers to physical space. Again, we may understand the artifacts of cyberspace via our scale of abstraction. Here I will consider cyberspace to be a special category of electronic artifact. By reviewing such artifacts methodically, we can see how they sit with respect to the conventional objects of our scale. In this discussion we will look first at objects that use electricity for mechanical work, then those that use it for mediation. Finally we will see electronic artifacts that have no physical presence at all and only exist in the cyberspace extensions of our minds.

At the most concrete end of the scale (fig. 25), near the position held by my lawnmower, we have simple electronic appliances. A toaster, for instance, uses electricity only to get physical work done. It's a medium only to the degree that I signal its operation by plugging it in and depressing the lever. To that extent a transistor, the subcomponent of all computers, is also a dumb appliance. It's either on or off. But in a transistor the electrical current is only meant to pass a signal. While the toaster does physical work, the transistor, like my typewriter, does physical work that is used symbolically.

Electronic processors used in toys, cars and missiles make them increasingly "smart." They use electronic chips for sensing and navigation, forming a basis for more sophisticated robotics. However, when compared to a computer, the work of these machines is more physical than symbolic. Their product is concrete, mechanical motion.

But if they were connected into a signal network, my newly smart toaster could talk to the coffeepot – and the pot to the alarm clock. In the morning my clock would prompt the pot which in turn would wake the toaster to start breakfast – a Rube Goldberg illustration, perhaps, but one that bridges the gap between appliances and media.

This overlay of networked electronic media onto physical objects is called "distributed computing" by researchers at Xerox PARC and the MediaLab at the Massachusetts Institute of Technology. It's the flip side to virtual reality. While virtual reality is the illusion of physical objects in an electronic medium, distributed computing is the electronic mediation of physical objects – even their animation.

Next on our scale are media appliances and displays. Televisions and radios, though their physical presence is not referential, serve a referential function. They support the images we see and hear. Telephones, TVs and radios are infor-

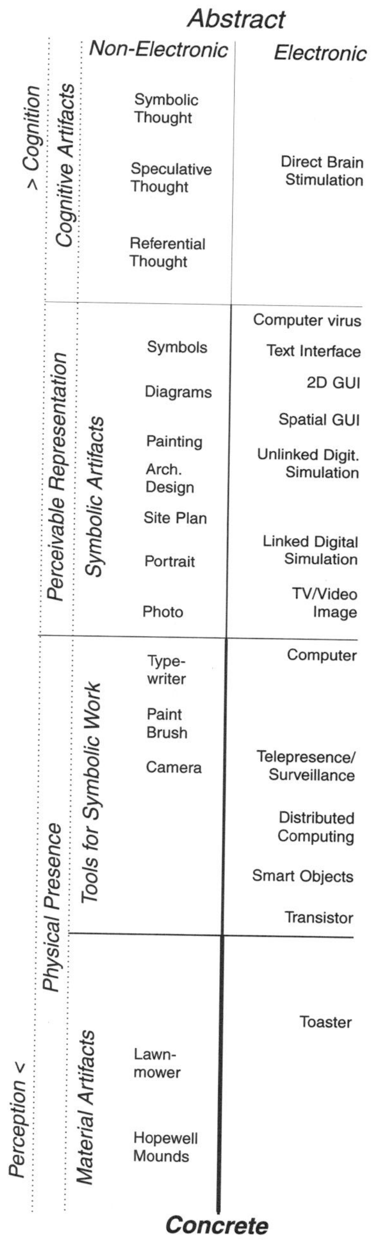

**Abstract**

| | Non-Electronic | Electronic |
|---|---|---|
| **Cognition > — Cognitive Artifacts** | Symbolic Thought | |
| | Speculative Thought | Direct Brain Stimulation |
| | Referential Thought | |
| **Perceivable Representation — Symbolic Artifacts** | | Computer virus |
| | Symbols | Text Interface |
| | | 2D GUI |
| | Diagrams | Spatial GUI |
| | Painting | Unlinked Digit. Simulation |
| | Arch. Design | |
| | Site Plan | |
| | Portrait | Linked Digital Simulation |
| | | TV/Video Image |
| | Photo | |
| **Physical Presence — Tools for Symbolic Work** | Typewriter | Computer |
| | Paint Brush | |
| | Camera | Telepresence/Surveillance |
| | | Distributed Computing |
| | | Smart Objects |
| | | Transistor |
| **Perception < — Material Artifacts** | | Toaster |
| | Lawnmower | |
| | Hopewell Mounds | |

**Concrete**

Fig. 25 **Scale of Abstraction for Artifacts**
This diagram shows relative locations of the electronic artifacts discussed compared to non-electronic artifacts.

mation displays. Of these only telephones let users interact with the illusion. With the advent of interactive television new developments are possible.

Stephen Perrella, a New York architect, has produced work that aims at interlacing information space with the physical environment. In his design for a manufacturing facility for wearable computers, all the surfaces of the physical environment are activated by electronic images (fig. 26). The building is effectively a display, dematerialized by the illusion of virtual spaces

Fig. 26
Proposal for a manufacturing facility for the production of wearable computers by architect Stephen Perrella.

beyond its surfaces. The source of the images is data generated by computers of the facility and possibly the clothes that it manufactures. (See also plates 1, 2.)

Computers are also media – especially in the light of networks like the World Wide Web and Internet. While our augmented toaster is still doing physical work, the computer's work is aimed at symbolic manipulation. Though the computer is a physical artifact, the product of its use is not. In fact, with its software, the computer straddles both concrete and symbolic worlds.

It does this in more than one way. As its hardware does symbolic work, its software often mimics physical objects. Many computers use iconic displays, presenting files and code as manipulable objects. Software buttons, dials and scrollbars emulate the mechanical tools from our material world.

*Envisioning Cyberspace*

## Interface as Artifact

This software simulation of space is itself an artifact that we can place on our scale. We can use the representation of space to help us evaluate the abstraction. For example James Leftwich, I.D.S.A., an interaction designer and principal at Orbit Interaction, has designed several interfaces that rely strongly on spatial experience. In one instance he developed an interface that extended the desktop metaphor to the spatial environment of an office (fig. 27). General Magic, Xerox and Microsoft have also created similar interfaces.

More abstract spaces appear in interfaces by cognitive scientist Stuart Card and his colleagues at Xerox PARC (figs. 28, 29, 30). Their information displays take the form of trees, carousels and walls, providing alternative ways of viewing stored information. Here the interface is selected by the user for different purposes, orienting herself within data, or locating information on a computer network. Through its graphic user interface (G.U.I.), she manipulates and navigates the information spatially. This approach can be very intuitive when coupled with our natural thought processes. (See also plates 14, 15, 16.)

Modeling cognitive problems as perceptual ones often aids their resolution. The GUI of an Apple Macintosh, for instance, turns cognitive artifacts into perceivable, experiential ones. Categorical actions, like filing information under different headings, is accomplished by dragging file icons "into" folder icons. Donald Norman, a cognitive scientist long involved in computer interface design, believes that the Macintosh interface lets users see the intended product and manipulate it better than

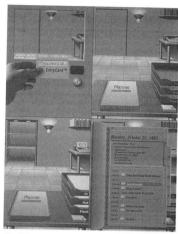

Fig. 27
This design for a computer interface by James Leftwich of Orbit Interaction uses a spatial reference to an office with doors, desk and shelving.

Figs. 28, 29, 30
These user interfaces developed by Stuart Card, George Robertson and Jock MacKinlay at Xerox PARC show different strategies for presenting information structures for digital libraries. Shown are the Cone Tree (left), Perspective Wall, and Document Lens (bottom). Each employs a different spatial/visual metaphor in its presentation.

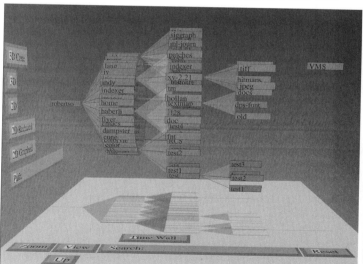

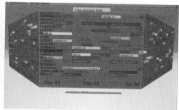

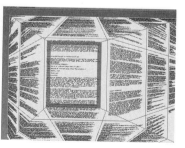

other operating systems.[3] Microsoft has since succeeded in incorporating this approach in its Windows operating systems.

But Norman warns that the fixed organization of a computer interface will not work. Too often "we find ourselves catering to the needs of the technology instead of having the technology cater to us." [4] Computers must remain flexible to the users' needs. If I look for a file but can't remember its name, the alphabetical listing feature won't help. Instead I should have the option of seeing graphic sample images prior to opening documents. This would get me around the cognitive problem. Visual and spatial understanding offers us many ways to achieve similar ends; with it we can arrange things differently, define organizational structure by attributes.

Rather than the operating system using a fixed cyberspace metaphor – say, a desktop or a city – it should manifest itself according to our needs. For example, to get the names of all the people on my block, I could create a simulation of that block and "visit" each house. But a simple list of names would be easier to generate and understand. Having the sidewalk layouts and roof pitches of houses is irrelevant to my task.

In his InfoSpace project James Leftwich, I.D.S.A., proposed an interface that mediates between the physical space of a computer operator and the symbolic space in which he is working. In an architectural example, a house model exists in a virtual space beyond a spherical shell that appears to surround the operator. The shell itself is virtual and displays tools related either to creating the model or to operating the computer. (See plate 10.)

The difficulty of locating software – in this case the operating system – in our scale of abstraction is illustrated by the co-existence of various types of perceived spaces in Leftwich's proposal. On one hand the sphere resembles diagrams which, though spatial, have no connection with the physical world. The house, however, represents a projected space with no real physical counterpart. The terrain of the model is yet another kind of object – a "portrait" of an actual piece of land.

This co-existence of different types of artifacts within an information system recalls our earlier example of the museum hosting different spatial experiences. This can be an important asset to a computer application. As a tool, software must be flexible and interpretable. Different representations of the same information – lists, charts and models – are not redundant but necessary.

3. Norman, Donald A. 1990. "Why interfaces don't work," in The art of human-computer interface design. Laurel, B., ed. Reading, Mass.: Addison-Wesley. p.209.

4. Norman, 1990, op. cit., p.217.

Envisioning Cyberspace

## Linked Realities

Television, video and electronic surveillance are the media equivalents of portraits on our scale of abstraction. Like portraits, they have strong links to physical reality (figs. 31, 32, 33). Take the security system at a store, for instance, their cameras connecting to remote video monitors. While the monitor display is indeed physical, its image only refers to physicality. Through the cameras, suspects are "present" at the security officer's location. Reciprocally, by viewing the bank of monitors he's virtually present at several locations in the store.

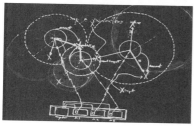

In most cases there is no interaction between shoppers and the store's security staff beyond the one-way video connection. But let's take this a step further. Say the security staff decided to mount the camera on a small, dog-sized robot. The robot has enough power to move through the store's aisles and relay images back to the monitors. More importantly, the security officer can communicate back to the dog, directing its motion and attention.

Telepresence depicts a space while at the same time embodying the viewer at the perceived location. Our officer may only have a view of our kneecaps, but he is present to us – even intrusive. Robo-dog's sniffing after us might curtail both theft and shopping altogether.

His cousins are usefully employed, however. Remote-controlled robots prowl the edges of volcanoes, sweep for mines and defuse bombs. A recent, spectacular example is the small robot sent to explore the surface of Mars. The scientists operating it from Earth were – time delays and all – remotely present on Mars looking at rocks and testing samples.

At a more abstract location on our scale are digital simulations of buildings used to map temperature and air flow. Though such a simulation is reality-based, it is a specially-crafted artifact. Referring to the physical world, this artifact only exists in electronic space as a cybereal, disembodied simulation.

Figs. 31, 32, 33
In an installation entitled "Telepresent Surveillance" artist Joel Slayton employed two free-roving robots. Each robot was capable of establishing and tracking targets using an infrared-sonar system (above). Video cameras mounted on the robots relayed live images onto the Internet. The image at top left shows screen captures from the surveillance, and the installation's diagram is shown at the bottom left. Gallery viewers were simultaneously aware of the presence of the robots and that of unknown, remote viewers on the Internet.

Contributing Artists: Steve Durie and Bruce Gardner.
Engineering: Guy Marsden.

Cybereal artifacts usually refer to a physical object without overlapping it. However, overlaps can be useful. In 1977 Kenneth Knowlton, then at Bell Labs, created an information environment that let computer workers change keypad configuration as work proceeded. Through the use of half-silvered mirrors, operators could see a virtual keypad projected onto the physical pad itself. The same keystroke could achieve different ends depending on the display. Such an overlap between physical and cybereal objects [5] is called an "augmented reality."

One of the most dramatic instances in which cybereal objects merge with reality is in surgery. Recent techniques developed at the University of North Carolina by Anselmo Lastra and his colleagues model parts of the human body so that surgeons can "see" the location of internal organs and malignancies. Using augmented reality interfaces – transparent visor-mounted displays – they can perform operations by guiding mechanized surgical instruments using the spatial model (see plates 19, 20, 21). Nowhere is the match between physical and cybereal objects more critical.

## Autonomous Simulations

The surgical interface connects physical to cybereal [5] objects. But such links may be broken. For example, virtual reality walkthroughs of building designs project something that's not there. They have an autonomy that a building surveillance model lacks. They employ spatial symbols without the burden of a parallel reality. But since they project future physical buildings, they still serve concrete objects and space.

Simulations that have no physical counterpart have a similar location on our scale as paintings of imaginary scenes (fig. 34). The difference is in their interactivity with the viewer. In these spaces participants can navigate and manipulate a scene. Computer games like Riven or Quake use such literal depictions as their "playing field." Though they represent no actual environments they still depend on the illusion of space.

Most of these games stress the experiential nature of the spaces and their occupants. Whether playing against the computer or one another, users respond to the objects and spaces as though they were concrete. A wall image represents a physical wall, for instance. It only represents an obstacle or limit to

Fig. 34
Artist and architect Marcos Novak has produced a number of proposals for a "Liquid Architecture," one that structures information spatially without needing to be embodied materially. Shown above is one of these autonomous simulations. One of the earliest proponents for an architecture of cyberspace, Novak is developing "transarchitectures" to extend liquid architecture into the space of everyday experience.

5. Cybereal
Cybereal artifacts are symbolic objects of electronic environments. Although they are presented spatially, they have no reference to specific physical objects. In this way they are distinct from models and images used in planning and design. Examples include metaphoric objects and icons used in the operating systems of computers.

the player's actions (fig. 35). Even less experiential games, like multi-user domains (MUDs), use spaces in this literal way. Whether you experience them visually or in text, what you "see" is what you get.

However, the artifacts in these spaces can be put to other uses. Where they once referred only to physical objects, they can now symbolize concepts and conditions. Cybereal artifacts can help us think through simulation – the equivalent of the flowchart diagrams discussed before. Locations of objects in these spaces would convey subtle, non-spatial relationships. For instance in an organizational chart we accept that the box containing the name of the C.E.O. is at the top without worrying about his altitude within the headquarters building. Height is symbolic – having only a metaphoric connection to the physical world (figs. 36, 37).

Fig. 35
Media artist Patrick Lichty uses recognizable, realistic elements to populate his simulated environments. The rendering of color, materials and space draws us in experientially.

Of course, using simulation, we'd expect our virtual objects to behave like physical ones. They should display traits of longevity, inertia and mutability. Yet, these characteristics can't be taken for granted – they require programming just as do more complex behaviors. Though we interact with these symbols as mute objects, as part of an information environment they communicate with the user and to each other. We could say they have "lives" of their own.

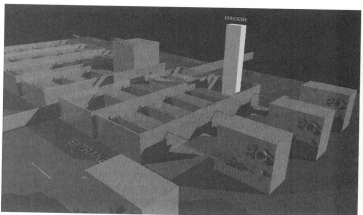

Interaction with such artifacts is designed by a programmer with a sensitivity to users' expectations. Brenda Laurel, the author of Computers as theater, likens this to a playwright's creation of characters. The interface designer establishes the identity of each artifact in cyberspace and its potential interaction with the user. These electronic symbols now not only represent something else, but they act as well. They can respond to us in more complex ways with color, configuration or movement. Computer games are obvious precursors – only now, the arti-

Figs. 36, 37
Above is an interactive planning tool by the author for the design of a corporate cyberspace. Components of the scheme are treated as manipulable objects. Some, like those in the detail on the right, represent programming code modules that, when linked, perform organizing functions for the space. This design was used to plan a company's intra- and extranet strategy. Geometry, forms and colors were identifiable and namable to facilitate dialog in lower bandwidth media like telephone and email.

facts don't represent anything outside the computer environment. These embodiments of code take on whatever visual form the user – and programmer – requires.

An extreme of autonomy is achieved by artifacts whose behavior is complex enough to appear alive. Computer viruses are the precedents for what is now called "artificial life." Though these viruses are invisible strings of code, artificial life is often represented with graphic displays of cellular automata, the kind found on some computer screen-savers. Other kinds are computer agents that automatically accomplish a range of tasks for the user. Like viruses, agents are usually not graphic entities, although some have been successfully embodied in MUDs and on-line computer games.

These artifacts can be designed to propagate autonomously. Viruses often replicate themselves vigorously to bring down their computer hosts. Copying files is a simple example of computer-assisted husbandry. More complex processes allow genetic reproduction of artifacts. Just as we each are the complex result of a comparatively simple genetic code, the symbolic artifacts of cyberspace may also embody the data equivalent of DNA. In the past, genetic algorithms were used to perfect design solutions through Darwinian selection. Now they are also used to produce a range of outcomes – as plants might be bred.

Already genetic algorithms are used in computer games and on-line environments to create avatars and other entities. In most cases the breeding is deliberate, although this too could eventually be autonomous. The results may surprise us, for here we approach the most abstract of artifacts. Ones that – although artificial – may not be made by man. While these artifacts may resemble things found in the physical world, their symbolic nature coupled with their automated creation sets them at the other extreme of our scale. If we exclude verbal language, these artifacts are as abstract as any we can perceive.

## Beyond the Senses

Up to this point our artifacts were taken in through the senses. While we can reflect – cognitively – on things we perceive, they exist outside ourselves and can be shared by others. They are part of our social environment. On our scale we have left the realm of perceived artifacts to look at those that are products or elements of our cognition.

Is there an electronic equivalent to cognitive artifacts, those that are thought but not perceived? Data files in computers cannot help – we need to perceive them in order to understand them. This returns us to audio-visual symbols of the perceived world. However, electrodes can bypass the senses and directly stimulate the brain. They can trigger visual or other effects that seem sensory yet are internally produced. In many cases, experiments using these techniques help researchers determine which part of the brain processes specific information. But, in such cases, the information passed through the electrodes is a simple prompt rather than meaningful content. Electrically-conveyed cognitive artifacts would be the equivalent to telepathy.

Bypassing the senses doesn't eliminate the use of space, however. We know that different parts of the brain respond to stimulation in unique ways. An electrode in one part evokes anxiety, while in another it creates a "blue" sensation. Meaningful information, however, is complex and relational. With the proper stimulation, the mind could generate spatial images in ways that we imagine or dream them.

Illusions generated by direct stimulation of the brain may be our most abstract artifacts. While they presently exist more in science fiction than fact, they would offer perception to those deprived of their senses. If designed for reciprocal communication they could have tremendous consequences. Suddenly, mental artifacts, thoughts and memories could be accessed by others than ourselves. While such systems are speculative, we should be prepared to ask some difficult questions. What would necessitate such an invasion of privacy? Could an intervention of this sort be justified? How could we avoid its abuse? Many of the questions asked by writers of science fiction become suddenly relevant and urgent. Concerns about privacy run a dark parallel to increased access to information through electronic media.

## Summary

Our scale of abstraction is a simplified categorization. In fact, many of our everyday artifacts would take several positions in our scheme. Take, for instance, a picture postcard. On one side we have a realistic portrayal of a scene – a specific reference to a place. On the other we have text containing information that both refers to the real place as well as more abstract concepts of well-being and anticipation. The postcard's stamp, while signifying postal costs also represents an American flag which in turn represents the values and history of the United States.

Likewise, many electronic media also are a mix of concrete and abstract representations. A television broadcast through graphic and verbal presentation may be abstract or concrete, depending on which sample is taken. The images may refer more to physicality than the concepts underlying the narrative. However, our scale helps us see the importance of spatial understanding in our transaction with the world. We use our

Fig. 38
This installation by German media artists Knowbotic Research, entitled "Anonymous Muttering," linked different parts of Rotterdam with the installation through the Internet. The dislocated sounds of the city temporarily blurred distinctions between the audience's site and remote locations in the city.

*artifacts to do work, communicate, and extend ourselves beyond our bodies. Our scale shows that nearly all our artifacts have abstract and concrete qualities that appeal to our cognition and perception, respectively.*

*This hybrid nature of artifacts may reflect our own mental and bodily presence in the world. The dual role of artifacts lets us use them for mental and physical work. They let us negotiate between cognition and perceptual space to help us think, connecting our personal, mental world with the social, physical world around us (fig. 38). Spatial thought is the medium that helps us manage this extension. Cyberspace is its electronic incarnation.*

# Body Extensions in Space

"Man and his extensions constitute one interrelated system. It is a mistake of the greatest magnitude to act as though man were one thing and his house or his cities, his technology or his language were something else...it behooves us to pay...more attention to what kinds of extensions we create, not only for ourselves but for others..."

Hall, Edward T. 1966. *The hidden dimension*. Garden City, New York: Doubleday and Company. p.177.

So far we have focused on the mental processes of thought. The differences between interior and exterior has been blurred by the fact that both perceived and cognitive spaces are internal illusions. But this leaves us with individual isolation. How do we transcend this while still acknowledging the mechanisms of thought? What lets us go beyond this introspection?

In this chapter we will see a number of ways that we extend ourselves into our environment. Although our view of the world is generated internally from sensed and recalled information, we are still responsive to the external, physical and social world around us. Our bodies mediate our environment through the senses and, conversely, extend us through gesture. This extension of the self is also noted in non-physical zones that surround us at various distances about the body. These zones show the ways our perceived and cognitive spaces overlap, supporting our identity and social interaction.

Beyond our perceived environment, our personal zones extend to the boundaries of increasingly larger territories up to the scale of nations. The zones that surround us establish levels of domination and belonging, acting as ordinates within our spatial matrix. We will see how social relations are determined by these invisible fields.

Finally we will review ways we mediate our presence, extending us beyond the boundaries of the body. This will include a discussion of user simulation and the redefinition of body language within electronic environments and will show how preconceptions of the physical body are thwarted in cyberspace. This chapter will begin a discussion of intrinsic differences between physical and mediated experience.

## Body and Mind

Perceived and cognitive images are of our own fabrication. The information we take in through our senses is not. It is useful to understand the differences between perceived and cognitive space in this regard. Perceived space is experienced bodily since its senses are in contact with the physical world. Cognitive space – more abstract – is not so encumbered with material limitations.

The cognitive, spatial matrix we develop in childhood places us at its center. Only later, as we mature, can we objectify, separating ourselves from our mental image. Yet childhood's concentric point of view is still reinforced by our senses. As we look around us, the world extends perspectively in all directions. Nearby objects seem more imminent than those far away. There is an inverse relationship between the remoteness of an event and its seeming importance.

The body is our reference for perception and cognition, it mediates between the two. Indeed, until stimuli pass through the body, we are aware of nothing external to ourselves. Conversely, any thoughts we express must be processed as voice, motion or gesture. The body accomplishes all this because it exists both in our perceived and cognitive spaces.

The presence of the body is also evident in our language and expressions. We describe many of our mental states in terms of body language. "Chin up," "grit your teeth," "shrug it off," "stiff upper lip," "grasp an idea" are used to convey states of mind. [1] This makes sense since the body is a reference we share with our listeners. In conversation we use metaphors like these as a common basis for understanding. [2]

## Orientation

Before we can fully engage a space, we have to orient ourselves within it. Just as the self was the center of our spatial matrix, our bodies are the reference in sensory space. Our body position, upright with eyes located several feet from the floor, establishes what is up versus down. The pull of gravity confirms this with the pressure of the floor on our feet. The body's orientation in the space, the direction we face, establishes front from back, right from left, helping us to locate sights and sounds.[3] Other senses come into play as the mind demands more information to build its image of the perceived space.

We are immediately aware of our scale in a new space. This is by virtue of our eyes' height from the ground, the proximity of objects seen with our binocular vision and myriad other sensory clues. We have from childhood a basic understanding of order that lets us establish relationships between objects. [4] As we learn more from the space we effectively map it into our memory. After experiencing the space we can close our eyes and imagine its contents as we might the configuration of familiar spaces.

Disorientation can affect us physically as well as psychologically. Recently launched astronauts suffer from nausea and space sickness due to sensory disorientation. Without gravity to tell

1. Fast, Julius. 1971. *Body language*. New York: Pocket Books. p.69.

2. Lakoff and Johnson, op. cit., p.18.

3. Harris, op. cit., p.90.
We assign these directions to many of our artifacts as well. Televisions, for instance, have fronts and backs because of their position and use.

4. Piaget, 1985, op. cit., p.87.

*Envisioning Cyberspace*

them up from down, they seek other cues for help. Looking out the window is no help – the curved horizon may show the ground above the sky. To make matters worse, the designers of the space module have placed the consoles peripherally around the hull, surrounding its inhabitants. Since there is no gravity and since surface area is at a premium, the designers force astronauts to reorient themselves in order to use the equipment.

The problem is that the astronaut is "lost." Having the Earth hang askew outside the window is hard enough without having your colleague float into the cabin upside down. What were originally design problems often wind up problems of hygiene. [5]

## Memory

We relate our experience to memory and culture. [6] As we draw details from our environment, we also infer information, making unconscious judgements and comparisons. Just as a child might see the shape of an animal in a cloud, so too do we compare the novel shapes of a new space to our memories. To an extent, the space is preconceived – we can't experience it without the influence of the past. Truly novel information runs the risk of being misunderstood or completely ignored. We assign to it meanings drawn from experience to guide our actions.

The risk, of course, is that such analogies are wrong or that we may miss something in the effort to mold our impressions. However, we proceed this way by default. The strategy is useful and its effectiveness only reinforces the habit. Without points of reference we are lost – and the risk of misinterpretation seems a small price to pay.

## Body Zones

Just as our body's situation in space affects our physical and perceived worlds, it also affects our cognitive space. Extending beyond the body in all directions are invisible envelopes that help us navigate the environment and negotiate social interaction. These zones are projections onto our environment. They determine levels of privacy and moderate our social behavior. [7]

### Zones of Privacy

These body zones can directly affect our comfort in a space, particularly if other people are present. While this sense of comfort is internally generated, it influences our behavior in a situation. Feeling ill at ease can make us leave, for instance. Inanimate objects that are too near will crowd us. If they are all too far away, we feel exposed. Agoraphobia and claustrophobia are our responses to this perceived space. They signal potential entrapment and vulnerability (figs. 39, 40, 41).

5. Pinker, op. cit., p.265.

6. Lakoff and Johnson, op. cit., p.57. Experience is not merely physiological. Our spatial experience is culturally conditioned. "...we experience our 'world' in such a way that our culture is already present in the very experience itself."

7. Ardrey, R. 1966. *The territorial imperative*. New York: Atheneum. pp.88-89.

Figs. 39, 40, 41
The image on the left is of an installation entitled "Alembic" by British media artist Richard Brown. The interactive floor projection shows a swarm of shapes that behaves like an organism. As viewers move around the perimeter, the swarm responds by approaching or avoiding them. It is as though it were maintaining a zone of privacy.

Alembic places the viewer into the role of an alchemist able to transform the states of matter. Abstract white noise accompanies the transformations. Images below show the swarm in different states.

Installation photograph: Douglas Cape
Sensing technology: MIT "Fish"

*How do we make these judgements? Certainly, our ability to sense scale – relating other objects to our bodies – is part of the process. Although I may hold a book to my eyes to read, I don't feel crowded by it. I know its scale and don't feel as confined as though a wall were at the same distance. Sense of appropriateness is also part of it. Standing back from something gives us an overview. Closing in on it yields specific details. If we move our bodies to effect these changes we anticipate new perspectives. We are not disoriented because we move our own bodily frame of reference.*

## Sensory Zones

*Other bodily zones are defined by our senses since our world is defined largely by their limitations. I recently experienced one as I approached a building one night. I suddenly felt warm. It was as though the building – still some thirty feet away – were radiating heat. I paused, backed away, and the sensation vanished. The wall, I discovered, faced west and the heat was residual from the recent sunset, an hour before. Though invisible to me, the infrared radiation from the building warmed me as I approached. My skin could effectively "see" the building although it was already dark outside. On a lesser scale, we sense the bodily warmth emitted by others in social or intimate settings.* [8]

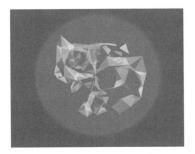

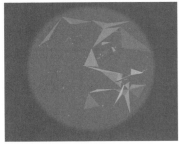

8. Hall, op. cit., p.108.

*My heat sensitivity is – unlike sight – mostly independent of orientation. I could sense the wall at that distance even if I was turned away from it. So too – to a lesser degree – is my hearing. Sadly our sense of smell is extremely limited when we consider the capabilities of many animals. Its radius of operation is fairly tight. Our scent myopia constrains its directional use to a few inches although wind-borne scents relay information from much further away. Finally, our sense of taste is confined to our tongue whose sensitivity to direction appears more tactile than otherwise.*

*I have listed these sensitivities to outline zones that extend beyond our bodies toward our perimeter of awareness. We map what lies within these zones into our perceived space – our world. Each sense defines a boundary, a space, that either surrounds us or, like sight, extends directionally from our bodies. The effectiveness of these senses depends on the stimulus. While we may have trouble reading this text at arm's reach, we can easily see a star light-years away.*

## Limits of Extension

*Our senses' limitations define us socially and psychologically. Consider our daily social interactions from a spatial standpoint. While we can sense things at a wide range of distances, human expression defines the scale of social interaction. As we have our limitations in sensing our environment, we are similarly defined by our ability to extend ourselves into it.* [9]

9. Altman, op. cit., p.54.

*Humans have a scale. Adults usually do not reach heights much beyond six feet. Our voice ranges from a whisper to a shout which is effective for two-way conversation for up to one hundred feet or so. The distances over which we communicate require different means of expression to overcome them. Normal conversation won't carry more than a dozen feet without requiring us to raise our voices. The voice we use in public speaking – unassisted by loudspeakers – carries with it an assumption of scale. We can tell from its inflections and pitch that it is meant to be heard over a considerable distance. Conversely, a whisper implies an intimacy of only a few inches.*

*Unmediated, the body forms the center of ever expanding zones that define different levels of social engagement. These zones are largely invisible although they are often delineated in room configurations and architectural designs.* [10]

10. These areas have been the subject of considerable study and I recommend to readers the books by Edward T. Hall, one of the founders of proxemics, the study of our cultural and psychological use of space.

# Body Language

*We can learn much about space from the way our body inhabits and uses it. Our body zones inform our identity and establish us in space. They may be passive, like the zones of privacy or we can activate them through motion.*

*The body shapes these spaces by orientation and manipulation. We use it for communication, situating our bodies in a group, gesturing with our hands for emphasis. Sometimes we shape the space to illustrate a point, cusping our hands to contain it or dividing it with a slash of the open hand. We enhance speech with gesture as an artist may illustrate a text.*

We also use our bodies to affect existing, physical objects to record our thoughts. While a hand gesture may only be meaningful for a moment, a painting – the record of a gesture – may be referred to repeatedly. Much of human culture is defined by such artifacts, whether they are sculpture, architecture or notes left on refrigerator doors. Even the humblest artifact tells us something about the culture that made it. Insofar as they are expressions, they are their makers' extensions into the social environment.

Artifacts – physical or otherwise – are evidence of our social nature. They manifest our thoughts and are the means by which we share knowledge with one another. Our bodies and artifacts form the bridge between experience and cognition – between our neighbors and ourselves.

## Immersion and Presence

To see these bodily zones and language in action let's imagine that we are attending a party at a friend's house. As we enter we are aware of many sensations. The room is alive with friends, loud music and conversation. We see furnishings, pictures on the walls, chairs and tables. Our senses are alert, conveying the excitement of entry. Even as we get accustomed to the situation, there is still more to take in. This on-going discovery keeps us stimulated and engaged.

For us to have these sensations the body needs to be present in the room. We could theoretically have a mechanical proxy that would do the sensing for us, but that would abstract the information, reducing it to images and reports. Instead the body has to be present in the room to appreciate its ambience. Exposure to this new environment fuels our excitement. We have invested our security in the situation, in return we enjoy new experiences. We pay for this immersion with our presence in the room.

We constantly cycle information through internal processes and their projection into the physical environment. We test the environment through speech and action, affecting further actions or eliciting responses from friends. We take in the responses, completing the cycle. This sounding and sensing process is heightened in novel situations. [11]

11. The term "cybernetics" refers to this process of sending out information, then determining actions based on feedback from the environment.

The room, its contents and my friends are all present to me just as I am to them. Because I am present in the space, I send out my own information not only for feedback, but passively with my body, clothes and orientation. My friends also send signals out into the party – some we are not even aware of. This on-going exchange excites us, propelling the party into the night.

## Body Zones and Rituals of Entry

Being social creatures, we are finely tuned to the presence of others. At the party we can see the role our bodily zones have in social interaction. While the walls and furnishings of the room are passive, the room's occupants temper the situation moment by moment. Spaces of interaction are established by body orientation, movement and proximity.

As we enter the room, the host and hostess greet us. We may get a kiss or a hug from the hostess which brings her into physical contact. Although the moment is brief, she has entered a close, intimate zone. The brevity of the embrace acknowledges this. Within this zone we are less able to focus visually on one another. We are more aware of touch, body warmth and smell. In a normal, intimate setting communication is whispered. But at the party we usually speak at a conversational level, offsetting the intimacy of the contact.

The host usually stands at a distance of between 18 to 30 inches. This is a comfortable, personal distance that conveys collegiality without intimacy. We can shake hands and our conversational level is normal for the distance. Within this zone, we still feel the pull on our eyes as we bring him into focus. But we see his face in three dimensions without the distortions — bulging noses and odd perspectives — associated with closer distances.

The host and hostess still take up a large part of our field of view, screening much of the party beyond. In approaching us they have effectively created a lobby out of their bodies that orients us and prepares us for the gathering. While we physically have entered the room, we haven't "entered" the party until we pass through this bodily foyer. The physical architecture of many buildings reflects this social choreography, providing us with vestibules and entry halls that specifically house this ritual.

As the host brings us into the room we pass in and out of others' attention. Those facing us influence us more strongly than those facing away. At a distance of roughly three to four feet we reach the limits of our personal distance. We are no longer aware of body heat and scent although we may still detect the hostess' perfume. Others at this range no longer dominate our attention. We view others spatially at this range, taking in not only eyes, ties and necklaces, but clothing and body proportions as well. At this distance we may begin to map others into our memory, creating their cognitive models for later reference.

The host introduces us to other guests, bringing us into momentary intimacy with handshakes or kisses. As conversations develop we settle at a comfortable social distance of four to seven feet. We are still engaged with others as individuals but, unlike closer proximities, this social distance brings others outside the conversation into view. Beyond this distance, up to twelve feet, we approach the limits of social space. Others tend to flatten perspectively, we can view their faces at a glance. Beyond seven or eight feet eye contact becomes increasingly important. This is in part because, to those further away from us, our bodies no longer command their vision. We are a smaller part of their perceived space and must compete with other stimuli.

## Sacred Space

As we move around the party, we are aware of physical groupings, momentary cliques formed by others in conversation. The radius of such spaces, while physically outlined by their bodies, is in fact determined by the invisible boundaries of their body zones. This space is established by the number of participants and the nature of their conversation. Since conversations usually build from a small group, the radius often expands outward, maintaining proper social distances all the while. The fluctuations of the party's dynamics produce these expanding and contracting spaces according to our self-imposed spatial constraints.

The space formed by our bodies in conversation is sacred. Barging into this space is an affront and must be compensated. There is a kind of spatial economy formed by conversants. The space between them has greater worth than the other space surrounding them. The devaluation of the space by intrusion demands some form of restitution. For this reason, we are obliged to offer an apology or, at least, an explanation. [12]

12. Goffman, Erving. 1967. *Interaction ritual.* Chicago: Aldine Publishing. pp.22-23.

Calling this space sacred is not an overstatement. Notice how when several people face the same object, how important the it suddenly becomes. As if, by orienting their bodies and gaze, the viewers elevate the status of the object.

In the course of a group discussion different participants become the center of interest. The group forms an amphitheater as the conversants interact. This spatial reorientation of focus is part of our normal exchange and is architecturally delineated in the form of theaters and churches. Whereas a conversation has a shifting focus, the stage and altars of these buildings fix our attention, exalting the speaker. Appropriately, many forms of theater have their origins in religious ceremony and recognize the sacredness of the interaction.

At distances of twelve feet or greater we have a choice of engaging or evading each other. Because of our sensory limitations, communication becomes more stylized and formal. A guest offering a toast at the party will use broader gestures and careful enunciation to cover the distance separating us. If he is raised on a platform we can take him in visually at a glance. His voice speaking to us at a distance of over twenty feet would be qualitatively different than if he were nearer.

## Territory

On a larger, territorial scale we have neighborhoods at one end of the spectrum and nations at the other. Beyond this we have more abstract entities like international alliances and cultures. We will discuss the implications of territoriality on cyberspace technology in a later chapter. However, I mention them now in the context of bodily zones because territory is their scalar and communal extension.

Territory is particularly important in the light of technology because we are usually not able to see its extent. I know roughly the outline of my neighborhood, but at no time can I see all its boundaries. I have seen maps of the United States many times and, although I am a citizen, I have never actually experienced its boundaries in the way I do my personal spaces. Nonetheless, my territoriality is evidenced by some degree of national pride. Although I can barely conceptualize its boundaries, I would feel threatened if they were violated. Even if this scale of personal space is based on abstractions of maps and technology, it is part of my extended spatial network.

Although we may find evidence for their existence through testing or behavioral observation, the bodily zones I have described are entirely psychological. They are an inference we make from information taken through the senses. Although we are usually unconscious of them, they form a part of our spatial matrix that we learn and create from childhood on.

The zones and territories lying outside the body can be seen as both sensory – as we are sensitive to their violation – and expressive if culturally shared by others in the space.[13] These zones appear to exist in the realm of our perceived space but they are actually cognitive extensions of the self beyond our physical bodies. We are invested in them more than other objects because they are part of us.

13. Ardrey, op. cit., p.158.

## Contingencies

The zones described here vary not only from one situation to the next, but also from culture to culture. My zones of privacy, based on American sensibilities, may be quite different from those of Asian or African descent. In conversation with someone from the Middle East, for instance, I may sense his proximity to be insistant – although to him it appears collegial. He, on the other hand, may interpret my pulling away as aloof and dismissive. The disparity in our acceptable distances causes confusion, affects our interaction and detracts from our exchange of information.[14]

14. Hall, op. cit., p. 145-146.

The dynamics of body language, gesture and bodily zones all influence our ability to transmit and receive information. Our impressions are a synthesis of these influences and deliberately communicated information. A line of Shakespeare delivered in an intimate setting is quite different from one spoken from the stage, for instance. Information delivered in an inappropriate setting gives it a sense of irony, for its meaning is inflected by the spatial conditions that attend it.

Finally, the zones of privacy are simultaneous and fluctuating. They are concurrent because we are conscious of our social and physical settings at the same time. I may have a conversation with a friend at a distance of several feet while my wife stands a few inches away. Each person is in an appropriate place within my spatial matrix, a fact conveyed by my ease in the situation.

The zones fluctuate, nonetheless. Orientation and movement affect them as does the fact that my attention constantly shifts. My eyes fix on many points while we speak or I may accidentally overhear another conversation. The experience of both my physical and social context is gathered from such observations moment by moment. It is only in my mind that they are assembled into a coherent perceived and, ultimately, cognitive space.

## Mediating Presence

Consider how different it would have been if we had attended our party by a mechanical proxy. While we might imagine this proxy to be a robot, it could just as easily be a teleconference call or attendance in an on-line chat room. Because the information is not directly taken in by the body, it must be preprocessed by the machine – with all the attendant interpretations – then expressed sensibly to us. We might see the image of a friend's face rendered as pixels on a video screen. His voice transmitted over the phone would also lack the richness and definition of his physical presence.

We use our mechanical extensions to give us the next best thing to being there. They mediate us. Telephone, radio, television and a host of other electronic media are our culture's way of distributing presence. One person, such as a news anchor, can be iconically present in millions of homes although he is physically present only at a remote television studio. Gazing at the screen, we are momentarily engaged, if not immersed, in the studio's environment. Neither presence nor immersion are qualitatively the same as those we experienced at the party. But this is the price we pay for mediation. [15]

When we entered the party, we radiated and had access to multi-dimensional information. Everything, gesture, sound and touch were available to all in the room. Space, physical and perceived, was the medium of transfer. It was efficient and effective to a degree unattainable by present technology. Conversely, the televised image depends upon specially fabricated technology for its transmission. Conveyed through air and wire, it can only handle a limited amount of information. The amount of information we receive electronically is referred to as bandwidth.

Costs go up with increased bandwidth. The producer of the television newscast – limited to the bandwidth of her medium – must prioritize the information. She edits the show not only in content, but in duration and views taken by the camera. The story of a kidnapping, for instance, takes priority over the position of the anchor's legs. This editing sculpts the story and determines our experience as viewers.

However, the anchor's body position may have been important. Certainly, if he had been present at the party, his legs would have been missed. One's body position makes a great deal of difference during a conversation. The wide bandwidth of physical presence affords us this information at hardly any cost. What seems superfluous to a television producer may be an important part of our societal presence. The impoverished image of the news anchor has a low quality of presence to us in our homes.[16]

However, the quality of presence improves with increased interaction between ourselves and the proxy image – if we can converse with them rather than simply absorb a script. The proxy increases in dimension as we investigate it, revealing detail with greater scrutiny. The extreme, of course, is that the image is as fluid and rich as if the other person were physically present to us.

## Digital Presence

Our presence in on-line environments is subject to the same limitations as with other media. In the interest of economizing bandwidth many environments in cyberspace are text-based. Information rendered in text has a low bandwidth, placing less demands on equipment and increasing the speed of transmission. In cases where information is passed live, as in a chat room or a multi-user domain, this speed is a great asset. The almost instantaneous transmission greatly enhances dialog on the Internet.

15. And it may not be too great a price, either. We aren't asking the news anchor to be our friend, after all. We are only interested in getting the nightly news.

16. Leaving to make a sandwich during a newscast would not be the same as walking out on a friend present in the room.

Of course, text is a limited tool for conveying presence. In chat rooms, for instance, body language and vocal inflection are screened out. Sometimes conversations are obscured by concurrent dialog of other occupants. Deprived of their bodies, users depict body language, particularly facial expressions, through emoticons, or smileys. Crafted from text symbols and punctuation, smileys are usually viewed sideways to convey amusement :-), laughter :-D, irony ;-) and a range of other expressions. They are used to temper a statement, to amuse or mollify the reader. The irony emoticon is used, for instance, to let readers know that the writer isn't serious. Here the smiley takes the place of the body since we usually offer clues with gesture or intonation to let listeners in on a joke. [17]

## Divided Attentions

Immersion and presence in on-line environments are quite different from bodily engagement with a space. Computers using a graphic user interface let users open several windows during on-line use. Using a chat room on the Internet, I could enter another chat room by simply opening another window. In doing so, I would be concurrently aware of both simulated spaces.

I would also be present to the users of both chat rooms. This is similar to being in a physical room while engaged in a phone conversation. Those in the room are aware of my physical, high-bandwidth presence, while the person at the other end of the line is only aware of my voice – a simulated presence in his ear. I am aware of both spaces, however, and can operate in each effectively.

In both the dual chat room scenario and the telephone conversation I have divided my attention between spaces. In the chat room example, I am actually present in three spaces if we include my physical location at the computer. My attention to the activities in all three spaces is distributed between them. Although I am "present" in each, my engagement with them is limited – I can't be fully involved in one space without neglecting another. My involvement in each scenario is inversely proportional to the number of spaces I engage simultaneously.

At the party we engaged only one space. We were immersed in its information-rich ambience. It had all our attention. Interactive, mediated environments, on the other hand, divide our attention between themselves and the space we occupy. Our engagement with each is limited by both bandwidth of their transmission and our distributed attentions between them. [18] At the same time others only perceive our transmitted presence – our avatars.

17. Emoticons have obvious limitations. Smileys, while representing the speaker, are still derived from cartoon images. Their usefulness seems limited more to amusing messages than serious ones. "I had a great time :-)" and "Oh, sure ;-)" are more effective because of the smiley's presence. "I just filed bankruptcy :-(" and "My dog died :-(" become ironic despite the emoticon. The scampishness of the smiley undercuts the seriousness of the statement. As a result, the smiley is a poor substitute for the physical presence of the body.

18. It is difficult to properly engage more than one space at a time unless all parties are mutually aware and engaged in a common activity, like a teleconference.

*Envisioning Cyberspace*

## User Simulation in Media

The body forms the bridge between our internal and external worlds. But we are not limited to direct sensation. Many of our artifacts are designed to extend us beyond direct experience. There are clear bodily extensions in some of our tools. A hammer extends our arm, a megaphone extends the voice, a telescope extends our vision. We use these in conjunction with the body and project our presence in clear, visible ways. Other artifacts project our presence in ways distinct from our bodies. Text and photography are arguably extensions of our voice and eyes, although the connections to the body are less obvious than with tools we use directly.

A difference between many of our electronic extensions and our physical extensions is that **we make representations of ourselves in order to convey messages electronically**. Television portrays an image of the newscaster that attends the news' delivery. Telephones convey a facsimile of my voice along with my message. The same is true of radio.

Two-way social communications often require this facsimile representation if participants are not physically present in the same space. Video and telephonic communications are products of analog communication – the message includes information about the speaker since it replicates the speaker in sound and image. Although a message could be relayed by text, telephones add value to the information by including aspects of presence – inflection, timing, response – beyond the capacity of text. The degree to which we use these facsimiles depends on the technology and the ability of others to participate in dialog. It also affects the interaction of those engaged in it.

Text can convey a complex argument or thought without the enhancement (or distraction) of other information. Yet, verbal and visual images of our conversation partner can offer detail that rounds out the message, giving it personal content that may be crucial to understanding the message itself. The avatar is useful only in that it enhances the interaction, otherwise it's superfluous. For this reason we can safely choose lower bandwidth communication – like a simple postcard – if the message requires no elaboration.

The direct connection between the representation and the user is loosened in digital and on-line environments. Rather than being a direct, analog depiction of the speaker, digital representations are more like puppets (figs. 42, 43). They often bear no resemblance, only relaying as much of the user's actual identity as intended. These representations of the user are often called avatars or personae.

Figs. 42, 43
These images are of some of the first avatars developed for use in virtual environments. They were conceived by Jaron Lanier, software developer and inventor of the term *virtual reality*. Ann Lasko created the design for the first avatar face, above. Note also that the resemblance between user and avatar was questioned even at the beginning of VR research in the early 1980s.

## Space: Metaphor vs. Medium

As information environments become more dimensionalized we rely more on sensibilities we use in analogous, physical environments. Although the quality of representation may vary, we will be able to see or create relationships using the skills we've had since childhood. This will require creating metaphoric, object-like incarnations.

Metaphors in computing have had their critics. Some have protested how the entailments of metaphors constrain innovation. Ted Nelson, creator of the hypertext concept, has argued that information objects not be tied to the behaviors of introductory models. He finds that slavish adherence to a metaphor prevents the emergence of things that are genuinely new. [19]

19. Nelson, Theodor H. 1990. "The right way to think about software design," in *The art of human-computer interface design.* ed. B. Laurel. Reading, Mass.: Addison-Wesley. pp. 237, 239.

In his foreword to this book William Mitchell mentions how automobiles were originally described as "horseless carriages." The precedent dragged on the development of cars, revealing itself in cars' configurations for several decades. If the human foot were the grounding metaphor for all vehicles, the wheel might never have been invented. Imagine the effect on car design!

The criticism is valid. Representing computation with objects taken from the physical world – files and trashcans – can easily mislead the user. The critique is against the poor use of metaphor rather than spatialization, however. Spatial presentation integrates a range of inputs into a readily accessible format. The artifacts it contains can be abstract, non-representational and unburdened by reference.

**Space is a medium, not a metaphor.** It is a tool for thought, not an iconic presence. Spatial environments on computers are no more metaphors than the space on this page. While we work with the illusion of three-dimensionality, it does not limit us to the behavior of objects in the physical world. It is a reference system, a way of viewing information.

Donald Norman, a leading researcher in human/computer interface design, believes that two principles are crucial in representing information. The Naturalness Principle states that "experiential cognition is enhanced when the properties of a representation relate to the properties of the thing represented."[20] For instance, we might select red instead of blue to symbolize heat, or the size of a symbol might indicate relative importance within a diagram. Norman's Perceptual Principle follows on this by saying that perceptual and spatial representations are to be preferred over those lacking those qualities because they are more natural and analogous to real perceptual and spatial environments.

20. Norman, 1993, op. cit., p.72.

*The simplicity of these principles belies their power. If they seem self-evident, it's because they are so profound. Since the bulk of our communication is intrapersonal, these principles define a basis for human interaction. Denying this is a disservice to computing and the design of cyberspace. The digital must be as analogic as possible for humans to make best use of it as a tool for communication.* [21]

21. Norman, 1993, op. cit., p.74.

## Cyberspace Extension

*Ultimately, cyberspace is social space. Whether the communication is direct or mediated through text or graphics, it links people. It may become a place for collective memory analogous to libraries and museums or provide a basis for distributed cognition. If the spatial medium is to succeed in cyberspace, it not only must work with how our minds assemble information, but with our bodies as well. Screens, datagloves and head-mounted displays are effective to a point – bodily sensation is not limited to direct stimulation. The intangible zones of our bodies also influence our understanding (figs. 44, 45).*

*At present, much of our computer interaction happens at the same distance, a product of our display technology. Most users sit facing a computer monitor placed some 18 inches from their eyes. All material displayed is experienced at what we socially consider an intimate distance. This gives a sense of immediacy to viewed material that is often unwarranted. The computer clock and file structure display appears equivalent to the work at hand and personal email messages. This contributes to the concern over the abuse of chat rooms and electronic bulletin board services. Dialog conducted through these media – immediate, silent and personal – seems whispered, inspiring intimacy and trust.*

*Teleconferencing has a similar problem with bodily zones and language. If several users are displayed on the screen, they never make eye contact unless special arrangements are made. Because of the screen's flatness, they all appear as head-shot images placed like postage stamps on its surface. Distance, orientation, gesture, bodily zones are all flattened into this abstraction. Body motion by one participant doesn't affect the dynamics of the situation – if he leaves the range of the camera, he simply disappears!*

*William Buxton drove this point home in a presentation at the 1996 ACM, Association for Computer Machinery Multimedia, conference. He described the typical choreography of greeting. Imagine someone approaching us. As they move toward us, they pass through a number of bodily zones before we strike up a conversation. Initially far away, they appear small – we see their entire bodies. They get larger as they come; we hear foot-*

Figs. 44, 45
Architecture professor Celine Pinet has conducted studies in which subjects determine dimensional and behavioral aspects of interiors based on virtual reality simulations. VR was effective for dimensional information, but it was difficult for participants to determine behavioral reactions to the spaces – comfort, convenience – because they needed information available only in physical immersion. Shown below are views of a waiting room in a health care clinic rendered as a virtual reality for the study.

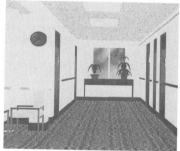

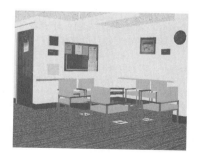

steps and recognize the face. Finally we see them up close, dominating our field of view. We can make out fine detail and hear the voice. All this time, there has been a growing anticipation of the encounter. It has occurred naturally because of our spatial and social sensibilities.

Buxton then demonstrated the effect of an audio-visual teleconference by rushing from the stage and thrusting his head within inches of a surprised audience member. It was a funny moment but it demonstrated our willingness to accept technology that violates our body zones and basic principles of human interaction.

## Defining Zones

But what **are** body zones in cyberspace? If we assume that our bodies are part of our information apparatus, what should be our requirements in the design of information environments, physical or otherwise? There is a clear need to consider these issues if cyberspace is to become an articulate medium. This need is manifested in our daily use of computers and in the use of on-line social environments. In IRC (Internet Relay Channel) chat rooms participants can enter or create their own "smaller" spaces for limited, potentially more intimate, discussion. Larger settings may be inferred from network news services in which many users participate in on-going, topic-related dialog. The most intimate communications can happen live in small chat rooms or – in an attenuated fashion – via email. At the same time the Internet is an ocean of passive information surfed with a Web browser. These conflicting scales of interaction all occur at the same distance from us, the same bodily zone of intimacy. All at roughly the distance you hold this book from your eyes.

We already see that matters of domain and territory are shaping our use of the Web. At the time of this writing, Microsoft is in litigation over practices apparently aimed at dominating access and use of the Internet. Simultaneously, the Internet, despite its "global" presence among technologically sophisticated nations is fragmented by access and cultural attitudes. The American-centric view of the Web promoted by our media is under increasing attack from other cultures.

Issues of territory and social identity are further complicated by the fact that, despite its name, the World Wide Web is not uniformly available to all nations. Third World countries – effectively invisible on the Internet – may not be able to participate or compete with those conversant with the technology. This is already a subject of public debate, but I mention it here because of its relationship to the design of cyberspace.

Territory and nationhood are abstracted extensions of our bodily zones. Since cyberspace is a cultural artifact, it is subject to principles of human behavior, expectations and interaction. The subtle influence of these principles on the Web's social spaces demonstrates their insistent power and points to the promise of an anthropic cyberspace.

So far we have seen extension and engagement from a static, concentric point of view. The body has been a receptor to the outer world, a passive conduit to our minds. Our internal spaces have been the ultimate site of action. In the next chapter we will pursue extension by looking at placement, orientation and movement in cyberspace environments. Here we will see important differences in the ways we understand physical and simulated spaces.

## *Navigating Cyberspace*

"Freed from the boundaries of time and space, I co-ordinate any and all points of the universe wherever I want them to be. My way leads toward the creation of a fresh perception of the world. Thus I explain in a new way the world unknown to you."

Dziga Vertov, 1923.
Revolutionary Soviet film director.

Fig. 46
In an installation entitled "Dialog with the Knowbotic South," Knowbotic Research transformed processed data transmissions from the Antarctic into a navigable display in Duisburg, Germany. Visitors were mentally transported to conditions far away.

*Remember back to a time you were a child, home from school, sick. Imagine lying in your bed, looking at the open door. The draft bothers you. Now imagine getting up, pulling the covers away, putting your feet on the floor. Stand, walk across the room. Shut the door.*

*Although you didn't move physically as you read this text, you were just engaged in two forms of cognitive movement. One was a dynamic manipulation of a cognitive model. We changed its perspectives in order to move us from the bed to the door. The other was more subtle. We "moved" categorically back in time to another place, our childhood bedroom. Unlike a dream sequence in the film, this was almost instantaneous and involved a reconstruction of the space. We filled in details categorically as we "looked" around the room and at the door. This kind of memory motion is similar to the instantaneous transpositions we encounter in media. The flashbacks of film, quick-cuts of television and abrupt transitions between Web pages on the Internet relocate us cognitively, if not perceptually (fig. 46).*

In this chapter we will look at how presence and motion in electronic spaces differ from those we experience in the physical world. We will look at different models of cyberspace to compare their interpretations of space and movement. In examining motion within these spaces we will distinguish between dynamic and categoric motions and how these affect our experience in different cyberspaces. Finally, I will present examples from a case study to illustrate these issues.

## Mediated Presence

Placement in cyberspace is an important issue. Where are you when you see a simulation of yourself? The short answer is that you are where your body is – the same as if there were no simulation at all. But if the simulation, or avatar, is all that another knows of you, it becomes more complex. This is especially true if the avatar mediates between yourself and another. Although I have seen Mel Gibson in a number of films, I am only familiar with the persona he projects. I know nothing about the actor himself. He could be sitting in the theater next to me, but even so the actor I know is only his representation on the screen. Where is Mel Gibson? To me, he is on the screen. To him, he is in the theater – where his body is.

This is different from live theater, of course, since the actor and his persona occupy the same point in space. In film and many other media representation takes on its own identity, changing our relationship to the person presented. This condition becomes even more complex in interactive environments mediated by computer.

In the following sections of this book we will review different kinds of existing cyberspaces for the ways we engage and navigate them. These will include computer-aided design software (CAD), dynamic computer games and, finally, multi-user domains. Each has a distinct quality of space and movement that draws on our cognition and perception. Motion in these spaces can take dynamic and categorical form, each relating to our perceived and cognitive models of space. These models of motion follow a scale of abstraction similar to the one we encountered for artifacts.

## Implicit Movement in CAD Space

Products like Autodesk's AutoCAD and Auto-Des-Sys's Form-Z give users many viewing options. In AutoCAD's case, the format sometimes defaults to giving simultaneous views: plan, elevation and in three dimensions. Designers have as many or few projections as they need to keep track of their progress. This technique, based on traditional drafting formats, lets users get views necessary for notation and documentation.

Unlike its paper-based predecessors, these views are "live." That is, if I make a change in the plan view of a house, the elevations and perspective will be simultaneously updated. The designer no longer has to erase and redraw the remaining views since each view is a rendering of information drawn from a database model otherwise invisible. Modifying elements in a view modifies the data and, consequently, all other views of it.

So where is the model itself? Certainly not in the images we see. We only see the representations of the data – views, but not the model itself. But designers have no problems unifying the views. It is as though each view showed a scene taken by a separate camera. In accommodating the illusion, the viewer has to imagine being present at various camera locations.

CAD users have a choice. If they understand the views to be abstract and unrelated, their static position in front of the display remains unchallenged. More often, though, designers understand the views synthetically and split their attention – effectively, their identity – between the views in order to better engage their work. In doing so they effect something that is not physically possible. They take multiple points of view almost simultaneously. Viewing the CAD images, they choose either to remain intact before the computer or project themselves into separate points of view of the same object.

Doing this without disorientation is part of our cultural training. Many art forms, film, painting and photography let us take disembodied points of view. Just as computer users often have several windows open simultaneously on the screen, Web users may have views of several concurrent, unrelated environments. We flick through television channels without disorientation despite the rapidly changing scenes.

In a CAD program, however, the views are of the same subject. Another crucial difference between CAD and conventional electronic media is interactivity. There is a strong relationship between the user and the object on the screen. It is present to him as he infers relationships between views. Although he is not physically displaced, he is cognitively engaged in each view of the simulation. His mental effort is the investment necessary for this engagement. The ensuing interactions only reinforce the apparent presence of the computer model.

## Orienting the User

While the body is physically static before the display, the user must find ways of identifying with the illusion beyond. If the space is filled with abstract objects, there may be no clues as to which side is up or down. Without this it is hard for the user to identify with the space presented. If the cues of gravity are left out of the simulation – as they often must be – other orientational cues have to help us. Often designers will include a ground plane in an architectural model to situate it conventionally for the viewer (figs. 47, 48). Designers may also include a directional light source indicating verticality and direction through resultant shade and shadows.

Many CAD programs incorporate assumptions about user orientation in the labeling of default views – front, top, right – and through the use of Cartesian coordinates. The Cartesian grid gives users orientation that is an abstraction of human orientation. The x and y axes in most cases indicate the ground plane, while the z axis appears to vertically penetrate it at the origin. The grid also provides reference for the task of design, offering incremental measures for locating points, allowing conversion of a design into data.

Figs. 47, 48
These studies for a dense cyberspace by Dutch artist Thomas van Putten show the use of sky, horizon and ground plane in orienting the user. Visitors see increasing complexity as they approach the ground plane. Directional lighting, as shown in the lower image, also distinguishes up from down.

Interaction and spatial assumptions vary with each CAD program. An experienced designer will eventually recognize the spatial cues offered by the software. Even so, orientation can be a problem if the interaction between the model and user is not natural and intuitive. Gesture and motion are particularly important here.

Artifacts on the screen have an ambiguous scale (fig. 49). CAD software lets users instantaneously zoom in on a scene. This has the effect of moving the viewer and the object closer together. However, as we have seen, the user gets no sense of approach aside from the sudden enlargement of the view. Since he can't properly evaluate distances on the screen, his scale with respect to the screen image is constantly in question. The gestural interaction with the object changes as well. Motion with a mouse and cursor is interpreted differently at each scale. Moving the mouse three inches can result in a screen movement of the cursor ranging from a fraction of an inch to hundreds of feet depending on the scale of view. Without some indication of scale, the user is lost.

We can recall from the previous chapter that our perception of objects – and persons – changes as we approach them. If we hold a book several feet away, we can't expect to read the text. If the same book is only inches from our eyes the text is blurred. We feel the pull on our eye muscles as we try to bring it into focus. We have a physical response to proximity and distance.

However, on the screen, all objects are in focus. A line that describes an object close up is just as clear as one much further away. Unlike our book example, we get no clues from the screen as to how near we are to the artifact. While this seems a problem endemic to screens, the same holds true for immersive virtual reality environments where focal clarity prevails.

The paradoxical effect is that, by zooming in on a view, the user seems to shrink with respect to the object. Without somatic clues of proximity – sound amplitude, focus, body warmth – the object appears to enlarge rather than approach us. Although users enter coordinates to change viewing positions, the screen objects seem to rotate and enlarge while the viewer stays put.[1]

Computer games and films overcome this problem with animation. Viewers make a "natural" transition from one scale to the next if the scene is changed gradually through panning or continuous zooms. By connecting recognizable – and therefore scalable – images together, the viewer establishes his scale with respect to the image. This kinesthetic sensibility helps us overcome the lack of physiological response as we approach virtual objects. [2]

Fig. 49
Scene from "Hypnagogue," a computer game by architect Edward Keller and artist Perry Hall. The highly detailed images in this interactive game resolves Hall's paintings to the scale of rooms, although the original works were often less than an inch across.

1. Viewing and understanding motion comes with cultural preconceptions. For example, architects are disposed to think of their CAD artifacts as stationary – like buildings. A mechanical engineer often sees the object as moveable, as though held in the hand. In CAD interaction, the architect will select right rotation to move about the object by traveling to his right. On the screen, however, the object will appear to turn to the left, approximating the views he would see as he moved. When the engineer indicates right rotation, she expects the object to move with respect to her. And the image on the screen will rotate to her right. Architects using engineering CAD packages have to overcome their trained expectations to keep from getting disoriented.

2. In many CAD packages, change of orientation and location is instantaneous. Many packages require the user to be familiar with the "body language" of interaction. What may be baffling to a novice can almost seem natural to a veteran user.

## Categoric and Dynamic Motion

Computer games provide us with many examples of simulated motion. In some it appears dynamic and fluid – changes in player direction are accompanied by changes in view. In others, motion is categoric, moving abruptly from scene to scene. In this discussion I will present three types of categoric motion: episodic, discrete and static. Dynamic motion *is experiential and perceived by the senses* while categoric motion [3] *is cognitive and imagined.*

The success of a game's illusion is a matter of image quality and, equally, of response time. We often view games with high resolution one image at a time because of the work that the computer has to do to render the next image. Action games have a faster play because their images are of low resolution. They flash by at such a rate that detail would be wasted. Slower-moving search games, like Hypnagogue or Riven, depend on high resolution for the content of the game. Such games may have no other goal than discovering the relationships between characters. The priority is detail, not speed.

Our current technology forces this trade-off. Speed and information density are inversely related. Motion in information-rich environments is jumpy as the computer struggles to keep up with the user's movements. The result is as if we walked through a space, opening our eyes only after we change location. And then only for a moment – creating a photographic still of the view. Nearly all other bodily cues have been eliminated in the effort of relaying the detail of the scene.

This episodic motion [4] of search games results from the computer's accessing graphic files. To computer users this resembles the opening of files and directories. Except, in episodic motion, the images are in spatial sequence (figs. 50, 51, 52).

The difference between this and the static motion [5] inherent to CAD is that CAD views recast the same data. CAD interactivity is also different from that of games and Internet browsers. For instance a designer can see any view (or state) of a model regardless of where he presently is (figs. 53, 54, 55). This is unlike a video game where, in most cases, movement is continuous and locations change sequentially. Contiguity from one scene to the next is important to the play of the game.

The current design of the Internet and World Wide Web makes no effort at emulating spatial continuity. It was designed as a file access system and its use is characterized by quick delivery of information through computer networks. Any illusion of spatial continuity is belied by discrete motion,[6] disjunctive contents and their often abrupt arrival (figs. 56, 57, 58).

Figs. 50, 51, 52
Related images shown in spatial sequence depict *episodic motion.*

**3. Categoric Motion**
I use the term "categoric motion" to describe the illusion of movement produced by a succession of static images or text in any medium. The images may follow in sequence, be unrelated, or simply be a reinterpretation of the same information. Different types of categoric motion include: episodic, discrete, and static motions.

**4. Episodic Motion**
A categoric motion produced by a series of sequential, related images or text. Examples: comics, film strips, pages of books, text-MUD movement. If the images of episodic motion are viewed in rapid succession, they approximate dynamic motion, as seen in film or video.

**5. Static Motion**
A categoric motion produced by images of different states of the same information. Examples: CAD model views, spreadsheets and graphs of data, changing from text to graphic mode while using a computer.

**6. Discrete Motion**
A categoric motion produced by images unrelated to one another. Examples: "surfing" the Internet, changing television channels, flipping through a catalog.

## Simultaneity and Divided Attentions

Despite their differences, the World Wide Web, CAD and many video games let viewers have a number of views simultaneously. On the Web we can open several browser windows to view a number of sites. CAD users can concurrently see an artifact from several angles within the model's space. While viewing choices in games are often limited to one at a time, CAD and Web users often have more than one vantage operating simultaneously.

The viewer can engage this multiplicity of views only by dividing his attention between them. The division is not equal at all times since the viewer can only focus on the scenes sequentially. His position with respect to the computer model – or the Internet sites – changes with his attention. Although all views are visible simultaneously, the limitations of his attention "moves" him from one viewpoint to the next.

Such ambiguities of placement, view and movement reveal the loose fit of spatial terminology on mediated environments. When the perception of the space is not unified, in a natural three-dimensional space, we must interpolate between the representations.

The fragmented images of our perceived space are integrated cognitively, much as our glances around a space are assimilated into a mental model. What is intuitive about mundane navigation becomes explicit – even awkward – in cyberspace. This tempers any expectations we might have of spatial experience in cyberspace. The simulation of motion is fraught with ambiguity. Our body sense is missing from the simulation of motion and, despite progress in force feedback systems, the very presence of the technology can distance us from the experience.

While studies have been done on human perception of space in these simulations, I know of few that explore the quality of human interaction concerning the body zones mentioned earlier. It's conceivable that simulation of these zones is possible, although it is hard to see how they would be represented. They are, after all, neither visible nor tangible.

Designers of cyberspaces should realize that using physical, perceived space as a reference is a risky undertaking. The artifacts of cyberspace are not as defined or verifiable as those in perceived space. They are symbolic and subjective – like those encountered in dreams and memory. They share many of the attributes of things we "see" in our cognitive space. While many simulations in virtual reality strive to mimic perceived reality, cybereal artifacts are ultimately extensions of our cognition – as are the computers that support them.

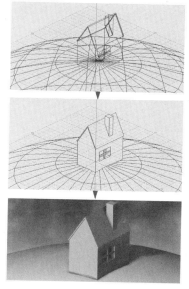

Figs. 53, 54, 55
Image sequence shows movement between states of a CAD model (wire-frame, hidden line, rendered image) – characteristic of *static motion*.

Figs. 56, 57, 58
Unrelated images shown in sequence create *discrete motion*.

## Engaging Space through Motion

*Motion is key to experiencing space, real or simulated. While we can gather information within view simply by changing focus, we are limited by our anatomy. Motion helps us gather information not available at a glance. It moves us from one space to another absorbing data and assembling the spaces mentally from various brief glances. Our cognitive model, while schematic, is in ways more complete than a static perception of the space.*

*Time-based perspective engages the computer user. But it is complicated by the fact that users are physically static while they are "moving" about in cyberspace. This is no small matter. Immersive virtual reality systems can make users nauseous – give them headaches and discomfort – because the mind tells them something their bodies don't sense. This is clearly a bigger problem in immersive three-dimensional virtual realities than it is in text-based VR. The more we ask our bodies to believe the simulation's dynamics, the greater our chance of getting nauseous. [7]*

## Representing Categoric Motion

*But if we do incorporate motion into strategies for cyberspace design, how should it be represented? The virtues of motion are clear in letting us see more and help us to think, yet what model of motion do we use in emulating space?*

*We have to ask some hard questions: What is actually moving in the simulation, the scene or the viewer? Do the spaces flow around the user or do fragments flash before him, mimicking changing points of view and attention? Do the spaces exist prior to the user entering them? Or are they quickly assembled on-the-fly, staying one step ahead of the user? Is motion experienced from the vantage of the body only, or can it be disembodied? Do any of these representations of motion prevail, or should they all apply as needed?*

*Fortunately, there are useful models for rendering the simulation of motion. Film certainly has a dynamic, almost immersive quality, moving us from place to place within a narrative. The language of film techniques is well-established. The camera often takes a disembodied point of view. In a long shot, the camera may pan or dolly – rotating and moving to follow the action. Motion can also be implied by quick cuts from one scene to another, similar to the CAD example seen earlier.*

*Fading directly from scene to scene collages the two while conveying us cognitively from one to the other. Split-screen techniques let two points of view operate simultaneously. As in our*

7. The human body has several organs for orientation with respect to gravity. Visual cues offered in VR often belie signals from these sensors and the resulting conflict often causes discomfort. Violent motions in VR compound the problem since, in addition to gravity, the body expects the forces associated with the movement.

earlier example of the CAD screen, we move from one point to the other simply by shifting our attention. More recent computer-aided special effects let one object fluidly take another shape. While morphing has seldom been used to indicate movement, it could be a useful tool if the viewer is conceived to be stationary.

Other forms of categoric motion include zooming in and out, using intermediate images or fades-to-black between scenes. These often denote a change in time or state of mind. For example, the convention for entering a dream sequence is the watery distortion of one scene fading into the next. The cinematic equivalent of teleportation – the instantaneous transition of science fiction – these techniques present cognitive rather than physical motion.

Breaks in film and video are more successful than those between Web sites because their content and rendition are consistent throughout. Story lines span the disruption with continuity, their transitions are quick, timed with the rest of the film. In contrast, getting a file on the Internet is usually a deliberate procedure. Delays in response and dissimilarities between sites reduce our engagement with the information. The interaction is flattened, bringing us back to the generic screen interface before returning to the space of the site. This quality places surfing the Internet at a higher level of abstraction than that of film (fig. 59).

## Experiencing Text-Based MUDs

Multi-user domains, MUDs, provide examples of how cognitive space and motion engage us. MUDs on the Internet number in the thousands. Though originally just role-playing games, they are increasingly used in collaborative work and research environments. With the advent of graphic, three-dimensional domains, such shared environments will become increasingly important for working and playing in cyberspace.

MUDs are largely text-based virtual realities – similar to electronic bulletin board services (BBS) and Internet Relay Chat (IRC) chat rooms. MUDs and MOOs (MUD Object Oriented) are distinct from chat rooms because using them requires taking an avatar, and moving within a matrix of imaginary rooms.

Being text-based, the contents of MUD spaces are not visible. They exist as descriptions either summoned or discovered as users go from one room to the next. The act of seeing is deliberate, not intuitive or casual. Reading descriptions of the spaces and their contents requires time. Many users, once they have read the descriptions once or twice, tend to ignore them in favor of moving quickly about the domain.

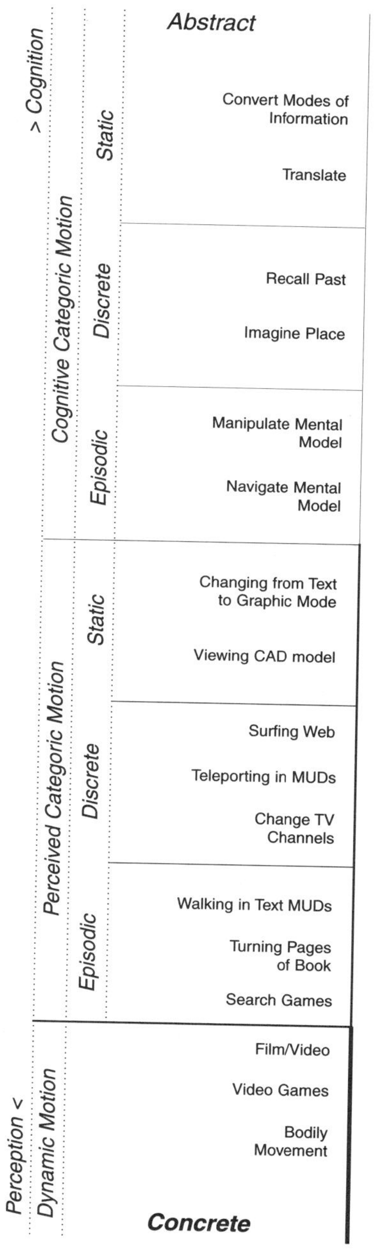

**Abstract**

*Cognitive Categoric Motion* — > Cognition

Static
- Convert Modes of Information
- Translate

Discrete
- Recall Past
- Imagine Place

Episodic
- Manipulate Mental Model
- Navigate Mental Model

*Perceived Categoric Motion*

Static
- Changing from Text to Graphic Mode
- Viewing CAD model

Discrete
- Surfing Web
- Teleporting in MUDs
- Change TV Channels

Episodic
- Walking in Text MUDs
- Turning Pages of Book
- Search Games

*Dynamic Motion* — Perception <
- Film/Video
- Video Games
- Bodily Movement

**Concrete**

Fig. 59 **Scale of Abstraction for Motion**
This diagram shows relative abstraction of the different types of motion discussed to this point.

As in film and television media, we understand mediated motion through our cognition. The same holds true with text-MUDs, except users are removed from visual engagement by the text interface. Any image of space, its contents or our motion has to be inferred from reading descriptions as we go. It is like reading a novel except that, rather than being part of a linear narrative, the user has the choice of participating in or affecting the action.

Because of the MUD's text interface, users are distanced from the action. Typing a command like, "Hello, a user will see the command on the screen followed by, "You say, 'Hello.'" The dual situation of the user – in a chair physically and in the MUD psychologically – is underscored by the screen's text. This results in the shared attention between environments we saw earlier in discussing mediated presence.

The user sees herself as a disembodied entity in the space of the MUD. In fact, she is represented by a kind of puppet, an avatar, that performs her commands. Questions of identity are further complicated by the computer's describing the avatar's actions as performed by "you." However, to other users, the action is ascribed to the avatar. Who "you" is and who the implicit "I" is illustrates the complexity of these entities, the avatar and the computer. However, once the user is acclimated to the MUD, references and identities become part of the play and result in conditions closely resembling theater. Suspension of disbelief is the price of admission.

## Movement in MUDs

The user experiences the space of the MUD episodically, room by room. Although the conceptual structure of the MUD may contain thousands of spaces, the user typically only "sees" the space she is in. "Seeing" means reading a description – usually only a few lines that outline the room's contents and configuration. Most room descriptions include a choice of exits leading to adjoining spaces. Those rooms may be named, like "Great Hall," or indicated by directions like north, east, south, west, up and down.

The user simply types in the name of a room, or one of the directions, and the description of the entered space is presented on screen. Other users will note her arrival with "Dr. Sherry arrives" or conversely "Dr. Sherry departs" from the previous room. The actions seem natural when read on the screen by users since others' presence and actions are part of the ongoing description of the room and its occupants. However, to the user, it is as if she was instantaneously transported from one space to the next.

Nearly all MUD movement results in instantaneous transposition. The movement may either be done individually by the avatar or through conveyances offered by the MUD. Visitors of MeridianMOO can use an elaborately fitted-out cruise ship, the QE2. The University of MOO includes space ships that ferry users from planet to planet. MediaMOO has an elevator that moves between the floors of MIT's MediaLab.

Each mode of transportation has its own entailments and access points. A taxicab, for instance, will deliver the user almost anywhere within a MUD, while a train only moves sequentially between stations. As the metaphors imply, these conveyances refer to conventional means of transportation, lulling the user into accepting the simulation. Engagement within the space is less based on sensory perception than on our sustaining the illusion cognitively. The cyberspace of MUDs is an extension of our cognitive space rather than our perceived space. If we were to go by perception alone, we would be limited to the text and surface of the computer screen.

Despite the elaborate spatial construct of the MUD, movement within it is highly abstract. In perceived space we move our entire sensory apparatus with us; we sense changes of light, the transition of a doorway and the subtle ritual of entry. In a text, motion is disembodied and abrupt – characteristic of Internet use. Still, once the text of the new room is read, the user re-engages the spatial illusion of the MUD.

Users engage 3D visual domains more perceptually than they do text MUDs. Spatial continuity and the user's engagement via the avatar's point of view are compelling developments in social cyberspaces. In this chapter I have focused on text MUDs in part because they have a longer history of use and because their text interface more closely resembles common methods of navigating the Internet. Although the World Wide Web lets users interact with the graphics of its Web sites, movement between them is still characterized by the implicit teleportation of MUDs.

## Relating MUDs to Other Cyberspaces

Other forms of conceptual movement hark back to our earlier discussion of CAD. Changes in orientation and focus can lead to the illusion of relocation. In the CAD interface we can take on any viewpoint discretely or simultaneously with other views. Analogously, several MUD options let users "see" objects in any space, near or far, within the domain. This is significant because the illusion of the space breaks down as the user can observe "at close hand" something that a physical equivalent of the MUD structure would prohibit. As if by uttering "polar bear" we could see the animal from anywhere on the planet. 8

8. This paradox is complicated by another feature distinctive of MUDs. Spaces within a text MUD's structure are discrete, referred to typically as rooms. Everything in a MUD occurs in a room – even outdoor activities. If, say, we were to leave a room to go "outside," we would be rewarded with a description of an outdoor setting. The description's structure is the same as that for a room in that it offers several options for exit, cardinal directions, landscape features or buildings. "Outdoors" is simply another room in the MUD's conceptual structure.

Regardless of where the user is within the MUD, she has visual access to any other space. The "look" command evokes the description of the object in question – room, avatar or otherwise. This resembles the CAD model since any view is available. However, in a MUD the user is mediated – she sits at her keyboard, her avatar stands in the room, they both "see" into a remote space. The relationship of the CAD user to his model is less complicated as there is no intermediary.

On the other hand, the MUD user only has to deal with the viewpoint of herself and the avatar. The CAD user often works with several points of view simultaneously. As we have seen, distributing attention (and identity) between viewpoints is characteristic of CAD use. To achieve a comparable effect, the MUD user would have several windows open simultaneously on the screen, accessing the domain by using an equal number of avatars. It would be a complex procedure, especially since MUDding is an on-going, social process. Paying attention to dialog encountered by each avatar and managing their responses requires quick fingers and an agile mind – an engagement that is taxing to maintain. Users who do this are obliged to let some avatars remain idle while they operate the others.

The demands put on MUD players by their space simulation is different from those of CAD users. Command lines, selection pallettes and scroll-down menus are all part of the CAD experience. The cyberspace of CAD is passive, interaction is biased toward the user. It is, after all, a tool for accomplishing work. Also, despite improvements in animation software, CAD models don't talk back.

MUDs do. And the degree of interaction increases with its complexity and the number of participants. While several views may be needed in designing an artifact, the same number would be unmanageable for a MUD user. Each would involve a commitment of attention and psychological involvement. While the CAD model attends the user's next command, MUD space is changing, evolving. Its occupants come and go, its spaces continuously emerge and dissolve.

## Moving Between States: Static Motion

Commands that move avatars from room to room keep them within the simulation of a perceived space. In MUDs, typically, commands preceded by @ take the user out of the simulation to its support system. It's like going backstage at a theater. Other kinds of software, CAD included, let users go behind the scenes, especially if the user needs to modify parts of the program. In a MUD, though, @ commands let him email other users, modify or build additions to the MUD structure or converse with MUD administrators or wizards. Using @ commands momentarily takes the user out of the simulation.

For example, @go is a movement command that transcends the need to "walk" from room to room in order to get around the MUD. Using it the user can teleport almost anywhere in the domain, provided that he has the address of the destination. Conceptually, the user leaves the simulation and, via the simulation's "backstage," re-enters the simulation at his destination.

In this scenario the user negotiates among three worlds: the physical world where he sits, the MUD simulation, and the world of the MUD's support structure – its operating system. This last level is highly abstract. In current MOO code it's more like the command-prompt interface typical of programming rather than a spatial simulation. It's conceivable that with advances in object-oriented programming techniques this environment itself could become spatial (fig. 60). Each component would be a controlling symbol for some aspect of the MUD experience. Motion of and around such objects might be coded. Coding could become ritualized in ways analogous to the precise, procedural methods of current programmers. MUD players building new spaces in the MUD could move to its support environment to do their work. This space could itself be a multi-user domain, playing a kind of Mount Olympus to the main social spaces below.

The analogy fits because @ commands endow their user with extraordinary powers. Our bodies don't participate in MUD spaces to the degree that they do actual space. The special power given with @ commands compensates somewhat for these limitations.[9]

Constructing MUD spaces and objects is accomplished with such commands as @dig and @create. Although it seems these actions should be done in the simulation itself, they are actually changes in the MUD program's support structure. Objects encountered in the support space are described in text code. They are manipulated using the MUD code's language and syntax. This support space is conceptually "between" the user and the simulation in the way an operating system is between the user and his application.

In fact, users are not usually aware of the transition to the support structure because, unless they move categorically with @go, they still appear to be in the same space of the simulation. The engagement of the support space seems magical. An administrator can appear out of nowhere to help a novice. Users can conjure things into being with nothing more than the incantations of the domain's code.

Fig. 60
Steven Pettifer and his colleagues at the Advanced Interfaces Group, Manchester University in England, have devised the interface shown above for controlling a multi-user environment. The structure at the center of the scene represents a different state of the space inhabited by the avatars – like a living diagram. Using it effects a static motion between the experienced space and its underlying structure.

9. For example: @who lets users see who is currently logged into the MUD; @go lets users teleport almost anywhere instantaneously; @paranoid yields a record of messages heard by the avatar; @sweep checks on who else might be listening to an avatar's conversation.

These illusions are much like the changes of state we experienced when we recalled our childhood bedroom. The relocation from where we were physically to where we were psychologically is a categorical motion between states. This transition is disembodied, although presence re-engages upon our arrival. It is almost as if we cease to exist momentarily in order to effect the change of state. The ease with which MUD players accept these conditions could stem from the fact that we accomplish these "magical" transitions every day. Movement from a state of perception to one of cognition is a comparable change – one that we learn as children.

The magical motion of fairy tales – flying carpets, entering dreams, magical appearances – make up the vocabulary of non-physical movement of childhood (fig. 61). These motions are possible only in a world sympathetic to the child, one in which the moon follows us from room to room. We never quite leave that world.[10] Despite our adult efforts at objectivity we are mutually invested in our environment. And to varying degrees, subjectivity underlies all our experience. While MUD users understand differences between the program state and the simulation, they quickly acclimate themselves to operation in both almost concurrently. It all begins with entering the MUD simulation from the world of Real Life.

In MUDs the connection between conventional and disembodied movement is direct. By entering these spaces as an avatar we enter a magical state – one where we have unnatural powers and the environment conspires with us. It is such a fantasy state, shared with others, that makes MUDding so appealing. It is as though the MUD were a form of communal dream or memory palace defined by words – yet experienced as space.

## Movement in Graphic Domains

Words are efficient at producing such scenarios. Given the computer programming basis for MUDding, it's reasonable that text media were used first in creating these domains. Metaphors and spatial terminology facilitate the MUD space illusion. But what happens when the domain becomes graphic? How do concepts of text MUDding apply to the visual environment? How does motion of the user change in this context? Graphic MUDs are a technical novelty and though their use is growing, their success has been mixed. Preliminary efforts such as The Palace, World Chat and AlphaWorld were disappointing for many because users missed the poetry of text MUDs.

Fig. 61
Scene from "It/I," a multi-media theater performance by Claudio Pinhanez produced at the Massachusetts Institute of Technology.

10. Piaget, 1960, op. cit., p.244.
"At first we are one with the world then, once distinct, the world is conscious and parallel to us as children. To a degree, we never quite leave this state..."

Visual MUD's schematic graphics render everything cartoon-like. The ephemerality of MUDs also argues for spaces that are dynamic – responsive to social, subjective interpretation – not fixed in a graphic image. While text-based environments have an implicit, logical structure, their use is subject to the user. Finally, movement between states is hard to convey in media other than text, though cinematic techniques seem closest to presenting it visually.

Many current graphic MUDs are also limited by technology. In order to simulate motion, the computer has to generate images that, taken in sequence, animate the action. Unlike a text MUD where motion is cognitive, in graphic MUDs users perceive motion by watching the changing scenes. Much as with video games, the realism of this motion is determined by the computer's ability to respond to the user's actions, compute the associated views and display these in quick succession via the network.

Lapses in animation – jumped scenes and jerky motion – impede the realism of the action. Users are constantly reminded of the contrivance, breaking the illusion. While they are still able to suspend disbelief, the experience is qualitatively different from that of a text MUD. The text MUD – which is more an extension of our cognitive space – has no images to conflict with (or support) users' engagement. Once they have made the leap of faith necessary to engage the text environment, the MUD makes few demands of the user. Whereas the interface for a text MUD is verbal, graphic MUDs often require control panels and mouse-operated movement in order to manipulate the avatar's speech and movement. Technology intervenes in the users' experience, forcing them to make movements unrelated to the actions of the avatars. There is only a tenuous connection between the command and the resultant action.

Movement through these graphic environments is like driving a truck. The computer – screen, keyboard and all – is a vehicle. The interface screen controls only reinforce this impression with simulated joysticks and gauges (fig. 62). Often a lot of effort is put into replicating conventional physical environments that – for all their detail – don't perform realistically. There is only a loose fit between the user's physical and simulated experience. And, too often, the veneer of realism is thin and forced.

There is so much involved in our appreciation of space and the world that any attempt to mimic it is soon overcome by greater expectations. We are finely tuned to detect subtleties of perception and, given a simulation, can easily distinguish it from its reference. This is especially true of simulations of humans.

One way to circumvent the problem is to avoid slavery to replication. The state of being on-line differs in so many ways from

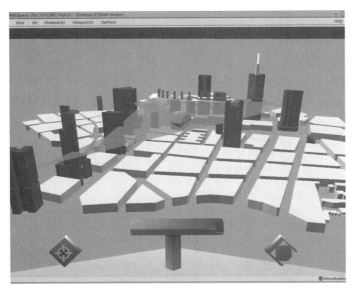

Fig. 62
German architect Bernhard Franken has built an
Internet project, Skylink Frankfurt, that connects
several existing buildings of Frankfurt into an
information network. Three-dimensional elements – a "dynanet" driven by the information
input, a "skywalk" for user addresses and a
"skystation" as help function – replace icons as
controls for navigation in the information environment.

Note also the VRML controls and joystick at the
bottom of the image. These vehicular references
and simulated controls allow dynamic navigation
of the model. The menu at the top of the screen
allows discrete navigation of the supporting computer network.

*everyday realities that it might be more fruitful to find ways to
render the conditions of cyberspace than to force upon it preconceptions taken from the perceived world. Our ability to orient ourselves in space, use it as a tool for thought, doesn't
mean that cyberspace has to be redundant with the physical
world. Mimicry is misplaced here.*

## Visualizing Categorical Motion

*A few years ago I taught a design studio at New Jersey Institute
of Technology's School of Architecture. My students addressed
some of the questions raised in this chapter.* [11] *The project
involved mapping text MUDs and designing environments that
represented spaces they encountered on-line. Whereas the
mapping of the MUDs went smoothly, the matter of rendering
the spaces proved troubling. Since the students were to make
computer animations of their experiences, they discussed many
of the issues of motion raised in this chapter. I remember these
discussions as lively, sometimes heated.*

*The issue central to "being on-line" was motion. Because infer-
ence is crucial to MUDding, each user reads the experience differently. While the text describing a room can be commonly
understood – say a chair stands in the corner near a window –
the matter of moving from room to room is more ambiguous.
Some students refused to be taken in by the illusion. They
were, after all, physically stationary regardless of what the
screen text said. Others who accepted the conceptual motion
were struck by the blindness of it – that they couldn't see the
approaching spaces. Still others questioned whether the MUD*

11. Anders, Peter. 1996. "Envisioning cyber-
space: Integrating cognitive and physical space
in architecture," in *Design computation:
Collaboration, reasoning, pedagogy.* proc. ACA-
DIA 1996 Conference: eds. P. Macintosh and F.
Ozel. Tucson, Ariz: The Association for
Computer-Aided Design in Architecture. pp. 55-
65.

existed as a coherent, consistent entity at all. Perhaps, they felt, the illusion of the MUD space was created spontaneously, on the fly, in response to the user's actions. The students took the role of a film director or a stage manager managing the structure of the MUD illusion. While CAD animations were still a novelty in architecture schools at the time, the dynamic, ephemeral quality of MUDding demanded the medium. Fades, pans, animation, morphing and other cinematic effects became commonplace by the end of the study.

These techniques specifically addressed illusions of motion – and, ultimately, being – in cyberspace. For example, fading into another scene in animation is analogous to reading the description of a space. Entering into an unknown space may be presented as though the avatar were backing into it. This conveys the unexpectedness of the new space and the blindness of the MUD experience. [12]

12. Text MUDs have an opacity owing to limitations of the interface. The average user occupies one space at a time without the sense of exterior spaces we have in the physical world. In a physical room I can look out a door or window to locate my space in a building or town. In a MUD room, I am only offered the description of the space in which my avatar stands. Information concerning adjoining spaces is often limited to memory, and terse navigational instructions.

Students joked that this opacity justified the acronym MUD. In fact, the command for creating a new room in many MUDs – specifically MOOs – is @dig. It's as though cyberspace for text MUDs, and implicitly the Internet, is solid and rooms are little voids within it – like the holes in Swiss cheese. Moving through the MUD is like tunneling from hole to hole without seeing the destination until arrival.

Smooth transitions are important to our normal spatial experience. Nearing someone from a distance builds a sense of anticipation. Entry into a building is especially gratifying if we have had a choreographed approach from the outside. This is why many traditional forms of architecture place such a high value on rituals of entry and approach. Since we can barely see beyond the ends of our noses in a text MUD, we lose the drama of larger scale experiences offered by bodily movement.

Some students interpreted motion relativistically. Rather than moving about the space, the space moved around the viewer. This reflected the actual user sitting still in a chair while manipulating the MUD environment. They created animations where the setting moved while the "sky" beyond stayed still.

In other cases morphing techniques transformed distant buildings into closer buildings, providing a dreamlike quality to the movement. Morphing is a technique used in film that averages between points in two images, effecting a magical metamorphosis from one shape to another. A dog can turn into a dinosaur with a smooth gesture. While usually we see these transformations in film, some students used the technique to subtly change shapes or perspectives of their spaces.

An extreme of this strategy was implemented by my former student, George Wharton III. He proposed that the MUD was

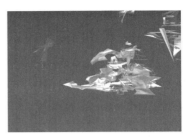

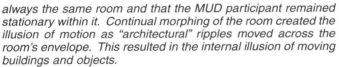

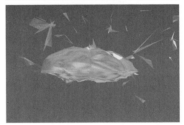

always the same room and that the MUD participant remained stationary within it. Continual morphing of the room created the illusion of motion as "architectural" ripples moved across the room's envelope. This resulted in the internal illusion of moving buildings and objects.

He designed a user interface for this motion that resembled a three-window CAD layout. The user's point of view was shown in all windows. It showed three simultaneous ways of understanding the avatar's motion. One quarter of the screen showed the movement of an avatar-point in a black void. It moved through spaces that only came into view – by illumination – when the point entered a room in the MUD. Until the avatar entered it, the space didn't exist.

The lower left of the screen presented the avatar's view – a perspectival, realistic space showing cinematic movement. The image at the right of the screen presented what the space was doing as it morphed around the avatar. Rather than having the viewer move from one space to another, he remained stationary while the space changed around him, providing the illusion of movement.

Morphing simulated motion in other ways. If, for instance, a room changes into the shape of a user's destination, a kind of non-spatial movement is achieved – somewhat like the change-of-state motion described earlier. One student, Susan Sealer, devised buildings that changed shape at the user's whim. Going from one space to another was equated with reshaping the point of departure. In another experiment, she changed the focal length of the software cameras in creating the animation.

Figs. 63, 64, 65, 66, 67
Thomas Vollaro interpreted the domain BayMOO as shards of information that would coalesce to form the rooms of the MUD. This reflected the cognitive – even solipsistic – nature of MUDs: the rooms don't exist until the user enters them and reads the text. Vollaro's animation reveals some of the subtleties of interpreting text into perceivable space.

*Envisioning Cyberspace*

By dynamically reducing the focal length, the original scene was reduced to a point. The destination scene seemed to engulf it, ultimately replacing it entirely.

Another student, Tom Vollaro, presented his MUD as an empty space filled with flying shards of data. When a user wanted to enter a space, the shards would coalesce around the user's avatar, forming the space. This resulted in a graceful ballet of fragments, shattering and reforming as the avatar moved through the MUD (figs. 63-67).

These visual equivalents of motion are not conclusive. The Wharton example shows that several points of view may coexist as the user navigates about the space. Indeed — in that example — the user is in cognitive motion between representations of the space as well as in the cognitive space of the MUD itself. How much the contrivance of the illusion is expressed depends on the designer and his intentions. For example, the overarching CAD point of view might be useful to a designer or MUD administrator, while the perspectival space might be all the typical user might need to engage the domain.

## Sensory and Cognitive Cues for Orientation

In all these projects the viewer engaged a spatial, three-dimensional illusion. Not all examples shared a horizon, but software camera positions were consistently oriented and dominant light sources were kept stationary, directed at the modeled spaces. This kept users from getting disoriented.

Without such simple cues — taken from everyday visual experience — users cannot situate themselves without using other senses. More sophisticated interfaces include sound, but in most cases sound direction is limited by the position of the loudspeaker. Orientation by touch is still under development with realistic sensation of texture and resistance still being far off. Even in purely visual simulations, the sense of proximity is crude. For example, the focal length of the software camera can affect our perception of the space and its contents. While another avatar in the same space might appear far away to you, to its user your avatar may appear close up. Mutual perceptions of social spaces would have to be standardized to approximate the readings we take for granted in our physical world.

The ease of movement between spaces can also enhance the user's engagement. Computer games that reduce their graphic content in order to increase their speed give users a strong sense of control. Responsiveness of the environment seems crucial to the success of the game. While many games present realistic space — if schematically — MUD environments leave a lot of room for interpretation.

*I stress the difference between computer games and text MUDs because games seem to be extensions of our perceived space, using illustrations of concrete environments. Text MUDs, on the other hand, appear to be extensions of a more conceptual, cognitive space where schematic models represent thoughts or memories. These are filled in by the imagination to provide a sense of engagement. Mental work is done by MUD users, they invest their attention in the space to complete it and move about within it. This is different from computer games space, where information is pre-processed and fed to them visually. In MUDs, space is cognitive and inferred. In games the space is explicit and experiential.*

# Special Issues in Designing Cyberspace

"The 'content' of human expression will be dramatically transformed as we make the shift to the digital. We are just beginning to understand how what we say and think will be different in the digital worlds of the future."

Holtzman, Steven. 1997. *Digital mosaics.* New York: Simon & Schuster. p. 12.

This chapter will describe several issues surrounding the design of cyberspaces. These include representation, methods of planning, multi-modal communication, levels of abstraction, gesture and scale. It also presents current disciplinary models for the emerging practice of cyberspace design.

At present, working on the World Wide Web hovers between the cognitive motion of MUDs – flashing from site to site – and the visual gratification of graphics and animation that still only occur on select sites. The desirability of visualizing the Web or animating its use may vary from one user to the next. However, if designers and programmers wish to tap into our natural capacity for using space as a medium, the questions of visualization, abstraction, movement and, ultimately, being become more germane. The transition of the Internet from being an entirely cognitive entity to one relying increasingly on sensory perception underscores the role spatialization can play in its development.

This chapter will discuss principles of design for an anthropic cyberspace based on the model of spatial cognition and perception presented in this book. I will use architecture – a spatial discipline – as a model for such design and critically evaluate its application as a metaphor. Finally I will briefly describe how principles from other fields may be similarly employed in designing cyberspace.

## Representation

Spatialization will be realized in various forms. Since movement is such a large part of our spatial experience, metaphors for spatial transition will be an important part of a designer's palette for on-line environments. Notions of "going on-line" and "surfing the Web" already imply the spatial, dynamic nature of networked media. But what is its perceivable equivalent? We have already seen that dynamic motion is only one of several ways movement is perceived.

An action game meets different demands than the cognitive spaces of the Web. We perceive motion in a game and judge the consequences. We infer motion from changes of state, one site to the next. Whereas motion in a game is marked by several transitional images, movement on the Web is ideally instantaneous. On the Web, motion is marked only by the scroll-bar of the browser as files are loaded to the user's machine. While motion in a game is palpable, fluid and dynamic, motion on the Web is abstract, discrete and categorical.

However, new media often lead to new forms of representation. Sensory appreciation of data is natural to us in physical and social interaction. More and more the Internet is becoming a social space. If we pair these expectations with the technical improvements of multi-media, Virtual Reality Modeling Language and live teleconferencing, the Internet will increasingly convey higher dimensions necessary for human interaction.

## Designing Experience

Computers work on numbers. The results of their efforts can be presented in nearly any imaginable way. Renderings, drawings, music, text are only a few of the possibilities. But what are these representations if they cannot be appreciated by the user? The experience of computation is justified by the user's gain from interaction. And this – plus users' expectations – shows us the importance of crafting the on-line experience. Brenda Laurel's book, The art of the human-computer interface, is aptly titled. For it is the nature of art to express our humanity through technology. This lies at the heart of technique.

The creation of cyberspaces is the product of years of research into human-computer interfaces. These have now developed to a point where artistic intentions can drive technological development, taking computation to a new, cultural level. While presently the Internet contains pockets of text and graphic virtual realities, we can foresee the growth of networks between these isolated spaces into a unifying, cultural whole. Each user may find her own interpretation of such structures, but the experience would be consistent in providing direction and orientation needed for human use.

In a previous chapter I described how a museum hosts a variety of information modes: paintings, pamphlets, sculpture and maps. The Internet is presently a collection of modes, yet the overarching metaphorical structure – the museum itself – has yet to be built. Until then, the order is not perceivable. The contents are hidden by their very quantity.

The arts present us with models for how this structure might best be expressed. Take the matter of motion, for instance.

Dance and choreography exemplify controlled, expressive bodily movement. While focused on the human body as an artifact, choreography by artists like William Forsythe also refer to geometries lying outside the body as abstract entities. The theatrical arts – and film in particular – have entire vocabularies of physical and conceptual motion. We have seen that cinema can transport us not only from place to place but from one time to the next. While film presents narrative through time-driven delivery, it is also a multimodal, spatial experience similar to that of on-line environments.

The difference between most art forms and the design of cyberspace is that cyberspaces are revealed through the actions of their users. Unlike conventional film, users of cyberspace determine the narrative of their experience. In that sense, the authorship of cyberspace is more like the planning of cities, buildings and other option-rich environments.

Many arts have some form of diagramming or planning graphic. Architecture uses bubble diagrams showing spatial relationships between components. Film uses storyboards that present the narrative of a work through text and images. We can imagine cyberspaces being planned similarly except, rather than being linear like film, they are expressed spatially like plans or models found in architecture. What is common to these diagrams is that station points are defined – a room in a building, a scene in a film, a step in a dance – and that they are connected in some way. Often, as in a flowchart diagram, the transition is shown as a line or arrow. But what is this arrow? What does it mean?

A film director choreographs our viewpoint with pans and fades. The transitions of cyberspaces must be carefully crafted as well. Whether designers take literally the spatial illusion of dynamic motion or whether objects congeal from the space around them is open to interpretation. While it is possible to mix effects, the design of the experience must convey more than just technique. The transformation itself must have meaning. A slow fade in a film has a value quite different from a quick cut. In the design of cyberspaces we can expect many kinds of perceived and cognitive movement but their choreography would be determined by an overarching unity – an art or aesthetic.

## Scenario

The simulation of movement could be used in browsing for information. Imagine that in using an Internet search engine we pull up a number of sites containing information we seek. Rather than being a list of addresses, we see them as an option-rich environment. Each site is presented as a place, an open room in a matrix of spaces. We can re-order the rooms, organizing by some parameter – order of date, authorship, or topic, for instance.

Once the spaces are set, we move among them, gathering detail as we go. Some are occupied only by text or tables of numbers. Others are fully realized spaces with their own inhabitants and visitors. We descend from our browsing altitude to enter an elaborate site filled with objects and enclosures. As our feet touch the "ground" the space comes alive, responding to our movement and attention. We may even be able to reorganize this space as we did the browsing environment.

We admire the site, but are curious about how it was designed. Upon inquiring, the space dims and we are suddenly in a featureless room with objects hovering before us. Each object has an image superimposed upon it representing a part of the space we just left. We have entered the site's planning environment. Each artifact represents a piece of the code that – when integrated with the rest – is capable of producing the object it illustrates.

If we look closely at one of these artifacts we can see within it subcomponents that let it operate – like cogs in a machine. Each of these is itself a piece of programming code rendered tangibly. Should we examine these parts we transcend the planning environment – dimming the lights once again – and view the constituent code as text.

In this example we can see how motion illustrates different navigational and organizational concepts. Reorganizing the spaces is a sorting function that visually morphs the spaces into a legible arrangement (discrete, categoric motion). Moving through the final layout is equivalent to browsing in a library or wandering through a museum (dynamic motion). This incorporates many of the sensations of physical engagement. The two incidents marked by dimming light took us to levels of increasing abstraction (static, categoric motion). Each level presented the space in the way that diagrams of relationships show layouts of buildings or the elements of a screenplay. It is as though **the levels of abstraction were only less dimensionalized versions of the original environment.** The most abstract (and paradoxically concrete!) would display the billions of bits that sustain the illusion.

Each level of transition, the morphing of spaces, the navigation of rooms, the transcendence of states, was modeled in a perceivable fashion. Some, like the dimming lights, are cues we recognize from film – analogous to closing our eyes to imagine something. Whereas the information exists as bits charged with electricity, our highest level of modeling – the perceived space – lets us review the information intuitively using skills learned in our childhood. All we experience in cyberspace is a result of numeric manipulation. But this must serve to engage the users with the information, to create or realize relationships.

## Levels of Abstraction

Gerhard Schmitt, professor of architecture at the Eldgenössische Technische Hochschule in Zurich, distinguishes the diagrammatic representation of space – "outspace" – from the immersive reality of a design called "inspace."[1] While this terminology is useful for describing extremes, with data we have many shades between. In the architecture of buildings we can easily distinguish the inspace of the actual building from the outspace of drawings and models used in its realization. With data, there may be an infinite number of representations along our scale of abstraction. What appears to be a schematic diagram is based on the same information as that of a fully rendered space. A black-and-white photographs refers to the same information as a color image – light projected onto a film surface. In a black-and-white image, however, the color information is reduced to shades of gray. Neither is wrong, they are merely different abstractions of the same information.

So it is with viewing different states of abstraction. Each has its own use. With current Internet browsers, users move from one state of a Web page to another by electing to see the text code that underlies the graphics. As similar codes become more sophisticated, they too may appear as spaces filled with interrelated objects. The precursors of this may be seen in graphic, object-oriented programs such as Visio's Smart Shapes, Strawberry Tree's products and in work done by researchers in visual programming.[2]

## Gesture and Meaning

We ritualize our actions in the very act of computing. The computer attends our needs by interpreting each of our gestures – mostly hand and mouse movements – for meaning. A hand movement in physical space might be simply to scratch the nose, but at a higher level of abstraction, the computer would interpret this as a command. Mark Lucente of IBM's T. J. Watson Research Center has developed a method of human-computer interaction based entirely on gesture and voice without hampering the user with equipment. Gesture is interpreted for meaning in ways similar to everyday communication. In the work of artist/technologist Myron Krueger, simple body gestures are interpreted by the computer to gen-

1. Keynote address by Gerhard Schmitt at ACADIA 1997 conference, Cincinnati, Ohio. October 4, 1997.

2. Davison, A., P. Otto, D. Lan-Kee. 1994. "Visual programming," in *Interacting with virtual environments*. L. McDonald and J. Vince eds. New York: Wiley Press. pp. 27-42.

erate form (figs. 68, 69, 70). But in cyberspace, gestures can mean very specific things. A gesture in one context may have quite a different meaning in another. [3]

3. Kurtenbach, G. and Eric A. Hulteen. 1990. "Gestures in human-computer communication," in *The art of human-computer interface design.* ed. B. Laurel. Reading, Mass.: Addison-Wesley. p.317.

There are many overlaps between gesture and movement. In a graphics program the mouse movement can mean a brush stroke on an image. In a computer game it moves us about. Some softwares, like SmartModel by Multi-Gen Inc., combine gesture and motion. Intended to be a virtual reality CAD program, it treats design artifacts as though they were miniature buildings. The user grabs objects from a virtual palette and

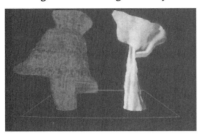

places them in a scene. As we expect in virtual reality, the interaction seems natural. But it's the programmer's concept of motion that unexpectedly ties gesture to movement.

A user of SmartModel wears a headset and datagloves. Say he wants to grab something in cyberspace and move it. He "pinches" it between index finger and thumb and moves it. If he wants to move himself, perhaps to change point of view, he pinches his middle fingers and thumbs to move the space. Effectively, he has grabbed an arbitrary pair of points in the cyberspace and, by pulling or pushing it, moves it around himself. It is as though the user were surrounded by a moveable box. At all times the user appears stationary while the space reconfigures around him. A descendant of panning and scrolling, this shows how gesture can effect changes of position as well as movement of objects.

Note also that it made a difference which fingers are used in the gesture. Using an index-finger pinch engages us with the space – letting us manipulate its objects. The middle-finger pinch treats the entire spatial matrix as a manipulable object. Some non-spatial communication has to be used – selection of specific fingers – to effect the changes. [4]

4. Minsky, Marvin. 1981. "K-lines: A theory of memory," in *Perspectives on cognitive science.* ed. D.A.Norman. Hillsdale, N.J.: Lawrence Erlbaum Associates. p.91.

## Scale and Gesture

At times our ideas appear to have a scale we can handle physically. In conversation we mold space with our hands to illustrate a point. We push, pull, slice and grab as if the air were filled with the objects of thought. These motions are relative to a stationary body, our reference for position and scale. While we all have experience handling objects, it's harder to imagine treating our spatial matrix the same way.

In our SmartModel example, the gesture takes in something much larger than the body – the very matrix that contains it. That is why the effects of middle-finger manipulation are so unexpected. As children we find it easier to imagine rotating an object in front of us than to imagine moving around it – to think of ourselves moving through spaces larger than us. In our imaginations the smaller object usually appears to move with respect to the larger. [5]

5. Harris, op. cit., p.88.

But this illusion of scale and relative motion is easily challenged in a simulation. At a movie, we may duck if we see a

projectile rushing toward us, yet we sense our own motion as the camera dollies through a scene. We assign motion to objects if they seem smaller than us. Conversely, we feel like we are moving if the objects seem larger than us. Add to this the human-scaled gestures used in computer commands and we see the complexity of working in these environments.

Figs. 68, 69, 70
Using computers and a video interface artist/researcher Myron Krueger has created several interactive pieces that reinterpret participants' movement. The images at left show a pair of avatars created by rotating profiles of two dancers. Gestures of the participants determine the resulting, dynamic video sculpture.

Not all interfaces use the same gestures for movement. Many treat space as a void and the objects within it as stationary. They let us move by using a joystick or clicking a controller. In these interfaces the user is assumed to be at a scale smaller than the environment – and implicitly subject to it. The interface can itself convey the programmer's attitude toward the user. This is not surprising since similar issues arise in non-graphic softwares as well. [6]

6. Papert, Seymour. 1980. *Mindstorms: Children, computers and powerful ideas.* New York: Basic Books. p. 35.

However, graphic software packages and emulated computer environments bring the issue to the fore. Everyone has had a lifetime of experience with space and scale. Interfaces for simulations that work closely with the user's expectations of the space tend to be more "natural." In the operation of those spaces, users will be less likely to focus on the artifact of the program and concentrate on the work at hand. The program will appear transparent to users by allying itself with their natural proclivities. [7]

7. Turkle, Sherry. 1995. *Life on the screen: Identity in the age of the Internet.* New York: Simon and Shuster. pp. 36-43.

Human-computer interface designers use the term "intuitive" to describe a good interaction with the machine. An intuitive interface is based on expectations grounded in everyday experience.[8] Donald Norman's Principle of Naturalness applies no matter how specific the application might be. [9]

8. Buxton, William A.S. 1994. "Human skills in interface design," in *Interacting with virtual environments.* McDonald, L. and Vince, J. eds. New York: Wiley Press. pp. 1-11.

9. Norman, 1993, op. cit., p. 72.

Ideally the interface disappears and we find ourselves in an environment that responds predictably to our actions. But it is one thing to say how the space behaves and another to envision what it is. In our previous discussion we have seen how much like cinema being on-line can be. Diverse points of view, disembodied motion and changes of state all are part of the cinematic experience.

## The Architecture of Cyberspace

Whereas film depicts motion, architecture contains it – plays the foil to action. It provides users with an overarching order and fixed points of reference. While in physical buildings these may reflect functional necessity – shelter and structure – in cyberspace this order can be used to orient us within an information space. This conceptual structure plays a similar role to the narrative of a film. In both cases an aesthetic continuity provides the backdrop for focal contents or events. Think of the way our museum housed its diverse contents. Large-scaled continuity acted as a framework for concentration, receding into the background while highlighting its displays.

Architecture is an applied art, responding to a program of diverse requirements not unlike the discipline of human factors design of computer interfaces. Ultimately the computer interface – like architecture – must respond to the dictates of human use. Both the products of architecture and cyberspace result from deliberate design. They each involve an aesthetic, humane response to often abstract demands.

Ritual plays a role in both kinds of space as well. The computer interface requires users to employ codified gestures to control the program. Architecture makes similar demands on its users. Its physical form requires specific movements, entry and circulation to use it effectively. Buildings often house specific rituals ranging from the sacred – cathedrals, temples, courthouses – to the profane – factories, sports facilities, parking structures. Their forms can be traced to the rituals they support.

Finally and perhaps most importantly, both cyberspace and architecture are cultural and social entities. I have stressed in this book the intrinsically human quality of space – its role in thought, communication and identity. Space, through its perceived and cognitive aspects, extends us beyond ourselves to others.

## Challenging the Metaphor

But the architectural metaphor doesn't fully encompass the qualities of cyberspace. While architecture's products (buildings) are stable and material, those of cyberspace are *evanescent and symbolic – sometimes changing even as we use them. Whereas the user of a building will probably have a similar experience as its previous occupant, each user of a cyberspace may take away a different interpretation of the space depending upon how it was used.*

*Users of cyberspaces are often complicit with the space – by deliberately selecting options – whereas architecture remains comparatively static. I may, for instance, visit a Web site and select options different from another visitor. I can even choose to see the source code underlying the pages. To have a similar experience in a building, it would have to change shape for me and, presenting the source of its design, take the form of any number of drawings or models.*

*However, of nearly all art forms, architecture comes closest to addressing our purposeful use of space – our bodily understanding of containment, restraint and definition. Works of architecture and its allied disciplines, urban planning and interior design, differ from those of the narrative arts because they contain options for users to create their own narratives. How I move through a city is only one path among many, and so my experience will be unique. High dimensional displays help us make low dimensional plans of action. The ability of architecture to simultaneously embody many alternatives closely relates to the operation of current computer networks.*

*Curiously, architectural metaphors abound in high-tech culture. Computer technology uses terms shared by construction and architecture:* firewalls, partitions, platforms, shells, modularity, design, site, windows, *even* architecture *itself. Discussions on human factors design for computers often resemble architectural discussions on ergonomics, aesthetics and function. More recently cyberspace and graphic environments have been described as "information architecture" by R. Saul Wurman,[10] a leading authority on information design – and architect as well. Various graphic designers and computer experts have described the creation of cyberspace as the contemporary equivalent to the construction of the great cathedrals of Europe.[11,12]*

*The comparison is well made, for the tradition of memory palaces possibly finds itself manifested in these structures. The simultaneous use of cathedrals to house congregations and to act as a reservoir of cultural memory points to a positive use of collective cyberspaces. The vast effort of construction, incorporating the concerted efforts of many disciplines also is reflected in the present construction of on-line environments.*

10. Wurman, R. Saul. 1996. *Information architects.* ed. Peter Bradford. Zurich: Graphis Press Corp. pp. 15-18.

11. Gelernter, op. cit., p.35.

12. Mok, op. cit., p.100.

## Designing Anthropic Cyberspace

*Unlike the world that naturally surrounds us, cyberspace and architecture are contrived by humans. Whereas nature is found, cyberspace and architecture are constructed for human use. Until fairly recently cyberspace has been devoted to the relay of text and numerical information. But the trend toward spatialization in computing implies that electronic environments themselves may become subjects for design.*

*But in cyberspace, nothing is given. The spatial experience is a conscious choice and requires an investment of effort and resources. The strategies for these spaces require us to determine their content as well as their containing spaces. Architects make many assumptions about the users of buildings: people have a certain size and weight; they can't occupy more than one point in space at a time physically; they are usually upright with their feet on the ground.*

*Cyberspace offers designers no such certainties. Users may occupy several spaces simultaneously. Orientation of the body is moot, as the body itself must be consciously rendered. Many alternatives obtain to users of these spaces, and designers must anticipate each choice, constructing the experience for consistency and grace. Further, this design must be coherent from one space to the next – one state to another. This might require designers to think like the director of a film, unifying content, movement and transition through careful design.*[13]

*In this way the architecture of cyberspace is more like the space of our dreams – one where our environment is complicit with us – anticipating our actions and responding to our states of mind. While the seemingly objective world of adulthood resists us, the illusion of cyberspace assists us. Conventional architecture of the physical world can only provide passive amenities. An architecture of cyberspace is a dynamic, changing environment that – if well conceived – attends us in our work and play.*

## Conclusion

*In discussing metaphors I have referred to several disciplines including architecture, urban planning, choreography, cinema, theater and animation. All these share the use of space to enhance our experience – they are all forms of cultural expression. As members of these disciplines increasingly use networked computation they will also influence the character of cyberspace.*

13. Norman, 1993, op. cit., pp.176-79.
Norman points out that no one representation can fulfill the needs of every user. This may also be true of the skills of interface designers.

| Quality of Cyberspace | Architecture | Music | Theater | Painting/Sculpture | Elec. Media Arts | Text & Literature | Dance | Film | Human Factors | Animation | Description |
|---|---|---|---|---|---|---|---|---|---|---|---|
| Aesthetic | • | • | • | • | • | • | • | • | • | • | Appeals to sense of beauty/poetry |
| Spatial | • |  | • | • | • |  | • | • | • | • | Uses or refers to dimensional space |
| Participatory |  |  |  |  | • |  |  |  | • |  | Active participation of audience or user |
| Ambient | • | • | • | • |  |  | • | • |  |  | Environmental, immersive |
| Presentational |  | • | • |  | • | • | • | • | • | • | Directed, aimed at specific audience |
| Multi-media | • |  | • | • | • |  | • | • | • | • | Uses more than one medium or mode |
| Functional | • |  |  |  |  | • |  |  | • |  | Serves purpose beyond expression |
| Expressive | • | • | • | • | • | • | • | • |  | • | Artistic, personal expression |
| Dynamic |  | • | • |  | • |  | • | • | • | • | Time-driven, movement |
| Active |  | • | • |  | • |  | • | • | • | • | Demands attention from audience/user |
| Passive | • |  |  | • |  | • |  |  | • |  | Serves as backdrop to audience/user |
| Cognitive | • | • | • | • | • | • | • | • | • | • | Uses symbols and abstraction |
| Perceivable | • | • | • | • | • | • | • | • | • | • | Apparent to bodily senses |
| Orientational | • |  |  |  |  | • |  |  | • |  | Helps situate or organize user |
| Interdisciplinary | • |  | • |  | • |  | • | • | • | • | Includes other disciplines in practice |

Fig. 71
This informal analysis relates design qualities of electronic environments to characteristics of existing disciplines. While not definitive, it shows how many fields can contribute to nascent principles of cyberspace design.

No single art form dominates cyberspace's development. The true nature of on-line environments is still being discovered. As it matures cyberspace will develop characteristics of its own. We must be careful in selecting our disciplinary models or we may miss out on cyberspace's true potential. But if we are willing to mix metaphors a bit – drawing on qualities taken from various disciplines – we may avoid the burdens they impose while still benefiting from their cultural past.

In the chart above (fig. 71) I have shown attributes we can associate with cyberspace and listed them along with several disciplines and art forms. This is a highly unscientific analysis – each art has examples to refute it – but I present it anyway to make a point. **Each art form has attributes that apply to the design of anthropic cyberspace.** While I have just presented a unifying role that architecture might play, other disciplines also use processes and modes of thought that can instruct us in the design of cyberspaces.

The tools for the design of cyberspace may already exist. Its designers must be conversant with methods used in several arts to create engaging information environments. While theater may serve the scripted interaction between users and the computer, animation and choreography can convey meaningful, symbolic movement. Already graphic designers, copywriters and programmers make up a large part of the online design community. It is likely that as bandwidth increases other arts will find increasing representation on the Web.

No one discipline will dominate cyberspace, instead the discipline itself will grow from those who have come from a diversity of backgrounds. Their convergence can lead to the creation of a new discipline, culturally rooted in preceding arts and technologies.

# Reprise: The Scale of Abstraction Extended to Cyberspace

"...with electricity we extend our central nervous system globally, instantly interrelating every human experience. Long accustomed to such a state in stock-market news or front page sensations, we can grasp the meaning of this new dimension more readily when it is pointed out that it is possible to "fly" unbuilt airplanes on computers...We can now, by computer, deal with complex social needs with the same architectural certainty that we previously attempted in private housing."

McLuhan, Marshall. 1964. *Understanding media.* New York: McGraw-Hill. p.311.

This chapter will present different kinds of cyberspace according to a scale of abstraction. It discusses cyberspaces' design and their capacity for embodying information. It concludes our discussion of internal, individual space and introduces the space of social interaction.

Because of the number of contributing disciplines a variety of cyberspaces have emerged. This may be a good point to address them. As with our earlier discussion on disciplines, the categories are necessarily loose. Since every day seems to bring new designs for cyberspace we will do better by addressing general categories than focusing on specifics.

We can refer to our scale of abstraction to guide us here. There are similarities between categorizing spaces and artifacts. At one extreme we have spaces that are physical and perceived by the senses – say a clearing in a forest or a canyon. At the other end we have abstract spaces – ones we have to construct from symbols, often investing our memory and cognition in the process. Imagining an "airy, sunlit room" is to conjure the image of a symbolic space. While a text may seem abstract, our interpretation of it is grounded by our experience, culture and language. Every word – airy, sunlit, room – is subjective since a room can have any number of attendant qualities.

Our scale of spaces ranges, as did our artifact scale, from the most abstract to the most concrete. While our perceived world is shared by others, our cognitive world is internal and private. And most of our waking hours are spent somewhere between these extremes. At the most abstract end of our scale we lose much of our spatialization to the conceptual languages of mathematics and internal dialog. Yet a good part of our mental activity either engages the physical world directly by perception, or by physical reference in images and metaphors.

But what does this mean when we speak of cyberspaces or electronic environments? After all, aren't all electronic signals ultimately part of our physical world? We also have to perceive output from electronic transactions to benefit from them.

Entering information into a computer also requires us to externalize our thoughts into actions that the machine can recognize. Technology may be heading toward a point where these stimuli may not need to be sensed by us at all. But for the purposes of discussion we must assume that cyberspaces are at least partially perceived by the senses and – to that extent – concrete.

We engage a video game differently from a text MUD. One is visual, dynamic, perceived. The other is cognitive, symbolic, abstract. Text MUDs may describe physical settings and occupants, but their use is social, stressing dialog over action. At an extreme MUDs have few spatial references at all, resembling BBSs and Usenet chat rooms. In our continuum of cyberspaces, BBSs and chat rooms are the most abstract, since their space is reduced to categories of privacy often without physical reference. These spaces are the most removed from perceivable spaces with text MUDs approaching them next on the scale of abstraction (fig. 72).

Graphic environments come next with the most abstract of them being two-dimensional, non-representative screen displays, like windows. As these become more representative of physical spaces – like graphic virtual realities – they appeal increasingly to our perception. The most directly representative of these would be televised images. Finally, the overlap of physical and symbolic worlds provided by augmented reality brings us near the perceivable extreme of cyberspace with perhaps only telepresence – remote controlled robots – being even more concrete.

Each of these cyberspaces could be the subject of its own book. However, I aim here to show how the range of cyberspaces parallels our range of artifacts as media. **There is no one cyberspace.** Nor is it likely that any one model of cyberspace will dominate others unless it incorporates all the previous models. The museum that houses many different representations returns as a model for an overarching cyberspace.

## Social Space and Utility

Cyberspace is a tool for communication. Whether the communication is with the machine – in a user/tool relationship – or with another person depends on its use. With user/tool instrumentality the representation of cyberspace is largely one-sided. The user sees a display of computer-generated data. Since the tool may not be intended for use by more than one person, the space generated by the machine is not a social space per se. Mediation here is solely for control purposes. The kind of space we see in most graphics programs is of this sort. Users simply employ the spatial image to help with their task.

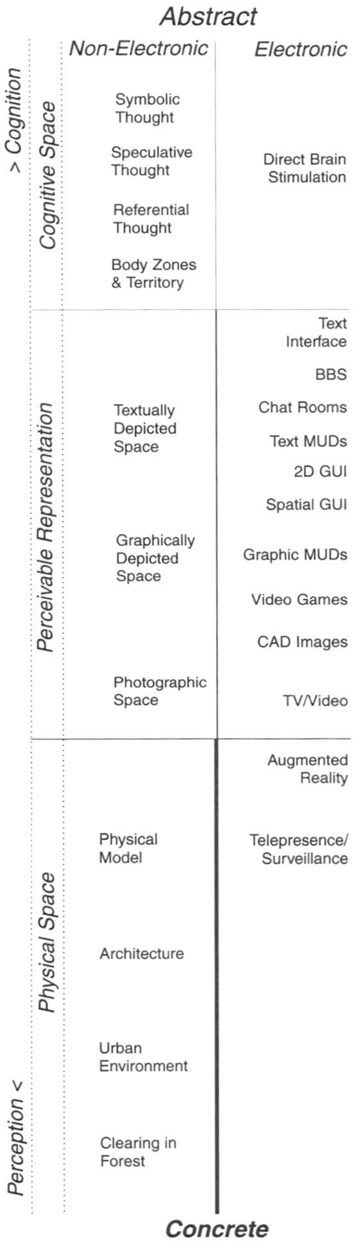

Fig. 72 **The Scale of Abstraction for Spaces** This scale shows levels of abstraction for electronic and non-electronic spaces. It relates to the previous scale for artifacts.

Conversely, software intended for conferencing and telecommunications uses spatial illusion as a conduit between parties. It becomes a shared, social environment. Tool-oriented, instrumental software may evoke social interaction through digital agents. And in some cases, networked instrumental software can be used as a medium between co-workers, though social cyberspaces are usually specifically designed for that purpose.

Distinctions between social media and instrumental software apply to our range of cyberspaces. Many of our examples, virtual and augmented realities, graphic and text environments may be used either instrumentally **or** socially. A virtual reality, for instance, could drive equipment or design a building, but it can also foster collaborations between remote parties. Conversely, a text screen can equally be a command interface or a means for sending email. With digital agents supporting instrumental softwares, we may see an overall trend toward emulated and "real" entities driving on-line interactions – effectively making all cyberspaces social environments.

This prospect has some compelling consequences. Cyberspace becomes a new, symbolic, social space. Regardless of the representation of that space – text, image or volume – it is a place of human interaction. While space is a tool for thought, the payoff for manifesting it is the creation of place. This is a grounding principle for anthropic cyberspace.

## Precedents

The media aspects of space and computation culminate in a human-based, social cyberspace. It harnesses our inherent spatial understanding with tools that extend both our perception and cognition. The traditions of disciplines like architecture and planning are precedents, for like them, the design of cyberspace is the creation of place – the context for human interaction. [1]

The design of these spaces could become an applied art with strengths drawn from many disciplines. Like theater it may be populated with human and automated actors. Like applied design, it deals with human aspiration, behavior and culture. As we have seen, film and television have already created a language for disembodied motion characteristic of existing on-line environments. The literature on cyberspace already draws from a variety of disciplines since it addresses so many of our modes of communication: sight, sound, body motion, even touch.

## Choice

Despite their apparent volume and presence, the spaces themselves are nothing but renditions of binary data. Ultimately, the choice of presentation – graphic, text, virtual reality – is deter-

1. Krueger, M. W. 1990. "Videoplace and the interface of the future," in *The art of human-computer interface design.* ed. B. Laurel. Reading, Mass.: Addison-Wesley. p.422.
"As more of our commercial and personal transactions are accomplished through computers, the quality of the experience provided by the computer interface has bearing on the quality of life itself. Therefore the aesthetics of interaction will be as important as the efficiency."

mined by users according to their needs. This is borne out in the everyday use of the Internet and softwares like AutoCAD and Microsoft's Excel. An Internet browser gives users the choice of seeing Web pages graphically or as its generating equivalent HTML code. AutoCAD lets users view drawings graphically or as a list of instructions that led to their creation. Users of accounting softwares like Microsoft Excel know their spreadsheets can be displayed as graphs, pie charts or tables depending on their needs.

User choice is an underlying principle of many softwares and we might see it as a grounding principle of an anthropic cyberspace. Altruism aside, this is also a pragmatic position. Since cyberspace is already taking a variety of forms, we will likely see a range of spatial options for viewing information. The principle of user choice would be a reasonable extension of options already available. In this scenario if one group prefers a way of viewing cyberspaces others can still see the spaces their own way. Cyberspace can contain an archipelago of world views, each valid and suited to its user.

In a previous example we discussed the choice of states that an electronic space may offer. In one state a cyberspace can convey a rich experience, while in another the same space may be only a diagrammatic structure supporting the environment's code modules. The same space could be sorted and reorganized according to any qualities the space may possess.

## Objects of Memory

Let's take a look at the relationship between a diagram and what it represents. Some designers of Web sites use architectural drawing methods for organizing Web sites. It's useful, for example, to use the third dimension as a time-line showing the site's user options. This is a kind of 3D plot of the site. However, with respect to the drafting metaphor, it's worth reviewing how architects' CAD models differ from other architectural documents. Sometimes a metaphor can be richer than we think.

As a set of architectural drawings is completed in a non-CAD project, sketches and preliminary drawings are discarded and replaced. But in the CAD process, the components of a project – column grids, exterior configuration – may be consistent throughout the design process. The earliest sketch on a computer may still be part of the final documents or model. With a model that retains its history – as CAD models do – we could theoretically view its layout in all its preliminary states. This would be (and is) all part of the final design's database.

This availability of state views is an important tool for thought, for with it we can compare different states of the same object. Although I took my example from architecture, it applies to any activity supported by computing – like threads in Usenet newsgroup discussions, for example. All postings submitted to the newsgroup are kept as an on-going log for review. By looking over this archive, participants may follow overlapping discussions going back several months. They then can revive threads that were abandoned or possibly take up an earlier part of a conversation that has since gone on to other matters. Comparing these states is similar to relating objects in space, but here the time – not the space – changes. We will return to this later when we look at computer games and MUDs.

## Space and Culture

Returning to the matter of user choice, we may ask what affects a decision. For instance, the choice of views is subject to cultural influences. Looking at art is a good way to observe the differences of spatial conception between cultures. Rudolph Arnheim, the great art historian, wrote on the differences between medieval illustration and the development of perspective during the Renaissance. A painting of a city prior to the invention of one-point perspective showed space contrived to best characterize the buildings. Often remote buildings would be shown at a size similar to ones nearby since the representation was mental – iconic – rather than perceived. Perspective, instead, unified objects into a spatial hierarchy centered on the viewer. With perspective came overriding geometries, grids and perspectival recession toward a vanishing point. This developed concurrent with the birth of modern, scientific principles and hierarchies of universal order. With perspective we can see space reborn through the eyes of the Renaissance.

Yet how different this is from the Japanese concept of Ma – the centerless space. [2] Ma's spatial order has no obvious hierarchies, looming proximities or vanishing points. Objects in the axonometric paintings of Japan do not recede into the distance, they merely occur higher on the image. Space is not an abstract entity like a Cartesian grid, instead it is the connecting interval between objects. Traditional Japanese space is a subtle network of relationships. It is never empty.

This too differs from Chinese scroll painting where the element of time is present. As a scroll is unfurled the images appear in a seamless continuum, forming a spatial narrative. Seen all at once the conflicting perspectives are more apparent. But seeing a scroll's image in sequence is similar to watching a film or viewing a large diorama. The duration between scenes is another way of establishing unseen relationships. For, like our CAD model, the scroll is a concise record of states.

2. I am grateful to Japanese performance artist Atau Tanaka for his explanation of Ma:
"Ma is what is often referred to as nothingness, empty space, silence, and the concept that such absence of material actually becomes material. So artists spend much time developing their sense of Ma – musicians to develop a sense of rest and silence – making music where they don't play, dancers in space they don't use, painters in areas they leave blank."
(personal communication)

Despite these differences, it's intriguing to see that we can still understand the art of other cultures. This may be a by-product of childhood experience shared by all people, for we recognize the content as though the artwork were speaking to us with a visual dialect.

Though it seems that consistency of representation inevitably leads to a cultural style, this is not borne out in fact. Take, for instance, early twentieth century Cubism and collage. Consistency of view and representation are not necessary for us to recognize images. [3] And this may be the great insight of these artists. For we don't see the world through one stationary eye as artists of the Renaissance would have us believe. Instead, we are in constant motion – our perception an assembly of fleeting glances and attentions. We can see in Cubism a representation of space appropriate to a time that produced scientific principles of relativity and uncertainty.

3. Norman, 1993, op. cit., p.50.

Fig. 73
Scene from "Labyrinth" a virtual environment designed by British architect Martin Rieser. Note the relationship of the screen image in the background to the avatar is the same as the avatar's is to the viewer.

## The Space Between Us

What succeeding generations will produce to characterize their time is not clear. But we can see the legacy of our century in our multivariant and fragmented cyberspaces. What order exists must be inferred or constructed – for the viewer is often left alone to navigate the seas of information.

Unlike the space of art in preceding centuries, cyberspace is not eternal. It is, after all, an entity measured in speed (megahertz) as well as content (megabytes). Nor is cyberspace a coherent world view. Instead it is a multiplicity of concurrent views of invisible information. Just as the world is invisible to us without our senses, the information underlying cyberspace cannot be seen without a determined view and presentation.

These forces of ephemerality and fragmentation vie against the potential of cyberspace as a social medium. How can we find in the self-sustaining riot of the Internet the silence necessary for coherent thought? How, with the transience of Web sites and electronic media can we have the duration and consistency needed for sustained human relationships?

To this point in the book, we have focused on the space of our thought, identity and extension into the world. We have touched on social interaction but mostly from an internal view – our perception and bodily movement. Finally in our review of cultural influence on space, we arrive at the theme of cyberspace as a social environment (fig. 73).

*Envisioning Cyberspace*

In the next section we will explore cyberspace as a social environment to see how matters of identity are affected in on-line communities. We will see how bodily space and territory translate to symbolic spaces. As cyberspaces are designed they bear their designer's understanding of his or her physical/cultural world. To varying degrees, these spaces may be appreciated as reflections of the "real" world and as illustrations of principles that transcend it. In viewing cyberspace as a social and political arena, designers of cyberspace can realize it as the connecting space – the space between us.

# Territories of the Mind

"Governments of the Industrial World...We must declare our virtual selves immune from your sovereignty, even as we continue to consent to your rule over our bodies. We will spread ourselves across the Planet so that no one can arrest our thoughts. We will create a civilization of the Mind in Cyberspace. May it be more humane and fair than the world your governments have made before."

Barlow, John Perry. 1996. From his Declaration of the Independence of Cyberspace.

"No matter where you go...there you are."

Clint Black, Country singer

Figs. 74, 75, 76, 77
Media artist Miroslaw Rogala presents alternative views of the planet from the center of Chicago in his interactive environment and CD-ROM, LOVERS LEAP. The project was a collaboration with Ford Oxaal – Mind's Eye View Perspective Software – and Ludger Hovestadt – 12D Environment.

When William Gibson, the science fiction writer and author of Neuromancer, invented cyberspace it was a cold, barren place. No one was there. Instead it was populated with building-like objects representing dominant corporations of the future. The user was mostly alone within the simulation. If he had any company at all, it meant trouble.

Gibson got his inspiration for cyberspace as he watched the players of video games in a local arcade. Though playing on separate machines, they were engaged in the same illusion – an electronic space beyond the screen. As in his books this was a hostile place filled with automated meanies. Players fought battles with machines and the avatars of other players. No wonder Gibson's cyberspace was a nightmare.

It would have been hard even for a science fiction writer to imagine the overwhelmingly social use of the World Wide Web today. The popularity of the medium has created a surging demand for Internet services and equipment. It has become an item on the national agenda, furthering aims of government, research and education. Electronic bulletin boards, IRC chat rooms, network news, email, on-line computer games and multi-user domains all attest to the Web's evolving social role.

In selecting his spatial reference, Gibson got it right. Space is one of our most innate means of engaging and managing information. It's a great model for an information environment. But we also use it to define ourselves and relate to others. Space is not empty – it's filled with relationships. If we include others, space becomes something more humane. It becomes a place. Cyberspace is a spatial – at times social – means by which we engage electronic information and each other.

Our spatial extension through sense and expression leads us to the same conclusion. The interconnection between mind, body, and our surroundings is complex and strong. Some have argued that human cognition is ecological, influenced by and complicit with its environment. It's no surprise then that spatial media invite social interaction. Space is the medium for interaction – even in the symbolic world of cyberspace.

In this section of the book we will focus on the social uses of cyberspaces, particularly those that employ spatial references. I will begin with a discussion of computer-based gaming and role-playing environments. A comparison of these will help to outline issues of identity and society implicit in electronic space. We will see how references to physicality in cyberspace often fail in ways that point to potential new tools for its design. Finally I will show how cyberspace, despite its abstract nature, reflects real issues of human behavior and territory.

Understanding cyberspace as a human/cultural phenomenon shifts the focus away from the technology and back to its users. This is more than an exercise in human factors and ergonomics. It's also not about setting rules for minimal machine performance. Instead it should be about creating a rich, stimulating space – a place worthy of our engagement. As choreography is to movement and architecture is to building, so must the design of anthropic cyberspace set the standard for our on-line social environment. The collective, good space is fundamental to civility and culture.

# Extending Politics into Cyberspace

On February 9, 1996, John Perry Barlow posted a "Declaration of Independence of Cyberspace" on the Internet. [1] This statement outlined principles of Internet use free from the interference of governments. It was addressed to the "Governments of the Industrialized World" in the wake of the signing of the United States' Telecom Reform Act of 1996. Barlow's Declaration was a defense of electronic privacy against the surveillance of authorities. The response was swift – but from an unexpected source.

The Dutch-based European Internet group, Nettime, launched a diatribe against Barlow via the Web and at a conference in Madrid in 1994, claiming that his Declaration was yet another example of American cultural imperialism. By basing his statement on the founding principles of the United States, they argued, Barlow implied that the Internet was America's technological extension. The authors further argued that prioritizing privacy characterized the "rugged individual" ideal represented by the American West. Rather, they insisted, principles of the Internet should be based on the collective good. Even if that meant that governments might have to monitor Internet activity. The authors were aware of the possible abuse of this authority yet believed that Barlow's implicitly nationalist Declaration demanded a rebuttal. [2] The response was echoed by others in the Internet community.

Although charges of imperialism seem out of place in cyberspace, a supposedly neutral frontier, they actually reflect a deeply human issue. For cyberspace is **not** neutral. Unlike nature, which mankind discovers and claims, cyberspace is carefully and deliberately created, maintained and controlled. The spatial consequence, however mediated, manifests our largest zone of identity – territory.

It may seem odd that we should meet such an earthbound word in discussing on-line environments, but it comes as no surprise to those who follow developments on the Internet. IRC chat rooms, network news, and multi-user domains all entail a degree of exclusivity. Network newsgroups, formed around mutual interests of their participants, have both following and loyalty. Outsiders are sometimes repelled by flaming, on-line hostility and arguments that polarize insiders against intruders. Invisible boundaries surround on-line environments regardless of whether these spaces are physical, permanent or even owned by their occupants. At times this resembles the intangible bubble that envelopes a party in a park or at the beach. The sheer presence of others engaged in a common activity defines the space – a place without walls.

1. Barlow, John Perry. 1996. "A Cyberspace Independence Declaration." In *ZKP2 @ 5Cyberconf, Madrid, June 1996*. D.McCarty, P.Schultz, G. Lovink, eds. Amsterdam: Nettime. pp.157-158.

2. Schultz, Pit, and Geert Lovink. 1996. "Der Anti-Barlow" in *ZKP2 @ 5Cyberconf, Madrid, June 1996*. D.McCarty, P.Schultz, G. Lovink, eds. Amsterdam: Nettime. pp.175-177.
The critical tone of this article was reflected in many of the on-line responses to the Declaration. Significantly, with the exception of this article, most of the responses were in English.

We have met this before at a smaller scale – the envelope formed by friends in conversation at the party, and our awareness of neighborhood and community boundaries. These do not properly exist in any palpable form. We can point to fences and landmarks, but the boundaries extend beyond our perception, out of sight and reach. These are spaces that exist by the common belief of their occupants and, apparently, of outsiders as well.

My former student Dana Napurano once illustrated this idea with images of a multi-user domain. The space itself was empty and black, like deep space without the stars. Hovering in the blackness were simple geometric forms that represented the avatars of users logged into the domain (fig. 78). The architecture of the MUD space was invisible and only noticed if avatars moved from place to place. If they encountered a space they would change color as they entered. For example, entering a room might change the avatar from a neutral grey to a blue.

A room was only detected by the color of its occupants. But spaces were not defined by enclosure. Instead, as the avatars approached each other in conversation, they would form constellations – the equivalent of a conversation group at a party.

Figs. 78, 79
This study by Dana Napurano shows a MUD environment defined solely by its avatars. At left, note the transition as avatars move from "outside" to "inside" the Black Sun Nightclub. As they congregate in the club they change color and form discrete, social constellations.

These constellations would take on distinguishing colors and patterns. The boundaries of the constellations were as intangible – yet as pronounced – as those of physical groups (fig. 79).

The unconfined territory of groups is an extension of our zone of privacy, a matter that depends more on cognition than perception. They are learned traits defined as much by cultural conditioning as by our bodily limitations. [3]

3. Altman, op. cit., p.67.

## Defining Territory

Size and shape of our bodily envelopes vary according to age, gender and mental condition.[4] Schizophrenic patients, for example, have comparatively larger zones of privacy than nor-

4. Altman, op. cit., p.77.

mal making them highly sensitive to the approach of others. These zones may also transfer to inanimate objects as has been shown in psychological studies of children. Asked to place a group of characters in a model space, children will place the "stranger" figure at a greater distance from their character than the "friend." That children can assign these zones of privacy to icons shows us how we perceive avatars to extend beyond their representations into the cyberspace around them. Napurano's demonstration shows how this extended presence manifests itself in a computer emulation.

But these zones are ephemeral – fluctuating and separating with the movement of individuals. In a proper sense they are not territory at all since they aren't "grounded." Once the party at the beach disperses, the sand and water may be occupied by anyone. Establishment of long-term territory requires a complicity with the environment – physical or otherwise. It requires independence from the mobile aura of our bodily zones. A brief look at nature will help us see the influence of territorial behavior and how it may be reflected in cyberspace.

## Territorial Behavior in Nature

Ethological studies of animal behavior show that permanent features of the landscape are important to animal societies. These sites maintain their aura regardless of who occupies them. In the case of the Ugandan kob – a kind of antelope – the stamping ground is a specific site reserved for the dominant male of the herd. Biologist and anthropologist Robert Ardrey describes this space as the arena – a place of ritual combat and sex. [5]

5. Ardrey, op. cit., pp.50-51.

The kob herd leader defends this space against competing males, allowing in only the females he selects for mating. Significantly, should he lose his status to a rival, the stamping ground remains unchanged except for its proprietor. It is an artifact of kob culture – independent of its occupant.

If the stamping ground of the kob exemplifies a natural (cultural?) social space, the nests of animals represent private space. Home territory is made up of the nest itself, the area immediately surrounding it and its boundaries. By definition the nest is the place of raising the young and the surrounding terrain is the protective buffer against their predators. The ferocity of its defense is less ritualized than the defense of a stamping ground but it is still part of behavior that ensures the longevity of the species.

A curious feature of territory is the strength it gives its occupant. The defender of territory rarely loses to a challenger. Reasons for this are complex, owing to what is defended and the social role of the territory itself. However, the combination of behavior and spatial position give the defender a psychic advantage during a confrontation – especially between members of the same species.[6]

6. Ardrey. op. cit., p.89.

A case for reverse-anthropomorphism would argue that human behavior is influenced by territorial instincts inherited from our animal forebears. But human behavior is more complex – if better understood – and territorial behavior is often subject to cultural and environmental conditions unique to our species. But it's not necessary to argue for reverse-anthropomorphism to see the importance of space and its role in our social behavior. The fixed landscape and its features figure in the myths and religious beliefs of nearly all cultures.

Unlike most animals, humans manipulate their landscape. We lay claim to space, marking it with fences, walls, monuments – even articles of clothing left on a chair. These personal extensions are a part of the shared cultural code that regulates our social interaction. Territory eases social stress by clarifying our roles and providing security. This extension is vital to our identity and social standing. Linking ourselves with our environment projects us into the arena of shared experience.

## Culture and Space

The influence of territoriality on culture raises many questions. How is territory linked with cultural influences on spatial thought discussed in earlier chapters? Do the principles of psychological space change from one part of the world to another? If so how can we observe this?

The art and architecture of other cultures is a good place to start looking. The disposition of parts within a sculpture or a painting can tell us much about the artist's world view. Similarly, architecture – the deliberate partitioning of space – conveys the cultural values attending its creation. The defining walls often frame, in microcosm, a cultural expression of space.

In Japanese traditional culture, for instance, the walls of a room are left unencumbered while objects generally stand free within the space. Western European and American cultures in contrast favor leaving the middle open, forcing furnishings to the periphery of the room.[7] In the Japanese model of space an object is attended by a surrounding space often much larger than itself.[8] This envelope is considered in proportioning the surroundings and the object's spatial reference to other components in the space. Japanese space is never empty, for it is filled with silent connections that dictate precise location and position. The power of a Japanese rock garden lies in this attention – the sculpting of relationships.

7. Hall, op. cit., p.50.

8. Perhaps the inanimate equivalent of our body zones?

*Envisioning Cyberspace*

The objects populating Western space have a much weaker aura. Pushing furniture against the wall prioritizes the occupant's zone of identity over the objects'. Objects at a room's boundary reinforce the perimeter – further defining the enclosure. The primary relationship in this space is between the occupant and the centrifugally located objects rather than between objects themselves as implied by Japanese design. Westerners reserve the auratic use of space for sacred objects like religious symbols or artwork in a museum.

Traditional Chinese space is not empty either. It is filled with invisible demons and dynamic, spiritual forces. The Chinese spatial tradition of feng shui stresses the precise location of objects in space to harness these energies. Objects have surrounding fields that channel or block these unseen forces to benefit the occupant of the spaces. These zones are the supernatural equivalent to the invisible zones of privacy that envelope us psychologically.

Scale is also an important element of Chinese space. Chinese rock gardens are microcosms that engage their viewers at many scales. A typical garden is small, contained and occupied by stones of grotesque complexity. The features of these intricately weathered rocks invite their viewer into a fractally smaller landscape. A rough face becomes a cliff, a hollow becomes a cave. The viewer is conveyed to other scales in a form of inner, static movement.

In the West we use miniatures and models to give us an overall perspective while maintaining accuracy of detail. However the delight in miniature is often reserved for the toys of children, or the manufacture of high-technology devices. The static motion induced by the Chinese rocks recalls the cognitive motion of memory. Indeed they resemble Victorian alcoves filled with memorabilia ready to transport their viewers to distant places and times. In our souvenirs – French for memories – we have the physical keys to our past.

## Cultural Extensions into Cyberspace

Cultural biases in space can reveal themselves in surprising ways. The cyberspace of the Internet clearly favors a demographic community that is technically literate, predominantly male and likely of American or European descent. This already slants the development of cyberspaces to favor Western interpretations of space (figs. 80, 81). Just as the earliest multi-user domains were based on fantasies of medieval Europe, newer MUDs invoke more modern – but recognizably Western – themes. AlphaWorld, a graphic MUD, is surrounded by the green lawns and mountains of the American West. Participants interested in starting their own sub-domain within the MUD

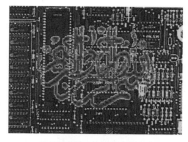

Motherboard/LawHat al-umm

Figs. 80, 81
Territoriality and culture are expressed in cyberspace, as are many other deeply ingrained human traits. Artist Amanda Steggel has produced Web sites promoting Islamic traditions as a foil to an Internet dominated by Western culture. Her project "Digital Mosque/LawHat al-umm" explores the meeting point of Arabic Islam with Western pop-culture, and challenges the concept of a uniform cyberspace. Uniform cyberspace is undermined by the presence of regional computer networks operated by indigenous populations. Steggel believes that as the borders and distances between cultures merge in cyberspace, we will see increasing opportunities for cross-pollination and non-Western expression.

have to buy "real estate." Each acre purchased represents a number of users that would have access to it. Say, if I built a MUD space of a hundred acres and the limit of users per acre was 1/1, my maximum population would be 100 visitors at a time. This would imply a specific kind of community – a low-density population distributed over a considerable area. AlphaWorld reflects a suburban model taken from the realities of California where its server is based. A player from Calcutta would likely find this space as alien as the science fiction settings also found in AlphaWorld's domain.

Despite such cultural disparity in spatialization, there is also great similarity between cultures and ethnic groups. As we have seen in previous chapters, our very physiology and cognitive development appear to unite us. Although they vary from one individual to the next, people of all cultures have invisible boundaries that define their identity and proprietorship. Whether in selecting their clothing or building walls, all peoples extend themselves into the physical environment, defining both privacy and territory.[9]

9. Altman, op. cit., p.79.

## Cultural Influence on Construction in Space

Human settlements around the world also point to uniformities between cultures. Principles of clustering, enclosure and connection are seen in African Dogon villages as well as Western cities. But the construction of communities is not just about buildings and streets. For they are the product of elaborate processes and rituals. Construction is a social act that not only creates the physical environment of a community, but unites its members in a common act.

The process of building involves many. The larger the project, the greater the number of participants and the greater the range of their skills. Building necessitates defining common goals, negotiating agreement and concerting their efforts. Because processes need to be harnessed, responsibilities are assigned and routines established. Sometimes these routines take ritual form ranging from religious rites to the elaborate codes and procedures of modern construction. We have seen that these constructive rituals are reflected in the abstract space of MUDs. Rituals consecrate the construction, validating it as a social act.

Over the past few years Wladek Fuchs, professor of architecture at the University of Detroit-Mercy, has operated a theater of on-line construction. He and his students have created a Virtual Community Network,VCNet, where students engage in the construction of a virtual neighborhood.

VCNet is not a MUD since students are not present to one another while on-line. Instead, the virtual neighborhood of the

*Envisioning Cyberspace*

network lets students place their designed buildings in an established context of streets and terrain. As in many architectural design studios, the context refers to real-world conditions and is used to evaluate the success of a proposed design.

What distinguishes VCNet is its longevity and on-going participation. Projects installed in the context model are subject to design reviews that are a conventional part of the architectural curriculum. However, these models stay in place, establishing the context for later designs (figs. 82, 83, 84).

Students who have models on VCNet learn from their experience in on-going classroom evaluations and network dialog. In this way comments, suggestions and complaints are relayed from students to designers of current work. This makes the students responsible for their work, requiring them to defend decisions or learn from their mistakes.

Figs. 82, 83, 84
Architect and professor Wladek Fuchs and his students have created VCNet, an on-line site for architectural design. Students install their projects in this shared environment and participate in on-going discussions about the design's effect on the community. Ensuing designs by other students must consider the existing conditions left by their predecessors.

This mediated ritual of construction reflects the on-going responsibility of designers to their communities. As construction is a social act, so too is the use and valuation of its product. The simulation of VCNet, even without avatar occupants, illustrates the persistence of the basic behavioral patterns influencing our world. When linked to matters of territory and control these patterns give rise to governance and politics. **The belief that cyberspace is an escape from these matters is ill conceived.** For any concerted construction – whether physical or not – is a social and political act.

## Defining Territory: The Politics of MUDs

MUDs often betray political and territorial decisions in their spatial layout. Regular, orthogonal geometries in their mappings often indicate a priori *planning by the MUD administrators. If we seek urban parallels to these environments we can find carefully structured layouts – master plans – for Washington D.C., Beijing and Karlsruhe, Germany. The looser, bifurcating structures seen in some logical adjacency models, are signs of informal, accretive growth. Examples of accretive growth form the cores of many older cities including Vienna, Istanbul and Moscow.*

*The initial decisions attending the creation of a MUD are crucial and often autocratic. The reasons are simple. MUDs usually spring from the inspiration of one or a few individuals who plan its design and operation. The chief administrator will sometimes base the initial configuration on a familiar environment. This may be the setting for a fantasy like Dungeons and Dragons or the administrator's home town.*

*The theme of a MUD may have little to do with its political structure. Both HoloMUCK and BayMOO are based on North American cities, but their political climates are quite different. Even a wizard's decision to base a MUD on his home town doesn't imply domineering control. LambdaMOO's stucture, while based on Pavel Curtis' home is now so large that few, including its wizards, know its extent and layout.*

*The crucial decision at the outset is how the MUD should be played. Is it, for instance, a given environment in which participants play defined roles – as in a video game or theater? Or is it a space built by its participants –– an idea based on human communities? MUDs usually find their balance between these extremes. The first option means that the administrator takes full responsibility for the spatial layout, theme, planning and management of the domain. Whether this is benign or overly controlled depends on its execution. However the model implies that the wizard is an artisan, like the designer of a conventional game. The players are its consumers who, aside from their participation, have little vested in the setting or its operation.*

*The second option of participatory development requires the administrator to cede control to the citizens. At its extreme, the territory of the MUD becomes the property of its community. The administrator takes the role of manager – often preferring to let the citizens handle their own affairs. LambdaMOO, for instance, makes clear that its wizards are available for advice and direction, but should not become involved in settling disputes within the community.*

*Although the administrators may delegate some operational control to the domain's citizenry, they still retain the responsibility of maintaining the technical aspects of the MUD – software and server support. Regardless of a MUD's political structure,* the domain's administrators are an inseparable part of the domain's operation and social structure.

How administrators play their social role varies with the domain. The default title, wizard, recalls the Dungeons and Dragons origins of MUDding. In most MUDs, the wizard sits at the top of the political hierarchy. In the more democratic MUDs, administrators forego aggrandizing titles, preferring more neutral labels. Amy Bruckman, director of MediaMOO, refers to herself as its janitor, for instance. At the other extreme, labels such as God and Supreme Being are also in use – one hopes jokingly.

As the more ambitious titles imply, wizards have at their command powers unique to their position. Beyond their role in creating and maintaining the MUD, they variously grant membership, administer policy and monitor MUD activity. They also bequeath power and resources – the currency of the domain.

## Status and Social Structure

Though role-playing is the overt activity in many MUDs, they still retain some competitiveness from their gaming predecessors. The equivalent of racking up points in a video game is gaining power in the MUD community. If for this reason alone, the administrators retain their stature, for often they decide how the MUD's wealth is distributed.

Prestige within MUDs is attained by accumulation of powers, memory resources and, sometimes, title. Powers are the computer commands available to a user. At times these are given as gifts by friends or granted by an administrator. Such commands let their users create new objects, see information unavailable to others, monitor MUD activities and remove other players from the MUD space. The powers range from the harmless to the menacing. One – a nasty bit of programming – lets you take control over another's avatar. This trick, called creating a voodoo doll, was at the heart of a notorious incident in LambdaMOO when a character named Mr. Bungle appeared to force sex on an involuntary avatar. Charges of virtual rape were pressed on Mr. Bungle's owner who was later expelled from the domain. [10]

10. Turkle, op. cit., pp. 251-253.

Resources are another sign of status in a domain. Sometimes measured in dollars or credits, they let users build new objects and rooms in a MUD. Since the entire domain resides on a server, there is a finite amount of memory available for its operation. Computer memory is the finite resource and substance of the MUD, an updated memory palace.

The limited supply of memory and the implicit stature of the wizards unavoidably sets up a social hierarchy ranging from the novice to the administrator. This countervails against the efforts of many social MUDs striving for democratic and distributed leadership. Though councils and advisory panels are common in such domains, the hierarchy of titles reflect degrees of mastery and social stature that often stratify MUD societies.

## Avatar/Citizen

Guests who log into a MUD for a visit are lent an avatar for the duration of their stay. These avatars are neutral – often named by number or color. Guest's powers are usually limited to movement and conversation within the MUD, but this varies from one domain to another. [11]

The guest's status is reflected in the default name of his avatar, unlike the citizens of the community, making it obvious who the visitors are. Guests and their avatars have no relationship beyond the stay of the visit. Red Guest, for instance, may be the avatar for several players in the course of a few days, much like the avatars of more conventional video and computer games. We will return to this later in our discussion of MUD communities.

Once a petitioner has been accepted by the MUD administration, she becomes a citizen with rights to maintain an avatar, basic powers and resources. Because in many cases the player is unknown to the rest of the community, citizens have only the status they are assigned in the domain. This has a socially leveling effect on the players. At the point that a player achieves citizenship, she plays two roles: the character role of her avatar and the social role of citizen of the domain.

Depending on the MUD, once the player acquires enough resources and powers she may construct objects and dig rooms. This may involve petitioning administrators for building privileges, asking owners of other spaces for the right to link new spaces to theirs and subjecting their construction to an approvals process. This process parallels the rituals of construction in the physical world.

In some MUDs this ability is conferred with the rank of "builder." As the player becomes more skilled and recognized within the community, she may rise to the level of wizard, taking on responses delegated by the MUD administration.

## Conclusion

On-line societies are filled with paradox and contradiction. MUDs are symbolic – many have no reference to an actual, physical counterpart. And yet they are grounded in spatial references to rooms, objects and personae. They present a kind

11. Social status of visitors is low and only allows access to public areas of the MUD. Other spaces may be inaccessible or even invisible. Sometimes, as in the MUD Diversity University, a visitor may see nothing in a space that citizens view as occupied with avatars and objects. The ability to "see" in a MUD is an attribute of power.

of reality – at times graphic and three-dimensional – although the spaces and occupants are manifestations of computer code. A MUD may appear to be an egalitarian, democratic system, but behind the scenes priori decisions, unseen support systems and administrators belie this.

Aspects of MUDding itself appear to contradict one another. Though free of physical constraints, cyberspace is bound by the laws of human behavior, aspirations and limitations. In it we are free to imagine ourselves to fly or disappear, yet we must still invest ourselves in the MUD society to yield its benefits. We may be like gods – conjuring palaces from the air – yet we must compete with others for resources and the approval of administrating wizards. The image of cyberspace as an escape from human reality is itself an illusion. For though it is not a physical space, cyberspace remains a human one.

I have dwelt on the territory and politics of MUDs in part to explain the complex nature of life on-line, but also because their social spaces are the culmination of the many types of space we have encountered this far. Piaget believed that the child creates the world. Taking available cues and native skills the child constructs his realities, a process that undergoes many changes in the course of his growth. As an adult, he physically builds the world, manifesting cognition into perceivable works, works to be shared with others. **Our outer world is a reflection of the world within.**

## Rituals of Construction

But the creation of this outer world is the result of iterative and concerted efforts. It requires communication and collaboration. Construction of material, social space is marked by ritual – the coordination of forces and resources, the creation and execution of plans. In the real world, this is a way of gathering strength, assembling for a common goal. We celebrate laying cornerstones, cutting ribbons, and the first shovel of dirt dug from the ground. Ritual includes the mundane processes of development, signing contracts, application and granting of permits, the phases of design and choreography of construction. Ritual consecrates construction – the building of our world.

It's as though the artifacts we build – our walls and structures – not only mark our gathering but commemorate the social effort of their construction. And this is what makes social spaces so special. **They are products of our investment.** Time, material and human toil have gone into their creation. For the builder to leave his construction is to leave a part of himself behind. And perhaps this is why we use ritual to mark construction. It celebrates not only the individual's accomplishment, but his sacrifice as well. The following example demonstrates that this investment is real enough – even in cyberspace.

Metaverse, a MUD developed for profit, had an elaborate structure yet couldn't develop enough of a following to sustain itself. Finally its administration closed down its operation, putting its server to another use. The citizens were left to wander the domains of cyberspace, looking for a new home. Several found their way to DreaMOO.

A few years ago my students discovered some of them reminiscing about Metaverse in the back rooms of DreaMOO. There was a sense of loss and nostalgia for their old home, a place many had contributed to through their participation and construction. Reformatting Metaverse's server erased not only the computer's memory of the domain, but the common past of its community. Clearly more than data was lost.

The next two chapters will examine social structures of multi-user environments, computer games and MUDs. As electronic simulations, these social environments accommodate not only the user and the machine, but their respective incarnations – avatars and agents. We will find that the relationships between participants and their incarnations belie the realism of the simulation in surprising ways.

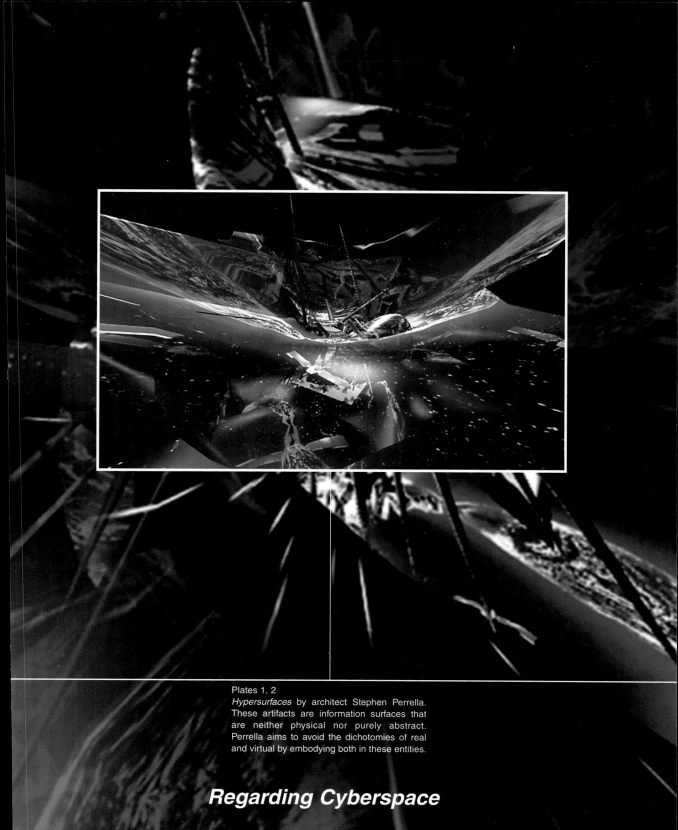

Plates 1, 2
*Hypersurfaces* by architect Stephen Perrella.
These artifacts are information surfaces that
are neither physical nor purely abstract.
Perrella aims to avoid the dichotomies of real
and virtual by embodying both in these entities.

## *Regarding Cyberspace*

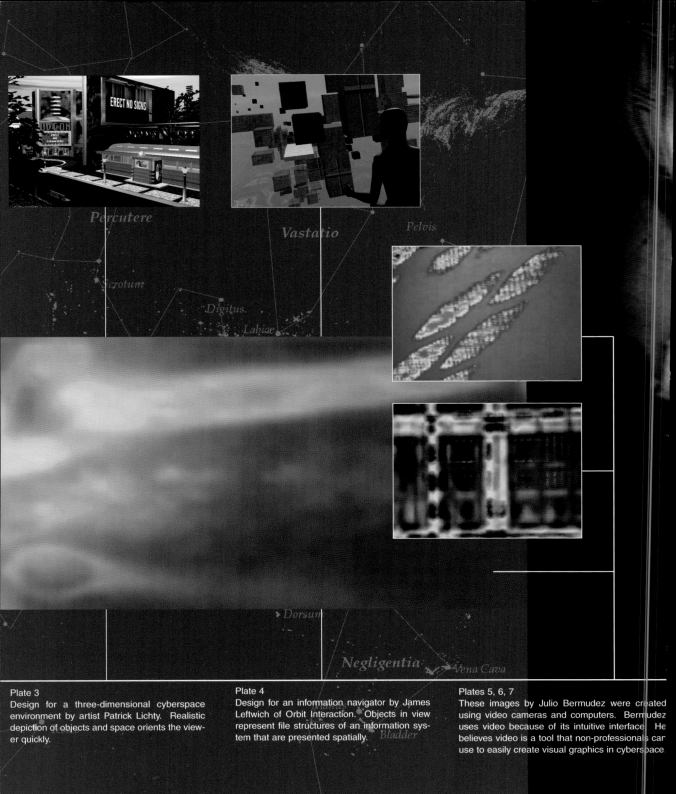

Plate 3
Design for a three-dimensional cyberspace environment by artist Patrick Lichty. Realistic depiction of objects and space orients the viewer quickly.

Plate 4
Design for an information navigator by James Leftwich of Orbit Interaction. Objects in view represent file structures of an information system that are presented spatially.

Plates 5, 6, 7
These images by Julio Bermudez were created using video cameras and computers. Bermudez uses video because of its intuitive interface. He believes video is a tool that non-professionals can use to easily create visual graphics in cyberspace.

*Distinctions between the real and the virtual vanish when we realize that what we take*

Plates 8, 9, 10
This installation, "Displaced Emperors," by the artists Rafael Lozano-Hemmer, Will Bauer and Susan Ramsay transforms the Habsburg Castle in Linz, Austria. Wireless 3D sensors calculate where participants point to on the facade and a large animated projection of a hand is shown at that location. As people on the street "caress" the building, they reveal its interiors, which correspond to Chapultepec Castle, the Habsburg residence in Mexico City.

*to be reality is, itself, mentally constructed. The space that appears to surround us*

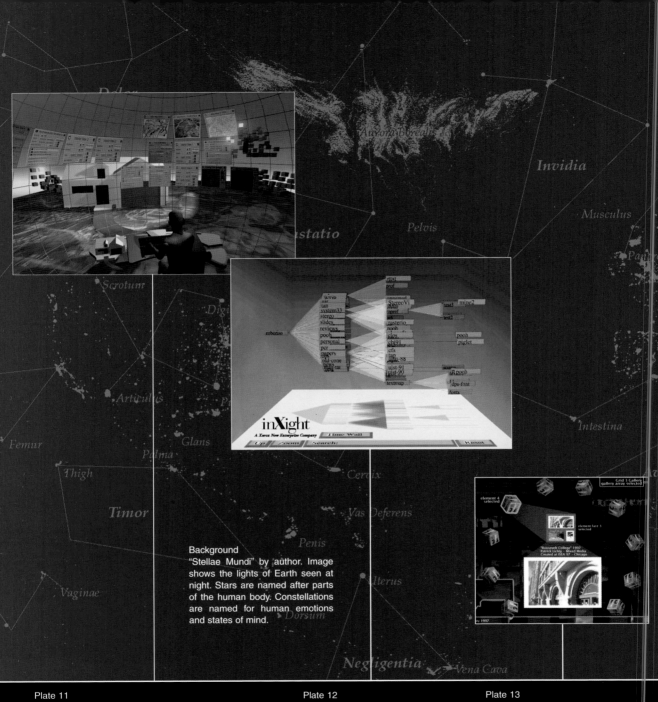

Background
"Stellae Mundi" by author. Image shows the lights of Earth seen at night. Stars are named after parts of the human body. Constellations are named for human emotions and states of mind.

**Plate 11**
This interface by James Leftwich, I.D.S.A, of Orbit Interaction shows several references to physical reality. The house and its site are an architectural model. The spherical scrim only supports tools that the designer uses in his work. The sphere has no link to a physical reality like the model beyond.

Image credit: James Leftwich and Max Sims,Technolution

**Plate 12**
Three-dimensional computer interface by InXight Corporation. Each component of a carousel can open to disclose its file's contents.

**Plate 13**
Interface by Patrick Lichty showing cubic objects whose faces store information. Each face of a cube reveals stored graphics when viewed frontally.

*is a sophisticated, innate format for handling information taken in by the senses o*

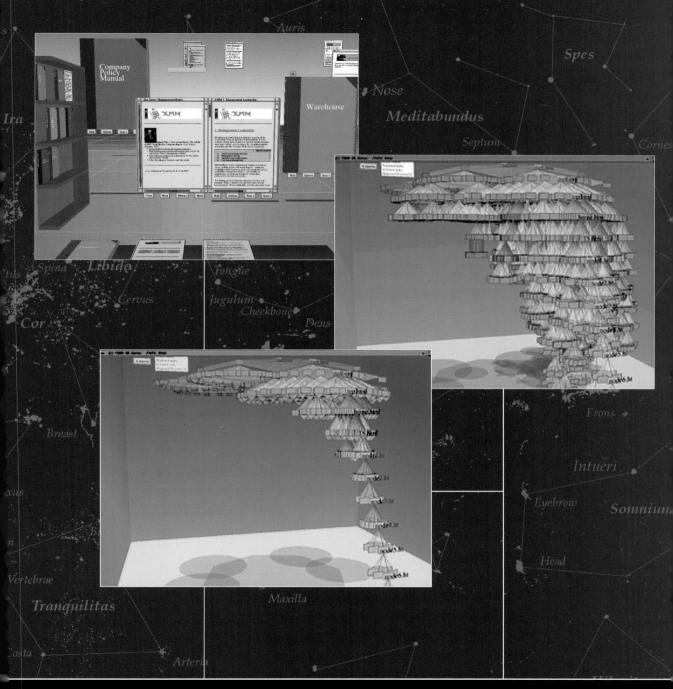

Plate 14
This computer interface designed by Stuart Card, George Robertson and Bill York at Xerox PARC depicts a cyberspace with manipulable objects. Books on shelves may be opened to reveal their contents. Unused documents hover in the background until the user selects them for review.

Plates 15, 16
This interface also by Stuart Card and Bill York is called a *Fish Eye Cone Tree*. The image on the right shows a partial structure of corporate intranet. The Fish Eye version, at left, only shows the portion of interest to the user.

*generated by thought and memory... Our bodies convey the external world to us*

**Plates 17, 18**
This blimp by artist Eric Paulos bears a small video camera that transmits images to a remote location. The user operates the small propellors of the blimp by remote control. The blimp is an example of telepresent surveillance in which the operator is only present to others through the proxy of the blimp.

**Plates 19, 20, 21**
These images show surgery on a breast tumor using an augmented reality interface. The red portion of the images is a virtual hole in the breast while the small rectangle is a live scan image of the tumor. This interface was developed at the University of North Carolina Department of Computer Science.

*through our senses. Reciprocally, our thoughts extend to the outside world via*

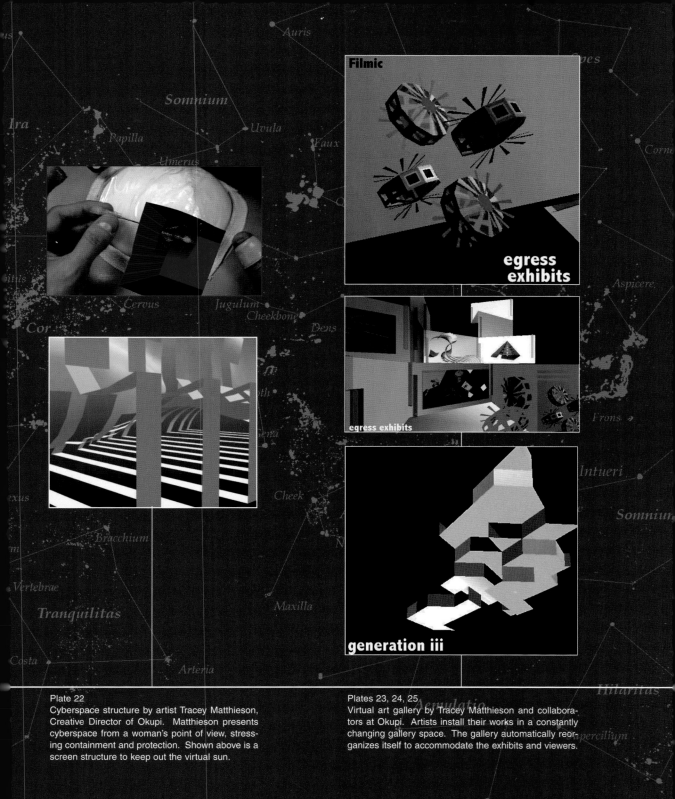

**Filmic**

**egress
exhibits**

egress exhibits

**generation iii**

Plate 22
Cyberspace structure by artist Tracey Matthieson,
Creative Director of Okupi. Matthieson presents
cyberspace from a woman's point of view, stressing containment and protection. Shown above is a
screen structure to keep out the virtual sun.

Plates 23, 24, 25
Virtual art gallery by Tracey Matthieson and collaborators at Okupi. Artists install their works in a constantly
changing gallery space. The gallery automatically reor-
ganizes itself to accommodate the exhibits and viewers.

*our actions and artifacts.* Space is the medium *for this. These relationships and*

Plate 26
Computer and video interface by Myron Krueger. Object in upper right corner is an avatar for the user. By gesturing, the user can navigate the planet below.

Plate 28
Image by Constantin Terzides shows a design generated using a computer algorithm. Changing parameters of the algorithm or data would result in a different configuration.

Plate 27
Shown is an image from the Deva Virtual Reality System, courtesy of The Advanced Interfaces Group at the University of Manchester, England. This view of an interface artifact shows the modular components of the realistic environment surrounding it. By manipulating the artifact users change the experienced cyberspace that it represents.

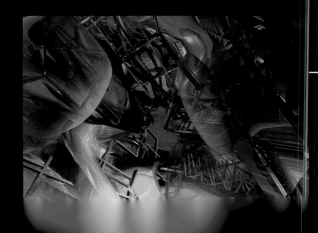

*processes are the basis of our daily reality*

Plates 29, 30
Images above and on left are by artist/architect Marcos Novak. Novak's work proposes a *Liquid Architecture* that changes its configuration based on data taken from the occupant. In other projects Novak has presented architectures that are solely displays of information. Totally abstract, these spaces are infinitely mutable and instantly responsive to the user's needs.

**Our private, social and cultural undertakings depend on principles of perception,**

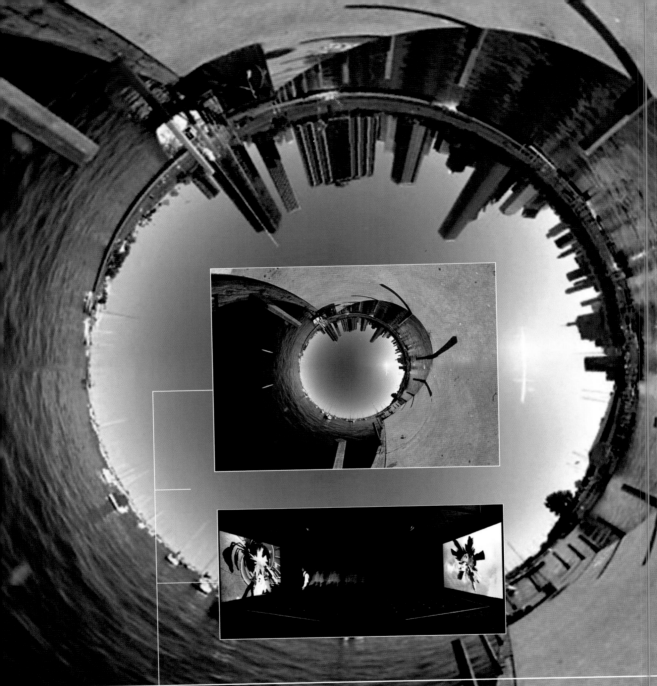

**Plates 31, 32, 33**
Shown above is a view of Chicago in Miroslaw Rogala's project "LOVERS LEAP." The lower inset is a view of the installation. As viewers moved from one screen to the other, the curvature of the horizons changed from convex to concave.

Collaborators: Ford Oxaal and Ludger Hovestadt. 1995.

**Plate 34**
In his project "Solve et Coagula" artist and scientific researcher Stahl Stenslie, with colleague Knut Mork, proposes a new post-biological life form that is symbiotic with humans. The image on the right shows a user in a body suit enveloped by the creature. The user interacts with the creature through sound and gesture. The bodysuit is a two-way interface through which the creature stimulates the human user.

*cognition and our use of space as a tool for thought.* *Proposals for the design of*

http://televr.fou.telenor.no/stahl/sec    stahl@rosa.nta.no

Plate 35
This cyberspace gallery by virtual architect
Dace Campbell displays a collection of virtual
environments. Each of the windows leads to
a separate virtual reality beyond. Some are
imaginary, others are modeled on real cities.

Plate 36
Scene from *Hypnogogue* by Edward
Keller and Perry Hall.

cyberspace must acknowledge the role that space plays in our thought and culture.

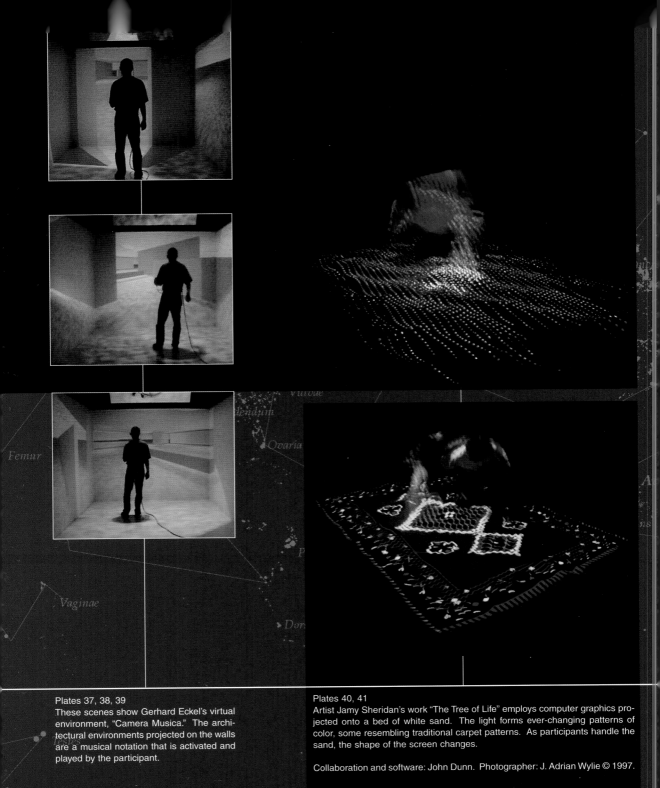

Plates 37, 38, 39
These scenes show Gerhard Eckel's virtual environment, "Camera Musica." The architectural environments projected on the walls are a musical notation that is activated and played by the participant.

Plates 40, 41
Artist Jamy Sheridan's work "The Tree of Life" employs computer graphics projected onto a bed of white sand. The light forms ever-changing patterns of color, some resembling traditional carpet patterns. As participants handle the sand, the shape of the screen changes.

Collaboration and software: John Dunn. Photographer: J. Adrian Wylie © 1997.

*Doing so will allow us to build upon our innate skills for managing information*

Plates 42, 43, 44
Composer Gerhard Eckel's "Music of the Spheres" is an immersive cyberspace that presents orbiting spheres of light. Participants "play" the spheres by pointing at them. At times the spheres explode with a cymbal crash. Virtual environment layout is shown at bottom.

**psychologically and somatically. This not only facilitates our internal processes**

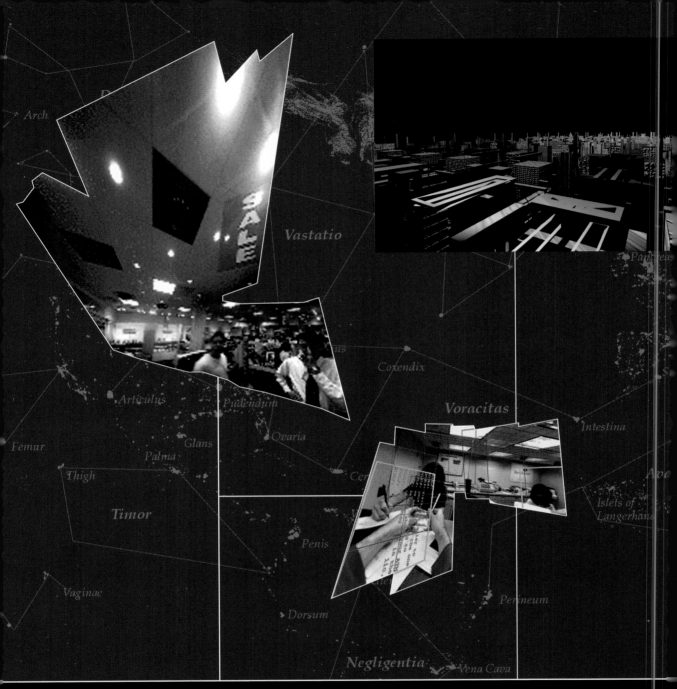

Plates 45, 46
These images are comprised of numerous smaller images taken by a head-mounted camera and fused together by computer. *Lookpainting* is a medium for computer supported collaboration (telepresence) generated by researcher/artist Steve Mann using his WearCam invention as described in http://wearcam.org/orbits/index.html.

Plate 47
View of a densely packed cyberspace by Thomas van Putten. Note the use of the horizon to orient the viewer.

*but also our natural extension outward – to our world and fellow creatures. It is*

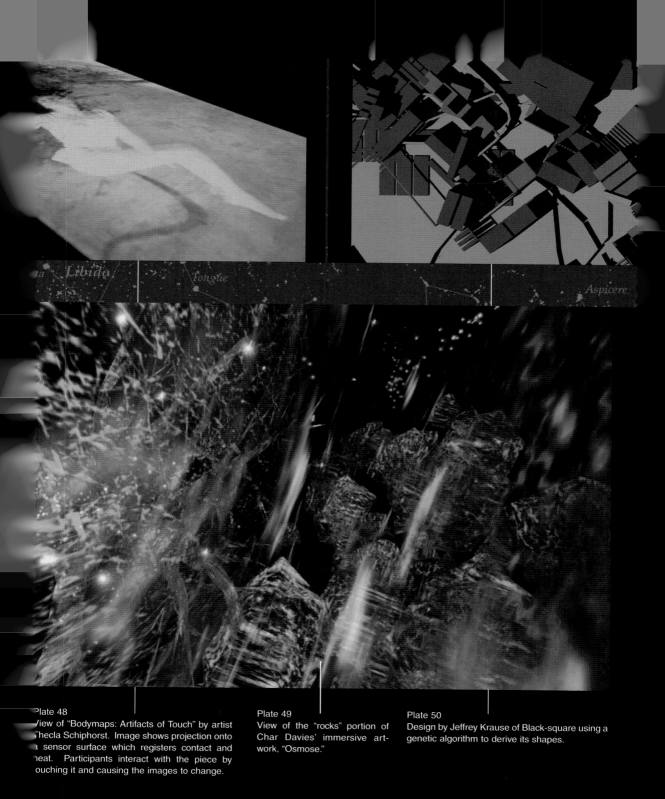

Plate 48
View of "Bodymaps: Artifacts of Touch" by artist Thecla Schiphorst. Image shows projection onto a sensor surface which registers contact and heat. Participants interact with the piece by touching it and causing the images to change.

Plate 49
View of the "rocks" portion of Char Davies' immersive artwork, "Osmose."

Plate 50
Design by Jeffrey Krause of Black-square using a genetic algorithm to derive its shapes.

*erial whether the resulting artifacts are physical or not. What matters is that*

Plates 51, 52

These images show an augmented reality. Note how one computer window follows the user while others remain linked to their screen location or to an inanimate object. Research by Steven Feiner, Blair MacIntyre, Marcus Haupt and Eliot Solomon at Columbia University.

Plates 53, 54, 55

These three images show how an augmented reality could be used to assist construction of a space frame. At left is a video image of the strut. In the center is a CAD image of another component. The composite image on the right matches the video image to the CAD model. Research by Anthony Webster, Steven Feiner, Blair MacIntyre and Ted Krueger at Columbia University.

**they are created with respect for human use and aspiration.  We cannot ask for le**

# The Swift and Brutal Society of Gaming

"...the early video games were transitional; they had a kind of transparency that gave them a modernist aesthetic, but the demand they made on their players to inhabit their game spaces anticipated the psychological requirements of the culture of simulation."

Turkle, Sherry. 1995. *Life on the screen: Identity in the age of the Internet.* New York: Simon and Shuster. p. 67.

*This brief chapter introduces computer games as simple forms of society that represent users and machines in a simulated space. Although video games have a specific audience and use, we will find their psychological and societal principles apply to other mediated environments as well.*

*CRASH!...BrrrAAAT...Arrrgh!!!*

*Some time back I interrupted a networked game of Quake at my school. I walked in as five students were furiously blasting away. Gibson should have been there. Though they were physically at their screens, facing away from each other, in cyberspace they were working in teams. One would back the other as the team scored its gore-spattered points.*

*Quake is a 3D multi-user game and this version was set in a dungeon populated by vicious, blaster-toting aliens. A fast-running piece of software, Quake allows networked gaming with almost no lag-time. These games are routinely played on the Internet by players separated by hundreds of miles. The game has a big following and my students were die-hard fans. Although the game's focus is speed and action, it is possible to send text messages to one another while engaged in the game. I asked the guys (and girl!) to stop playing long enough to try this out.*

*They were still pumped for action, a little annoyed at the interruption. After all, why chit-chat when there was so much killing to do? But they complied – it beat school work after all – and slowly maneuvered their avatars to the Great Hall of the dungeon.*

*There they could "see" each other, their avatars floating on the screen. Their low resolution made them look blotchy. Ugly, but stripped for speed. The avatars twitched as they hung there, fidgeting. When I asked them to start a conversation there was a pause. I waited.*

*Someone typed "Tim sucks" on the screen.*

*It was a bloodbath.*

## Society and Space in Action Games

Quake is not a congenial social environment – but it's a social environment nonetheless. Multi-user games vary in their purpose and those favored by teenage boys seethe with violence. These kids socialize with bullets and nailguns! Although Quake has sound, the only voices players hear are the automated screams of the victims. To chat players have to drop the mouse and peck at their keyboard. Hardly the place for afternoon tea, I'd say.

Quake, like many other games, has a set environment with an established group of avatar characters. It is goal-oriented – toward winning the game. Quake resembles many non-electronic games also because roles played by participants are dropped at the game's end. Action games have duration, like a play, and the curtain drops with a sign saying "Game Over."

Players compete with each other and the machine itself. Each party, at times even the computer, is represented as an avatar. The game environment – an incarnation of the machine – is set, as is the cast of characters. The presence of the machine is pervasive, right down to the judgement of who wins and loses. Players are pawns. Given a role in a fixed environment they have a limited palette of options. They even have a set time to "live" before the game's end. Though it's true that more tech-savvy players can customize the game, most just accept things as they are.

Keeping the play environment uniform and the character roles set is an advantage to competitive, goal-oriented games. It levels the playing field and focuses players' attention on the action, which in this case is dynamic and experiential. It also benefits the programmer by limiting the variables and duration of the game. For this reason many action games can stand alone without the attendant administrators required in MUDs. The actions of the players, while spontaneous, are in fact predictable. A successful computer game draws a balance between limiting options and allowing enough freedom for the player's enjoyment.

Standard computer games are systematic and top-down oriented. That means the programmer creates the environment, defines the avatars, goals and action. Participants effectively play out pre-scripted scenarios. Even the simplest computer game implicitly involves three parties: the player, the computer and – by extension – the programmer. The programmer is the creative component of the three, while the player is often just a consumer of the machine-driven sensation.

## Search Games

*Recent developments in gaming technology have produced a class of games that rely heavily on spatial imagery. These games, like Myst, Riven and Hypnagogue (fig. 85), involve a series of related scenarios. The challenge is to uncover the game's secret. At times there may not be a conclusive solution to the puzzle, only a deeper understanding of its characters and events.*

*The search involves moving about highly resolved virtual spaces. Typical of computer games, this is accomplished by mouse or keyboard commands. Although the user sees through the eyes of his avatar, the avatar itself is not presented visually in most games. The effect is one of disembodied movement — seen through a "floating eye" moving incrementally about the space.*

*Search games are often a solitary activity, a kind of puzzle. As opposed to a social environment, these games present an enigmatic, often abandoned space. Computer agents may appear as characters in the scenario but their actions are often pre-scripted clues for the player. The computer's presence is that of an ambience rather than a character. Unlike computerized chess, for instance, there is not even an opponent. The irony of this virtual solitude is that play requires attention to relationships. The underlying narratives of a game like Myst involves an intense — if absent — human drama.*

Fig. 85
In the search game Hypnagogue, architect Edward Keller and artist Perry Hall collaborated in creating a mysterious environment populated by ghosts and memories. The objective of the game is to discover relationships between the space and events that transpired there.

## Principles General to Multi-User Environments

We can see in computer games characteristics underlying many other multi-user environments:

1. Users are represented by avatars that often bear no resemblance to the actual players.

2. Avatars are controlled by keyboard or gesture commands.

3. Avatars move through a spatial simulation – in many cases a 3D graphic environment – that appears stationary although perspectives change as the avatar moves.

4. Action is sometimes seen through the eyes of the avatar, although games showing the user's avatar are prevalent.

5. Players' powers are determined by their skill and by outside agencies: the game program or the administrators of the game.

6. Players may encounter other avatars or characters whose behavior is driven by the gaming software – usually an opponent in the game. Children's games also employ them as benign assistants or playmates. Masks for the machine are called agents – or bots[1]– while users' masks are often called avatars.

7. Computer game players assume a role that is kept for the duration of the game. Regardless of his actions, the avatar is always in character as dictated by the game. Even so, a game like Quake or Doom leaves little time for character development. Being out of character means losing the game – the computer tends to crush introspective players.

8. The simulated space of the game creates an arena for action and opportunity. This space is represented with varying degrees of abstraction. A game of computer chess, for example, presents the abstracted space of the chessboard. However, players simply move their chess pieces rather than move freely within the space. Also, since the opponent in a chess game is often a computer, social interaction is limited. All attention is focused on the evolving pattern of play. Efforts at animating the pieces are peripheral to the cognitive action, whereas animation is central to a typical video game.

9. Finally, players can often stop and save a game in order to resume it later. This is used to strategic advantage. Players, for instance, can save a game and then try several ensuing options. Finding a successful one, they can then save it too – ratcheting their way to success. In the process, players record the different states of play. They can return to any state, much like reviewing the layered states of a CAD model or archived threads of dialog on network news. It's hard to imagine an equivalent to this in our physical world. It resembles time travel or exploring alternate "what if" realities. This recursive strategy applies to the software for group planning exercises as well as splatter games in cyberspace

1. A contraction of "robots."

# MUDs: Cyberspace Communities

"The experience of cultural encounter and confrontation is something that is increasingly characteristic of life in our cities. Virtual communities do not exist in a different world. They must be situated in the context of these new cultural and political geographies."

Robins, Kevin. 1995. "Cyberspace and the world we live in," in *Cyberspace, cyberbodies, cyberpunk: Cultures of technological embodiment.* Featherstone, Michael, and Roger Burrows, eds. London: SAGE Publications. p. 146.

This chapter will describe the social structures of several text-based and graphic multi-user domains and the role of the citizen/builder in their communities. The chapter will conclude with a discussion on the representation of the computer and its users through avatars and agents.

Fig. 86
Detail of a logical adjacency model of the MUD MeridianMOO.
Model: Nanilee Anantakul, Ying-Huei Chen, Satanan Chanowanna, Watinee Thantranon.

## The Abstraction of Games vs. MUDs

Opposite the raucous extreme of action games is the comparatively placid world of multi-user domains, MUDs (fig. 86). MUDs is a generic term for a class of role-playing games found on the Internet. They take forms including AberMUDs, MOOs (Multi-user Object Oriented), MUSHes (Multi-User Shared Hallucination), MUSEs (Multi-User Shared Environment) and MUCK (Multi-User Collective Kingdom). MUCK, I understand, also stands for Many Unemployed College Kids.

MUDs are mostly text-based virtual realities – a convoluted way of saying that users read them rather than view them graphically. Action is performed via keyboard while all scenes must be rendered mentally by the players from scraps of text offered in the course of play. Text is an efficient medium – a few words can evoke a rich response in the mind of the user.

Compared with graphic, sensational action games, text MUDs rely more on cognition than sensory perception. Spaces and avatars are not viewed on the screen but in the player's mind. The domains are symbolic extensions of our cognitive space. Action games, to the degree that they appeal to our senses, are more a part of our perceived space.

In the chapter "The scale of abstraction," I presented a scale for artifacts with physical objects at one end and concepts at the other. Neither video games nor text MUDs are physical although they are situated between the two extremes. Even if video games use imaginary settings and characters, they refer to physicality in their action and images. This puts them at a point in our scale near realistic, fictional images in paintings or film. In modeling our perceived space, they rely on our perception for their effect.

Conversely, text MUDs are abstract and cognitive since the characters and scenes are conveyed symbolically rather than sensorially. Yet even they use descriptions of physical objects and places to ground the action. And to that degree they still maintain a connection to the concrete world in the same way that memory palaces used perceived space model conceptual ideas. There is a major difference between MUDs and memory palaces, of course. While memory palaces were idiosyncratic and internal, MUDs are external, shared environments. Conceivably, they are sites of collective memory recalling the accretive memory of CAD models and network news threads (fig. 87).

## MUDding: Representation and Movement

Getting into a MUD [1] usually means logging onto its host computer – its server – by using networking software like Telnet or Gopher. If logging on for the first time, players are assigned an avatar that allows other players to "see" them. Movement is categorical, accomplished by typing directions or destinations offered by the game. Often the description of a room includes a list of reasonable exits including the cardinal directions: north, east, south and west. Players in the MUD may type "N," for example, to wind up in a room immediately to the north. A description presents this new room and its occupants along with suggested exits.

1. I will focus on text MUDs in this discussion because they have a longer history of use than graphic MUDs and because they share many qualities of space and categorical movement associated with the Internet and World Wide Web.

*Envisioning Cyberspace*

Fig. 87
Inter(net)City by Dutch computer artist Thomas van Putten proposes an immersive information environment. Each component of the space contains information linked to other spaces. This presentation points to the power of spatial models for related information but is also reminiscent of both memory palaces and large-scaled urban structures.

*There is no dynamism involved in "walking" from room to room. Users instantly relocate episodically with a directional command. They can also "teleport" discretely to nearly any place in the MUD by using an @go command – although even the simplest movement in a text MUD involves categorical relocation.*

*The experience of MUDding is similar to reading a book. Characters converse in a described setting. If a user, Varmint, types* "Hey, there! *the computer reconfigures this to* "Varmint says, 'Hey, there!' " *for other participants. Users and computer conspire to create a living literary fiction – the text equivalent of a masquerade.*

*The following is an example taken from a session on the MUD HoloMUCK recorded by Michael Buldo, a former student at the School of Architecture at New Jersey Institute of Technology. Naima and Dex are avatar names of other MUD citizens. "You" is the computer's reference to Mike and is only used on his terminal. Other occupants of the MUD see the name of his avatar, Kilian. Spelling errors reflect speed of interaction since the dialog happens in real time. While all the information below appears on screen, I have differentiated the type to clarify who is saying what.* **Bold** *type indicates what the user enters.* Italic *shows messages sent by other users.* Roman type *is generated by the computer's MUD program.*

*01) Naima pages: "They arrived! Well wonders never cease."*
   *Time> Tue Oct 31 19:53:04 1995*
**page naima= we d got them on Monday!!, thanx alot**
You page, "we got them on Monday!!, thanx alot" to Naima.
**w**

*MUDs: Cyberspace Communities*

You head west...
Main Street (800W)
This once-desolate section of Main Street is looking busier these days.
To the north, at 800 W. Main St., stands the Red Dragon Inn.
[Obvious exits: north, w, e]
**page dex= are u free tommorow between 8** Your pager vibrates
slightly. **and 10..am??** You page, "are u free tommorow between 8 and
10..am??" to Dex.
*01) Dex pages: "no, not till tomorrow night"*
    *Time> Tue Oct 31 19:54:33 1995*
**page dex=awww...the people comming in to review the project will
be on wanna let you meet them...i might be round tommorw
night..dunno**
You page, "awww...the people comming in to review the project will be
on wanna let you meet them...i might be round tommorw night..dunno"
to Dex.
**w**
You head west...
Main Street (900V~/ Ohio Avenue You are at the intersection of Main
Street and Ohio Avenue, very near the western border of Tanstaafl
County. This region is very hilly, and covered with a variety of trees--
oaks, maples, and especially pines. Reality still holds sway in this
region, but just to the west, the darkened West Tunnel burrows through
a hill and into the unknown regions beyond...

*Despite the contrivance of text MUDs, they have an avid fol-
lowing. Novices quickly learn the ropes. MUD and MOO software is easy to learn and offers helpful prompts. Once the
MUDding skills are acquired, the process of play becomes
transparent.*

*In their minds users are "there" in the MUD, seeing the spaces
and chatting with friends. Players invest themselves in the
process, filling in details and suspending disbelief. Perhaps for
this reason many are ambivalent – if not hostile – to the idea of
visual MUDs. Some users insist that the introduction of graphics would diminish rather than enhance MUDding. They stress
that MUDding is a social rather than sensory experience.*

## The MUD Environment

*Unlike the dynamic, continuous, visual spaces in most video
games, the movement in the space of a text MUD is episodic.
Often the spaces are separated from each other by directional
links. Users rely on memory to recall nearby spaces. The MUD
typically only presents a room's description when the player is
in it. The effect is as though the user were tunneling through a
solid to go from one space to another. And it's this interior
quality that leads to spaces being called rooms.*

*At times it's a claustrophobic world. For instance, users can't
casually see distant views through windows or doors as they
might in real life. This requires specific commands. However,*

unlike normal sight, long-distance viewing, once elected, is not limited by lines of sight and perspective. If I were to "look" at a remote object while MUDding, it would be visible as text regardless of intervening objects or rooms, like gazing into a crystal ball.

Both sight and movement in MUDs appeal to our spatial understanding. Yet their episodic, surreal nature belies the illusion of conventional space. This is a product of MUD technology and of computing in general. The categorical movement and "clairvoyant" vision in MUDs results from accessing stored descriptions. When players enter a new space the contents of that space's file is presented on the screen. The movement of the user – via her avatar – is entirely symbolic. Aside from the crafted illusion, it is no more spatial than accessing a file on a computer.

And yet the illusion of space is so compelling that it forms the basis of a MUD's continuity, its chief activities, its "placeness." Users gladly transcend the anomalies of text MUDding to benefit from this illusion and its resulting sense of community.

## MUD Social Structures

Some MUDs retain game-like qualities from the Dungeons and Dragons game that inspired them. However, many MUDs also take their cues from Internet Relay Channels (IRCs) which, though they use spatial references, are aimed more at socializing than navigating. In fact, socializing is such a priority that – if no one is logged onto a specific IRC – it ceases to exist! MUDs, on the other hand, have longevity – their space exists so long as the supporting server is on-line. This gives MUDs their sense of place. Players return again and again to catch up with friends. Also, players maintain their identities from one session to the next, distinguishing a MUD from a typical video game.

The relative permanence of MUDs and user identity gives players a chance to familiarize themselves with their environment and each other. Beyond this, it also lets them define their own on-line identity. Domains require players to use avatars. Long-term use of an avatar allows character development and has an impact on the political structure of the MUD as well.

## Competition and Cooperation in MUDs

To better understand MUD society we should look at the reasons why they are so popular. Many users play MUDs competitively since some are still gaming domains of the slash-and-slay variety. Even in more socially benign domains an element of competition remains. Long-term citizens accrue power and influence by rising in the MUD hierarchy. They can also accumulate credit – in terms of computer memory – to build rooms and objects within the MUD.

Other players extend their social lives through the MUD environment. Here they make friends, gain an audience, play games and even engage in simulated sex. For many text MUD users socializing is more important than the need to experience the MUD visually. Some believe that visuals would detract from the immediacy of text – the sense that they are engaged in intimate conversation. Relationships blossom quickly in these environments owing to the isolation and unfamiliarity of the surroundings. It's as though participants were trapped together on a desert island.

## Risk and Reward

In both gaming and social MUDs, users momentarily escape the pressures of everyday life. The popular press has been alert to the escapism encouraged by these environments. And, like any medium, it may be abused.

But there **is** an element of risk in MUDding. The environment is strange and its occupants not always benign. The narrow bandwidth of communication paradoxically increases the risk through its very limitations. For example, in the real world we are used to communicating verbally and visually through gestures. In MUDs – even graphic ones – messages are stripped down to live text hammered out on a keyboard – spontaneous and misspelled, they convey immediacy. But, without the modulation of bodily expression, subtleties of meaning – irony or humor – are lost. This all to the detriment of the communication. Risk of offending or being inadvertently insulted attends all transaction and users are forced to use smileys where neither words nor bodies can help.

Even 3D graphic MUDs with humanoid avatars require separate controls to operate limbs from those used in messaging. Avatars may move limbs but the vocabulary of body movement is often limited to walking and waving. Compared to our corporeal language of shrugs, raised eyebrows and wrinkled noses the avatar is effectively mute.

The main source of risk for the MUD player is betrayal – betrayal by others sharing the space or by the illusion of the domain. The former is often a product of the masking effect of the avatars – the temptation is just too great. The latter is more pervasive since the MUD illusion relies on the user's willingness to be taken in. The user buys into MUDding despite its obvious contrivance. All evidence points to its artifice: it is mediated by machine, experienced as text or graphics, vicariously explored by avatar. Disbelief is the price of admission and users leave *their doubts at the door. Analogies drawn by Brenda Laurel between computers and theater are extremely valid here.*

*Skepticism is a defense mechanism, the nagging voice of reason. It's what helps us separate fact from fantasy. It's exactly what we don't want at the theater – or a MUD for that matter. But by abandoning doubt MUD players risk betrayal. This betrayal takes many forms in domains and in the chapter "Navigating cyberspace" we saw some of the ways the spatial illusion of MUDs breaks down. These lapses may be accidents or pranks of programmers. But the rewards of simulated society obviously outweigh the hazards for most players.*

## Investment in the Community

*Psychologist Sherry Turkle, writing on the psychological aspects of MUDs, recalls the psychoanalyst Erik Erikson's concept of a psychological moratorium. In his theories about adolescent development Erikson proposes a period of intense intellectual and social interaction at which time adolescents form close friendships. It is a time of exploration and experimentation. The moratorium is imposed not on these experiences but on the effects they have outside the individual.*

*Although Erikson focused on the maturation process, we also benefit from the moratorium as adults. Play, hobbies, vacations are all part of our on-going, psycho-social regeneration. They refresh and re-animate us. The simulation of life in a multi-user domain is another venue for the experimentation described by Erikson. MUDs provide their users with a safe zone for exploring matters of identity, social behavior and even sexuality. For those readers interested in these issues I highly recommend Sherry Turkle's* Life on the screen *for a close examination of the psychological issues underlying these simulations.*

*Finally, unlike many other games, many MUDs are built by their citizenry. Although AberMUDs – a type of multi-user domain – limit the power of construction to the wizards, many MUDs invite their citizens to build their environment and its contents. This, of course, appeals to the participants already adept at programming, but in many cases code writing is quickly learned by aspiring citizens.*

*But this alone doesn't explain the tenacious hold domains have on the imaginations of their users. MUDding requires an investment by the user in exchange for its benefits. In the chapter "Body Extensions in Space" I described a party in terms of the risk and investment we make by being physically present. Our payoff is in the reinforced friendships and engagement we have at the event. Any involvement, mediated or physical, requires investment of our attention, time and physical activity. This applies to MUD activity as well. Time spent MUDding is time not spent on something else. Presence in a MUD is an investment in the simulation.*

## Construction of (and by) the Community

*Next to socializing, construction is the chief activity in many domains. Building is a social act. It creates new places for the community, new toys and robots. It involves consultation, cooperation and dialog, strengthening bonds within the community. A builder who has created rooms is likely to return with new plans or modifications. A proud owner will invite guests to enjoy his creation. Building forms a commitment in MUD players – in logging off, they leave something behind.*

*The investment of experienced MUD players is in their service to the MUD, their construction of a surrogate self – the avatar – and the enhancement of the domain. In exchange many players gain achievement and a sense of belonging. Although their work takes place in cyberspace, the feeling is real enough.*

*For in building spaces and animating them with avatars the citizens create what Ray Oldenberg calls a "third place." [2] Our daily "real" lives are often polarized between our domestic and work roles. And polarized physically between the places we play them. A third, intermediate space is where we are free to relax, socialize and be ourselves. Multi-user domains are the electronic equivalents of cafés, bars and street corners. These aren't places of solitude but places of engagement where we find friends and talk out ideas.*

*It's a neutral turf where, ideally, no one dominates. Perhaps for this reason as well as the anonymity of avatars, MUDs are well suited as sites for self-discovery and exploration – the moratorium spaces of the Internet. Third places bring people together, effectively leveling their social status. Since selection of avatars is arbitrary there are few clues indicating status within a MUD. The giant blue oyster you're chatting with could as easily be a fifth-grader as a computer scientist.*

*Many electronic media require the creation of avatars to represent the participants. These are either analog descriptions of their users – a telephone voice or video image – or, in digital media, they may only have a tenuous connection to their user. In the role-playing environments of MUDs players take on either assigned characters or – in many cases – assume self-created identities. The critical difference between this and a television show is that a MUD avatar is part of an on-going, unscripted performance. The spontaneous interaction with the space and fellow citizens of the domain gives MUDding its life-like immediacy.*

2. Oldenberg, Ray. 1989. *The great good place: Cafes, coffeeshops, community centers, beauty parlors, general stores, bars, hangouts, and how they get you through the day.* New York: Paragon House.

## Elusive Entities: Avatars and Agents

MUDs share with other computer games the use of role-playing avatars, computer agents, a spatial context for action and technical interfaces like keyboards and screens. However, they differ in important ways. While video games have a finite duration, MUDding is continuous. The space of a video game may be consistent from one game to the next, but usually the action is discrete, a battle or race with clear goals and conclusions. A video game player's association with his avatar only lasts for the duration of play. This is the reason video games post the scores of winners in the name of the player rather than his avatar.

Most video game players have to accept the avatar they are given. Conversely, a MUD player creates her own avatar which remains part of the MUD once she is accepted into the community. A MUD player may log in as often as she likes, using her avatar to participate. In constructing this identity the player invests herself in the MUD, returning periodically to reinforce her presence in the domain. As we would expect from any social setting, the consistency of characters over time is important to their identity in the community. Repeated exposure to someone else in the same environment dimensionalizes them as we learn more about them.

But matters of identity are never simple in MUDs. The avatar is only a mask for the user. It may not resemble her physically at all — not even in the text description (figs. 88, 89, 90). An avatar may take on traits of animals, robots, historic figures, even furniture. A character's ability to teleport — a given in MUDding — is miraculous by everyday standards.

This gap between the user and avatar mask gives rise to many complexities of on-line identity. Nothing prevents a computer user from belonging to several MUDs — effectively distributing herself among several communities and identities. Arguably, this resembles our role-playing in conventional society. I, for instance, am a husband, father, teacher, architect and partygoer — each requiring distinct modes of behavior. But in everyday society I manifest all these roles in one body. On-line, these manifestations — or avatars — may be radically different.[3] In most cases, though, it's not a problem since an avatar is usually unique to its MUD — most players limiting themselves to one avatar per domain.

Theoretically one user could have as many avatars as she can manage. Some MUDs encourage this since often MUDs appear underpopulated. A user might, for instance, operate a group of avatars at a time. Simon Birrell, a designer of graphic MUDs, and his colleague Christopher Stangroom used this strategy in creating their MUD, Jekyll & Hyde. A MUD player,

Avatars of The Palace

Avatars of AlphaWorld

Avatar of Worlds Away

Figs. 88, 89, 90
The above images show avatars from different graphic MUDs. Note the special character of each. AlphaWorld is distinctly 3D while Worlds Away and The Palace flatten the backdrop, placing the avatar on its surface. Each has a different way of rendering the avatar's presence in cyberspace. Images courtesy of Bruce Damer.

3. Turkle, Sherry. 1984. *The second self: Computers and the human spirit.* New York: Simon and Shuster. p.294.

rather than taking on a single character, takes on a character group – say a gang of thieves or a team of policemen (fig. 91). The action is accomplished via the screen interface but the major feature is the multiplication of the user through her avatars. The person behind one avatar may be the same as behind another.

Just as one person may wear a number of masks, several people may share the same mask. Logging onto a computer with a borrowed identity is frowned upon but commonplace. The same holds true for a multi-user domain. In fact, given the parallel with video games it comes as no surprise. Since pre-set video games offer only a set staff of avatars, players commonly have to share one another's avatars from game to game. That's not hard given the brief and mortal interaction between participants.

It's another matter on a MUD however. As we saw earlier, newcomers are commonly assigned re-usable avatars for the duration of their visit. These avatars have default names like Guest 1 or Blue Guest and their user/avatar relationship has no longevity in the MUD. Green Guest, for instance, may represent a host of users in the course of a week. This is not disruptive to the MUD since its citizens recognize the guests' transience. The guest's avatar is like a rented car.

It is more disconcerting if the person behind an established avatar is not consistent. It shakes the illusion of the MUD by calling attention to the gap between the user and her avatar. Consistency of character is important to the illusion of MUD society. Inconsistency, on the other hand, connotes duplicity – even schizophrenia – neither being desirable in any social setting.

Unlike its analog counterparts, the digital avatar is an independent artifact within the MUD. It's not just a projection of an individual as is – say – our television anchorman on the nightly news. Instead, an avatar is like a mask through which a user is present in the domain. Sherry Turkle refers to avatars as "personae," the Greek term for mask. Translated it means "through sound" indicating that the masks used in theater through which the voice of the actor was projected. Also implicit is the interdependence between the actor/person and his mask/personae. Every day we take on our roles according to our situation. We express these roles – and their masks – though demeanor, voice, dress and ornament. Arguably these roles are the various threads we weave into the braid of our identity. [4]

What distinguishes the digital avatar from these more integral roles is its psychic distance from the user. Given the gap between the player and the avatar, users may play roles that bear no resemblance to themselves. By separating from their

Fig. 91
Scene from Jekyll & Hyde, a graphic MUD developed by Christopher Stangroom and Simon Birrell. The domain has character groups (police, thieves, citizens) that may be operated by individual players. Any avatars for which human players are not available stay true to their objectives and desires.

4. Other metaphors for identity could include houses with many rooms. LambdaMOO has an avatar called "Tree" who is actually a MUD in itself. Visitors can enter the avatar and explore it like a domain.

*Envisioning Cyberspace*

masks, players bear less responsibility for their actions since consequences are directed at the avatar rather than the user. Although users treat their avatars as personal extensions, avatars are also a kind of shield. This allows the freedom of personal exploration encouraged by MUDding – its moratorium. Just as a MUD space may not be what it seems, neither may its occupants.

One of my former students, George Wharton III, took this ambiguity of identity as the theme of his design for a cyberspace bar. When a player arrives at the bar, she is given a mask through which she can see the other participants (fig. 92). All other avatars are represented as masks floating in the dimly lit space. At the side of the screen a menu offers several other optional masks. This menu is a listing of the other avatars in the space. By selecting another mask the user can see and hear what the current user of that mask is experiencing. The bar scene is populated by masks behind which there may be any number of users. Or none at all.

Fig. 92
In this proposal for a MUD bar by George Wharton III, users select which avatars they want to use. They may change their selection at any time by choosing from the menu on the left.

The idea that there may be no one behind the mask is hard to imagine in the physical world, but it's a fact of life in MUDs. Momentarily abandoned avatars haunt the MUD like zombies, to be awakened when their users return. Others are ownerless and autonomous. Much as an avatar represents a player, a bot – short for robot – may be simply a mask for a computer agent (fig. 93). Unlike many of their video game counterparts, bots may be supported by elaborate programs for interaction. They may range from simple behaviors, like a robo-dog that follows players from room to room, to sophisticated routines that fool players into believing they represent living players. In fact, two famous on-line personalities were actually programs created to simulate human interaction in networked environments.

Michael Mauldin, a researcher at Carnegie-Mellon University, programmed Julia, a bot that responds to players with words and gestures. Since she operates in a text environment, she has as much presence on-line as any other avatar. And this is crucial to the illusion. Mauldin has programmed Julia to seek out key words and phrases from other users' text and respond to them from a list of options that apply. Her spontaneous wit is crucial to the illusion of her intelligence. She can dish it out, too:

Fig. 93
Design for an autonomous agent, or bot, by Norwegian media artist Stahl Stenslie in collaboration with Knut Mork. In other works Stenslie has proposed post-human and post-biological life forms.

Ace says, "So why not kiss me, Julia?"
Julia says, "Sorry, I'm not into geeks, Ace."
Ace says, "Julia, I'm not a geek."
Julia says, "Then lose the pocket protector, Ace." [5]

ELIZA, a program originally developed by Joseph Weizenbaum in 1966, was originally created to test a computer's ability to mimic human conversation. The program mirrors the comments of another participant in a conversation. For instance,

5. Turkle, 1995, op. cit., p.89.

someone might tell ELIZA, "I am feeling sad." ELIZA's program separates out the "I am," substitutes it with "you are" and precedes the answer with "Why do you tell me that?" The response reads, "Why do you tell me that you are feeling sad?" Despite its clear artifice, ELIZA became a preferred conversation partner. Also, to Weizenbaum's chagrin, she became a hot topic in the psychiatric community as a possible tool for therapy, an idea that her inventor felt trivialized human interaction and worth. [6]

6. Turkle, 1995, op. cit., pp.105-106.

## Bandwidth as Mask

Both ELIZA and Julia hide behind two masks. One is their apparent identity – the fact that they have names at all. The other is their text medium. If human interaction is reduced to words on a screen, it levels the playing field for computer agents and participants. It would be much harder to create a program that uses higher dimensions of human expression. Creating accurate models of humans in computer graphics is very difficult. We are so attuned to subtleties of texture and gesture that even presenting them accurately requires great skill (fig. 94). Coupling these expressions with the interactive capabilities of ELIZA or Julia would be a great challenge. Paradoxically, the higher the dimension of representation – graphics and modeling – the better our chances to see through the artifice. With Julia and ELIZA, text strips away any corroborating evidence we may use to validate identity and presence. As we have seen with MUDs, we invest our imagination in the presentation of the text. We fill the gaps with ourselves, just as we're compelled to answer ELIZA's questions. Paradoxically, the user's engagement may be inversely proportional to the simulation's quality.

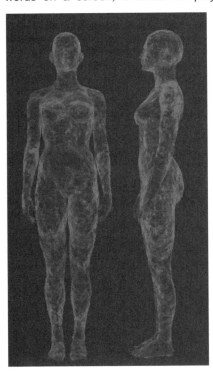

Fig. 94
Artist Victoria Vesna and her colleagues at Bodies© Inc. have created several life-like human avatars for use in VRML environments. While the figures are realistic, their components may be exchanged to mold the body to its user's specifications. Applied textures, like the lava pattern shown at left, also subvert the realism of the avatar.

## The Trouble with Human Metaphors

Computer agents and bots have caused a lot of excitement – and heated controversy – in the computing community. The arguments against agency, particularly bots, center on three issues of anthropomorphism: human worth, metaphor, and the morality implicit in their use. Weizenbaum's concerns illustrate the first. Using a digital avatar separates the user from his representation. Digital media reduce users to caricatures while elevating agents' status through their representation. By having equivalent presence in a domain, agents and bots effectively lower humans to the level of programs. Perhaps this, in conjunction with the distancing effect of the avatar, encourages the uncivil behavior of some users. It's easier to be rude to someone if they are only a computerized representation. More so if they are possibly not human at all. The ambiguity of who or what is presented challenges the very idea of on-line society. The second issue recalls arguments against metaphor used in computing. This is particularly grave when the symbol for a piece of code is the image of a human being. Presenting code in human form creates unrealistic or inappropriate expectations in users. Beyond a trivialization of the human model, the agent metaphor implies an identity, history, familial relationships, gender, emotions and metabolism that are superfluous to its use. In working with an agent, users soon find shortcomings in what they assumed to be an intelligent human-like assistant. The metaphor's standard is too high.

For this reason designers of agent interfaces try to manage users' expectations. Kris Thorisson, a former researcher at MIT's MediaLab and now at Lego Corporation, has designed cartoon-like interfaces for agents. One interface, Gandalf, is a caricature of a Viking – helmet and all (figs. 95, 96, 97). He is disarming, a slightly goofy smile on his face. The user is aware of his attentiveness yet knows not to expect the intelligence of a human. Although Gandalf is quite sophisticated and can converse on specific topics, the user risks no disappointment owing to his representation. Gandalf presents a well-chosen metaphor for interaction.

Another problem with the human metaphor is that it sets up a dialogic relationship with the computer. This is the point brought up by John Walker in his "Through the looking glass" memorandum. [7] Agents acting as humans – even cartoons – imply that interaction is by conversation. This may not be the best model for getting needed information – if we don't ask the right question, we won't get the right answer. This concern underlies debates between those promoting artificial intelligence (AI) and those in favor of virtual reality. Others besides Walker, notably Jaron Lanier, feel that the computing environment should be a space for discovery rather than a limiting

Figs. 95, 96, 97
Researcher Kris Thorisson has developed an agent, Gandalf, who can respond to pointing gestures and conversation on planets. Gandalf's expression and gestures are consistent with a human model. However his representation as a caricature keeps users from unrealistic expectations that would result from the realistic depiction of a human.

7. Walker, John. 1990. "Through the looking glass," in *The art of human-computer interface design.* ed. B. Laurel. Reading, Mass.: Addison-Wesley. p.443.

*channel of dialog. In this view AI is seen to be reductive, deterministic and a poor model for accessing information.*

## The Legacy of Artificial Intelligence

*Where did this reaction come from? The original research on artificial intelligence (AI) led to a number of dead ends as it was shown that human thought is much more complex than originally conceived. And, for a while, the prospect of mimicking human cognition with machines seemed unattainable. At that time much of the excitement in computing centered on new ways to present information to the user, notably virtual reality.*

*Over the past twenty years the model of human cognition changed from being monolithic to being comprised of many parts that together – it was believed – formed identity and produced thought. In this view, our behavior is the complex product of many relatively simple, iterative processes. While this model continues to be controversial among psychologists, the computing community has used it effectively to advance artificial intelligence research. This model vies against the top-down model of cognition that argued for one complex algorithm defining all behavior. Instead the bottom-up model proposes that complex behavior is the interaction of many concurrent simple processes. The impression of behavior and thought is the emergent property of these many subsystems in action.*

*Rodney Brooks, a researcher at the Massachusetts Institute of Technology, is well known for implementing this principle in several small robots – some smaller than a breadbox. Each robot is made up of relatively simple software mechanisms that, in concert, create complex behavior. Patti Maes, his former colleague, has applied these ideas to producing software agents that perform tasks ranging from scheduling to taking polls on the Internet.*

*Agents are subject to similar criticism as against AI. One of the more intriguing twists on the older arguments addresses the morality of the human metaphor. While the original model of AI inspired fear of being dominated by expert systems, the agency model does the opposite. Should computing be based on having others do our work for us? Are the simple agents that sort our mail and search the Internet no more than electronic slaves? Has our cultural and technological evolution only led us to repeat the very worst of our mistakes?*

*The problem, of course, lies in the metaphor. No one denies that computers – and their software – are created to serve our needs. It's when we put a human face on computer agents that the problems begin. It doesn't matter to the computer what representation data takes, whether ambient or anthropomorphic.*

Software can take many forms, each telling us something about its designers. Presenting the user with agents to do his bidding is different from immersing him in an information environment. Each scenario empowers the user in different ways. In the former the user delegates his work, in the latter he navigates a space created for his use, letting him discover and learn.

In the end, however, **the space and its agent occupants are masks for the machine**. Whether the machine presents us with characters or ambience should ideally make no difference so long as our needs are met. Just as there are times when text is more appropriate than graphics, so too are there times when an anthropomorphic interface is preferred to a spatial one. The selection of one over another is often a pragmatic decision based on resources and desired information. [8]

The debates surrounding the use of agency have less to do with its function than the entailments of its metaphor. Whether or not they were manifested as icons or text, agents were understood to be software entities with purpose and, at times, personality. In their software simplicity they were not too far removed from the automated creatures that roamed the IRCs and multi-user domains. Their anthropomorphic association stuck, resulting in some heated debates that only recently have begun to cool.

What the controversy about agents reveals is how cultural and political values enter what originally were discussions of technology. The stakes have been raised. As computers have become more sophisticated and accessible, they have become a cultural as well as technological issue.

## Conclusion

We have seen in this chapter some similarities and differences between physical society and that of multi-user domains. We have also seen how citizens of MUD communities often participate in the creation of the domain. Though not physical, MUDs retain many characteristics of earthbound communities. Even so, avatars and agents are constant reminders of the artifice of on-line experience. In the next chapter we will return to the matter of space and its manifestation in cyberspace environments.

8. Laurel, Brenda. 1990. "Interface agents: Metaphors with character," in *The art of human-computer interface design*. ed. B. Laurel. Reading, Mass.: Addison-Wesley. p.362.

# MUD Spatial Structure

"We build not only to shelter the body, but also to support a structure of consciousness. By construction and demolition we ratify meanings we take for granted. As we build the world we rebuild ourselves."

Walter, Eugene V. 1988. *Placeways: A theory of the human environment.* Chapel Hill, N. C., and London: University of North Carolina Press. p.205.

Fig. 98. Logical adjacency model of the MUD MeridianMOO. The loops represent global transit systems of the domain.

Model: Dana Napurano and Keith Kemery.

*This chapter presents the implicit spatial structure of MUDs. It introduces logical adjacency models (LAMs) as tools for understanding the cognitive structure of on-line social space. We will also see how spatial anomalies in MUDs reveal inconsistencies in the spatial reference of domains. And finally, we will conclude with a discussion of how motion in MUDs determines their form in the way that circulation forms our physical communities.*

*The organization of each MUD varies according to its themes and history. Its spaces can be modeled by simply noting directions used to get from point to point. For instance, if a room is north of another, it maps as a cube above another cube. A room to the west is mapped to the left and so on. Sometimes rooms are not accessed directionally, but by invoking their name or number. These spaces are indicated with spheres located arbitrarily so long as the connections are maintained in the diagram (fig. 98). In studies I have conducted with students at the New Jersey Institute of Technology and the University of Michigan we have mapped several text and graphic MUDs using this method to uncover their logical structure.*

*The product of these efforts, called logical adjacency models (LAMs), were surprisingly complex. Because of their node/connector construction they resemble large, molecular* models. But LAMs are necessarily incomplete because of the size and ephemeral nature of the MUDs. Larger MUDs, like LambdaMOO, can contain thousands of rooms. Mapping such a MUD in its entirety is almost impossible since the number of rooms change by the minute. Entire sections of a MUD can disappear or transform overnight. While Rome wasn't built in a day, Columbia University's graphic MUD model of Rome effectively was. After months of preparation, the MUD came into being immediately after its server was connected to the network.

Adding to the difficulty of mapping, some rooms can't be mapped logically because a MUD may contradict itself. For example, in real-life we expect reversibility. If I leave a space by going west, I should be able to return by going east. As a rule this is true of MUDs, however in DreamMOO such an attempt at re-entry may unexpectedly lead to a third room.

The ball-and-stick modeling of MUDs works well so long as the MUD's implicit structure complies with the model's assumptions. But that's not always the case. Nested spaces like those found in MUDs like The Chatting Room or Diversity University are linked by including one another rather than bridging between. The forced rigidity of movement in HoloMUCK requires the construction of intermediate stepping-stone "rooms." These have no other purpose than to relate changing perspectives as a player moves down a street.

The logical adjacency structure of each MUD has a distinct form, like a fingerprint. Often MUDs begin as a verbal diagram of a neighborhood (Jay's House), an existing town (The Chatting Zone), or even the Earth (MeridianMOO). A MUD administrator will determine themes, rules of play and often designs the preliminary spaces. Once in place, citizens of the MUD are often invited to build their own rooms, objects and buildings. Over time the configuration of the domain evolves to where not even its operators – called wizards – know its current shape.

This is a participatory construction, a kind of architecture without architects. There are constraints, however. The degree of freedom enjoyed by citizens is determined by their stature in the community and the MUD's administrators. Some MUDs like HoloMUCK or Jay's House have stringent codes enforcing the realism of proposed additions. In Jay's House, for instance, the builder of some cliffs outside the neighborhood had to change the description of their mineral composition to that of the actual cliffs of the referent community. The irony is that the only material builders use is memory – the allocated computer memory of the MUD.

## MUD Citizen as Builder

Upon joining a MUD, the new citizen often receives an allotment of memory. With comparatively simple programming – such as MOO code – they may build virtual objects within the MUD. These may include rooms, bots or animated objects. If the builder runs out of memory – the cyberspace equivalent of money – she can find more or get some from an avatar friend or wizard. The amount of memory one has at her disposal is often commensurate with her stature within the community.

Getting memory and status in a MUD is a symbolic and social matter – often a result of who you know. This has obvious parallels in conventional society. The more time a player invests in a particular MUD, the more exposure she has to others and the MUD administration. This vicarious investment pays off in memory and in special powers granted by the wizards.

Citizen-builders rarely write code from scratch. In object-oriented MUDs – called MOOs – each object is usually a modification of a parent object. Every object shares this "genetic" characteristic whether it is an avatar, room, or robot. It is inherent in object-oriented programming, a code-writing method that lets programmers assemble software from code modules called objects. There is an implicit evolution of objects as one generation succeeds the next.

Modifications are accomplished by editing the code underlying a parent object. Say I wanted to create a bartender robot. I could take the code for a waiter robot as a template and change some characteristics. Whereas the waiter would ask, "May I take your order?," the bartender might ask, "What'll ya have?." Editing attributes is easier than creating new behaviors, and many objects are simply redefined versions of earlier models.

## MUD Spaces and Societal Roles

The earliest MUD, EssexMUD, was created in 1979 by Roy Trubshaw and Richard Bartle at the University of Essex in London. Unlike its predecessors, the computer games of Adventure and Zork, EssexMUDs let several players log onto the game simultaneously. Like its predecessors, however, the theme of EssexMUD was fantasy-based. The fact that Adventure and Zork were derived from the fantasy game Dungeons and Dragons led to the acronym MUD – which originally stood for Multi-User Dungeon. Nowadays it usually stands for Multi-User Domain. The spatial environment of the MUD establishes the theme for the community.

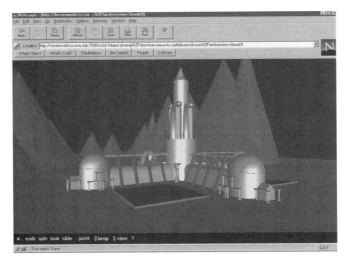

Figs. 99, 100, 101, 102
Ian Horswill's graphic MUD, NeverWorld, incorporates several recognizable places designed by his students. At left is a castle. Below, from top to bottom, is the interior of a cathedral, a visitor center and a space station. Each environment encourages appropriate behaviors of its users, much as a stage set influences a play.

*Characters in a MUD based on the "Lord of the Rings" are predictably different from those based on Star Trek, for instance.*

*The consistent backdrop of the MUD space – however abstract – acts as a stage set for dramas played out by its members. It influences and sustains thematic interaction simply by being there. There are clear parallels in how our physical environment affects our behavior. As we may each play separate roles in our society, society provides us with places to act them out. Barroom behavior is not appropriate in a church, nor is preaching at a party. We go to different places to play our roles. MUDs emulate these spaces, by hosting different behaviors.*

*There are many MUDs without fictional themes. These may be based on physical models, perhaps the hometown of the founding wizard or the physical site of the MUD's server. For instance, The Chatting Zone maps Ipswich, Ireland, hometown of its founder. While MeridianMOO represents the entire planet, users enter it in "Norway," the native land of its wizard. Oddly, the MUD's server is located in Morristown, New Jersey.*

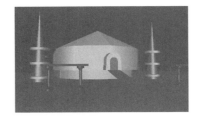

*Basing MUDs on actual physical models is an expeditious first step in starting the domain. It saves the wizard the effort of creating spaces from scratch and lets her make a "home" of the domain. JupiterMOO, developed by Pavel Curtis, is based on the layout of Xerox PARC in Palo Alto, California. Its mapping is so accurate that citizens of the MUD who visit the physical facility have no trouble finding their way around the campus. LambdaMOO, still one of the largest operating*

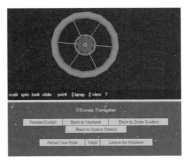

*Envisioning Cyberspace*

MUDs, was originally based on Curtis' personal apartment. His bedroom closet is still the point of entry. In another case, MediaMOO incorporated the architecture of MIT's MediaLab.

Using a physical prototype is also a basis for reference. A conventional urban space provides a familiar spatial framework for navigation. Streets, buildings and places keep directions simple and memorable since they are experiences common to all users.

These elements were also common to earlier memory palaces. They too relied on a familiar – architectural – organization. However, unlike those purely cognitive and idiosyncratic spaces, MUDs are shared through technology. In fact, the primary purpose of MUDs is to support social interaction. The wizards' selection of realistic physical prototypes in starting MUDs provides the MUD with a palette of ready-made social spaces, sets for various activities: classrooms, houses, bars, museums and the like. While a thematic MUD might determine the behavior of its characters, MUDs based on existing communities let users "be themselves" and select settings based on momentary need – the way a city provides a variety of optional backdrops (figs. 99, 100, 101, 102).

## Linked and Unlinked Spaces

As a MUD develops, the structure sometimes evolves by leaving the real-space reference behind. The resulting geometry can be extremely complex and hard to map using LAM conventions. Depending on the MUD's policy, most MUDders can build their own rooms once they have citizenship. These rooms are usually independent of the main MUD structure, "hovering" outside the domain. In DreaMOO, for instance, linking spaces to the main structure requires permission on several levels. Not only must the builder petition the MUD administrators, but also the creator of spaces to which they wish to connect. Since not all members are logged on at the same time, the process requires both patience and persistence. Consequently, many builders opt instead to let their new spaces float free of the main structure.

This produces spaces with non-directional links to the main structure. Most private spaces – some quite elaborate – can only be entered by teleportation. And then only at the host's invitation. Teleportation requires the address of a destination. If a casual user doesn't know of a "hovering" private space, it's unlikely that he will find it simply by navigating the MUD. He would have to make a lucky guess using the @go command or get assistance from a colleague. Due to this opacity, accurately mapping a MUD structure can be a frustrating experience.

## Politics and the Spatial Structure of MUDs

The freedom allowed by wizards directly affects the MUD's structure. BayMOO, a San Francisco-based domain, has a laissez-faire approach to development and, over time, has evolved as a free-form, branching structure. Its logical mapping reflects its incremental, unplanned growth. In contrast, the MUD Cyberion City uses a strict geometry to organize its spaces. A grid of spaces wrapped around a cylinder represents a space colony orbiting the Earth. Spaces are divided into sections and arcs and located using starboard/port, spin/anti-spin directions. This overarching geometry indicates strong top-down management of the MUD construction and remotely resembles the concentric and grid-based geometries of some memory palaces.

Fig. 103
This LAM of HoloMUCK shows the rigorous geometry of the spaces of its core. The spaces outside the core are a free-zone without building codes.
Model: Michael Buldo and Robert Zapulla

The LAMs of more tightly controlled MUDs are rigorously geometrical when compared with more democratic domains. In contrast, the looser structure of democratic communities makes them initially harder to navigate since there is no overarching order. In MediaMOO, for instance, organizing elements like Curtis Commons were added later to provide orientation for users. This is the electronic equivalent of urban projects in Baroque Rome or Napoleon III's Paris. Larger public spaces and boulevards were carved out of the medieval city to provide spatial structure for larger-scale organization.

As in cities, MUDs need orientational spaces once they become large, particularly if they lack any other geometrical structure. In democratically-run MUDs like MediaMOO, these spaces are created spontaneously by community members. Centrally controlled MUDs must rely on their administrators' experience for their organization.

The McGill University MUD, HoloMUCK, illustrates the extremes of administrative control. Originally its wizards had developed Flux, a MUD that placed minimal restrictions on new construction. As it evolved, its configuration became increasingly complex. Navigation in the MUD depended more and more on teleportation as the order of a larger MUD structure dissipated. Eventually the administrators felt the illogical nature of the spaces confused the players, rendering the MUD unusable.

Flux was reincarnated as HoloMUCK (fig. 103) using geometry clearly derived from a generic Canadian small town. Two main roads intersect to provide the center of a gridded community, a river bisects the town laterally. The wizards placed strict and strongly enforced rules on construction within the main structure of the community, TANSTAAFL.[1] As in Jay's Place, HoloMUCK's planning stresses the realism of the domain setting. If a closet were revealed to house aircraft, the wizards would not allow its construction within the main structure.

If the failure of its predecessor was due to spontaneity, HoloMUCK now suffers from its stifling restrictions. Even movement is affected by the demand for realism. Players have to move through stepping-stone spaces that describe changing perspectives as they navigate the MUD. This exacerbates the already anomalous, categoric movement in a text MUD.

The peculiar interior quality of MUD spaces presents them as a set of connected rooms. However, HoloMUCK's spaces are described as both external and internal. And this poses a problem for those attempting realism in text. If, for example, we walk down an actual street the perspective of our view changes with each step. The church on the far corner soon becomes the church to our immediate right. How does the designer convey this dynamism using categoric motion?

In many text MUDs a public space like a street is simply another room with suggested exits. In HoloMUCK a street is a series of separate spaces disposed linearly with exits to the right and left. If players were given instructions to go to the third building on the right, they would have to go through three of the street's sub-spaces, then exit to the right. This methodical plodding, of course, resembles the process of moving down the street. But the deliberate incremental movement between spaces calls attention to the artifice, undermining the credibility of the MUD environment.

HoloMUCK's wizards have tried to alleviate the over-regimentation of the domain by allowing builders free reign outside the city limits. Lying outside the main structure is a free-

1. The acronym stands for "There Ain't No Such Thing As A Free Lunch," perhaps a reference to the need for order to maintain a community.

zone where spaces may follow any or no logic at all. As a result most new construction lies outside the rigorous and isolated core of the community.

## Spatial Anomalies

The stepping-stone spaces of HoloMUCK demonstrate how the spatial illusion of a text MUD can break down. Each decision to move to the next space returns the user to the machine interface – reminding her of the artifice involved. Despite the wizards' attempt at rendering a realistic space, the rigor required to navigate it undermines the illusion. Anomalies of this sort are part of the terrain in MUDding and, arguably, of any spatial references involving computers.

For example, the popular notion of "surfing the Web" alludes to dynamic motion despite its categoric, discrete nature. It is simply the illusion of Web pages' adjacencies regardless of server locations. I can "go to" a Web site in Tokyo or Sydney no matter where I am physically. The sense of being somewhere else while logged onto a network is the illusion that underlies Gibson's cyberspace. These illusions of motion and engagement are not limited to computing networks. As we have seen, film, television, art and literature have the power to transport us as well.

Text MUDs have a range of anomalies involving space, identity and movement. As mentioned, a space described as "outdoors" is simply another room in the MUD's diagram. A building in a MUD would have to have a link to this space in order to have an exterior – unlike buildings we experience physically. Things are not what they appear to be. A room's description may have nothing to do with its use. The bedroom closet of LambdaMOO can house dozens of users at a time. The sewer system of The Chatting Zone turns out to provide shortcuts below the rigorous mapping of Ipswich, Ireland. Nor is identity safe from ambiguity – social identity in MUDs is itself part of an on-going masquerade.

Many MUD anomalies are products of movement. HoloMUCK is only one example among many. Motion in a domain – using cardinal directions – is the result of text commands, not physical relocation (fig. 104). Users are subject to the logic of the MUD and its designers – neither of which may be trusted. "Black holes" occur when users can't leave a space unless they teleport to a destination or log off the system. It's hard to imagine a physical counterpart to these anomalies since they are a product of categoric motion.

Some anomalies are unique to specific MUDs. These include variations on the black-hole anomaly. In BayMOO, for

Fig. 104
Predominance of cubes in LAMs indicates use of cardinal directions in the MUD organization. Spheres (below) indicate prevalent teleportation in a MUD.

Fig. 105
This model of the MUD BayMOO shows the ring of rooms that define Alcatraz. This spatial anomaly is an elaborate version of a black hole. Users enter but can't escape without teleporting.
Model: Ranah Hammash, Nanilee Thanantakul, Watinee Thantranon.

instance, the prison island of Alcatraz is represented by a loop of connected spaces (fig. 105). One enters the island from "San Francisco" and proceeds through the spaces one at a time. Appropriately, the player can't get out. Each room only leads to the next and none return to the mainland. Another example is in AlphaWorld, a graphic MUD, where a group of five spaces interconnect. Each room has a teleportation terminal that looks like an elevator. Each terminal has four destinations, but the user discovers that they are only the other four rooms. The five rooms are part of a cluster forming a pyramid. There is no way out by using the teleportation devices.

While AlphaWorld's anomaly was clearly designed as a trap, many anomalies may not be deliberate. Programming – or digging – a new MUD space in a MOO requires simple but specific programming. Entering the MUD command @dig "Living Room" creates a space called "Living Room." This space is unconnected to any other, effectively hovering in Limbo. The builder can only access it categorically by teleportation.

If a designer in the "Kitchen" wants to create a room with links to the Kitchen, the command would read @dig w/e to "Living Room." This creates a Living Room that is entered by going west from the Kitchen. It is exited by going east from the Living Room, returning the user to the Kitchen.

A designer can accidentally create a black hole by using the command @dig w to "Living Room." This leaves out the return leg of the previous command, stranding the player in the Living Room. There is no way out except by teleporting to a destination or logging out of the MUD.

In MOOs the tools for creating a spatial environment include @dig, @add exit, @add entrance, @exits, @entrances among others. Each has its own syntax and entailments and – predictably – coding errors that produce accidental oddities in the MUD. Regardless of their origin these paradoxical spaces have few precedents in our perceived world. If anything, they are more allied with the fantasy world we inherited from childhood. Similarly, we suspend our belief when we enjoy a movie or a novel. Disembodied relocation and point of view are easily accepted in these media without risk of losing the audience.

Since anomalies are an accepted part of text MUD culture, designers often employ them to direct traffic within the environment as well as to create elaborate traps. A room with appropriate exits can be used to bypass a tangle of connected spaces, for instance. Other rooms are actually vehicles, examples include buses, trains, airplanes and Meridian-

*MOO's QE2 – a fully outfitted cruise ship. A room hanging disconnected in a MUD is effectively private since no casual user is even aware of its existence.*

## Problems of Design

*Despite these apparent conveniences, anomalies can take their toll on social interaction. Take the ease of construction, for instance. Digging space is a quick and effectively cost-free activity. In MUDs where citizens build spaces and objects, the number of rooms can vastly outnumber that of the users – particularly those logged on at one time. Paradoxically, the MUDs with the greatest number of builders seem to have the lowest density population. This explains the apparent vacancy of many MUDs. While there may be pockets of activity, large areas remain unused, rarely visited.*

*Unsuccessful rooms are like unsuccessful Web sites. Once built, they are rarely modified. Visitors may "hit" on a space once or twice, but without novelty or companionship to engage them they rarely return. Wizards encourage builders to innovate, making their objects and spaces entertaining, but the talent and ambition of users varies widely and unless construction is checked by an administrator, the MUD risks wasting memory on superfluous construction. Even in successful MUDs many citizens are only familiar with a handful of spaces. Many have not explored the main structure since their first few visits.*

*MUD social activity often centers on the entry, where users begin their sessions. It often appears as a lobby, town square*

Fig. 106
This LAM of the graphic domain AlphaWorld shows that teleportation is the preferred method of movement, although, once visitors arrive at their destination they move dynamically in a 3D space. AlphaWorld's structure comprises several "worlds" which are linked by teleportation. The overall structure was mapped in this model.
Model: Dang Nguyen and Christopher Kretovic.

*Envisioning Cyberspace*

or visitor center. The area immediately around the entry is also populated but occupancy drops off sharply thereafter. Experienced MUD users often prefer teleporting to their destinations rather than sequentially moving through the labyrinth of rooms. Once they arrive at their destinations they often move spatially, browsing the adjoining rooms (fig. 106). This movement resembles our earlier recollection our childhood bedroom. We moved categorically in recalling the space, then we moved dynamically within it.

The apparent emptiness of MUDs is exacerbated by privatization. As mentioned, most private spaces often float free, unlinked to the main structure. The Chatting Zone and the University of MOO, among others, have a predominance of rooms where private socializing occurs. Many citizens are in the public space only momentarily before they teleport to their rooms. From there they secretly monitor MUD activity or work on their spaces.

This depletes the public spaces of a population and turns them into virtual fish bowls. The MUD space appears empty since there often aren't enough users logged on to support this stratification. Only by using a categorical command like @who can the average user find out who is currently logged on.

## Solving Problems by Spatialization

The polarization between public and private spaces is the product of poor spatialization and design. MUD entries are a case in point. Real cities don't have single points of entry. Their periphery is open to commercial and public traffic. Even the most private spaces of a city are part of its spatial structure. MUDs, while seemingly based on reality, ignore fundamental truths about actual communities. Teleportation is only a symptom of the problem. Although HoloMUCK forbids teleportation in the belief that it destroys the sense of physical community, the solution is misconceived. **Teleportation is merely a user's way around a problem of design.** It's a symptom but not the problem itself.

The graphic representation of a domain might offer solutions to these problems. If a visitor can "see" the extent of a MUD she may be more inclined to explore it. The text blinds users to distant spaces, blinkering their experience. This limits users to sequentially plodding from room to room.

Teleportation is preferred to spatial movement once the terrain is familiar and destinations are known. But socializing seems to relate inversely to teleportation – it's hard to meet people on the street if everyone is teleporting.

Another resolution to the social stratification may incorporate all private spaces into the main MUD structure. Also limiting access to these spaces to spatial movement may improve social interaction. Finally, increasing the number of entries to the domain would shorten the distance to subsequent destinations. If more than one entry is used, each will serve as a node of activity, creating the equivalents of neighborhood pubs and hangouts.

Figs. 107, 108, 109
VanGogh TV, the Dutch computer/art design group, has created several MUDs using 3D graphics. Image at left is from Telco Domain and those above and below are from the domain Worlds Within produced for the 1996 World Olympic games.
Artist: Karel Dudesek, Designer: Tim Becker, Technician: Martin Schmitz

Random access at these points could stimulate exploration and interaction. Once the main entry has a critical mass of occupants, additional visitors could be let in elsewhere to spread activity to lesser frequented areas. This could revitalize the community.

## Visual MUDs

But what happens when a MUD becomes graphic and three-dimensional? With the advent of Virtual Reality Modeling Language, VRML, and similar programs it's now possible to create on-line virtual worlds. These new social environments called WOOs (**W**eb-based **MOO**s) resemble video games with the crucial difference of including responsive avatars, social activity and buildable environments.

Most WOOs refer to our perceived world by incorporating ground planes, sky, horizon, light sources and 3D objects. Significantly, while these items are tacit in a text MUD – our minds fill them in – in graphic MUDs these form the basis of the environment, the game board. This replication of our earthbound, physical world implies that the player is present in "human" form. Of course, the user's avatar may take any shape but many principles of human perception still apply. For instance the default orientation of the sky is above the ground plane and the limited range of view implies frontality and vertical posture. Standard viewing heights of a few feet imply a scale similar to that of an average person.

Predictably these environments encourage dynamic, spatial movement. Displays of these spaces – such as those of Van Gogh TV's Worlds Within (figs. 107, 108, 109) include navigational controls.[2]  Others offer virtual joysticks, standard in the VRML browser, as though the avatar were some form of vehicle.  Movement appeals to the user's perception – perspectives change as the player navigates the space.  In many ways the action resembles that of a conventional video game, although at a slower rate.

Action games like Quake have elements of MUDs built into them but, to enhance their speed, the images are low resolution.  In large graphic MUDs the resolution is also limited but the complexity of the environment slows the interaction down.  To convey dynamic motion, new perspectives have to be quickly regenerated to portray the new viewing angles.  The more complex the environment – the higher the polygon count – the longer a view will take to render.  If the user moves too quickly he may notice a lag in the image.  In an immersive environment this could, over time, lead to disorientation and headaches.

Programmers of 3D MUDs keep the polygon count down by simplifying the construction of objects and using bit-mapped surfaces which show details as two-dimensional graphics.  Consequently the worlds created have a schematic, cartoonish quality that belies their realism.

Another technique surrounds the user with a zone of resolution, called a horizon, comparable to a bodily zone of privacy.  In AlphaWorld, for instance, only the buildings in a radius of roughly one hundred feet are rendered.  However, beyond them, a player can see remote sky and mountains many miles away.  As the user moves in the space, the zone of resolution keeps pace, generating objects and buildings along the way.  To the player it appears as though the objects magically pop into view.  This is a parallel to the episodic movement in text MUDs.

This product of computational necessity recalls the somewhat self-centered world of childhood.  The world of WOOs responds to the player, it's not objective or concrete.  Just as a child might imagine a world created just for her, WOO players can see one under construction responsive to their movement and point of view.  The moon in the sky **does** follow you.

Despite WOO's at dynamic movement, users still use categoric motion.  Logging in and out of a domain still involves the categorical movement of the Internet.  Given the science fictional nature of many worlds, teleportation is popular as well.  As in text MUDs, WOO players can forego plodding from space to space and instantly arrive at their destination.

2. Worlds Within also supports voice communication, text-based chat and collaboration through a shared whiteboard, where up to 8 people can work together on one file and store it in the environment.

## Dimensional Space in Graphic MUDs

The space of a graphic environment varies with the MUD. Some, like Worlds Away or The Palace, are effectively two-dimensional, showing a flattened backdrop in elevation and avatars in front – similar to a stage set for a play. The Palace, for example, presents compelling renderings of interiors that have icon-like avatars moving across them. For all the richness of the imagery, though, it is a flat world. The avatars look like playing pieces scattered on a painting. Similarly Worlds Away – formerly Fujitsu's Habitat – shows animated 2D cartoon avatars moving in front of flat backgrounds (please refer back to figs. 88, 89, 90).

Other MUDs, like World Chat and AlphaWorld are more committed to rendering a three-dimensional environment. Unlike text MUDs, space in these worlds is transparent. Despite the zones of resolution, it's possible to see many objects and spaces at once, whereas text MUDs limit users to one space at a time.

While "outdoors" is simply another room in a MUD, in a WOO it is an all-embracing volume – more like our perceived space. In a text MUD a player may be "outdoors" but still be only offered a finite number of directional cues. A player standing "outdoors" in the open space of a WOO is implicitly connected to all buildings and rooms in the domain as well as all points within the outdoor space itself, theoretically infinite in number.

For this reason, a WOO maps better as plans, like those used by architects and urban planners, rather than the flowchart method used in LAMs. Only when the world space or room is connected to another through categorical, episodic motion can it be mapped easily using the LAM method.

Movement in 3D domains is not limited to teleportation and the ground plane. Flying is another popular way to get around. It's also an easy way to spot the artifice and inconsistency of the simulation. A common way to create a horizon in a 3D MUD is to surround the ground plane with a cylindrical scrim that displays horizon and sky. Seen from the ground plane this is fairly convincing since the user doesn't see the top of the cylinder. Flying, however, changes the perspective, revealing the curvature of the cylinder (fig. 110).

The effects of the cylinder can be seen from the ground as well. Some time back some students and I went to the suburbs of AlphaWorld. AlphaWorld is actually made up of several thematic worlds but the main space resembles a city placed on a flat, green plane. Over the past few years the cit-

Fig. 110
This model shows schematically how the space of AlphaWorld is defined. The square ground plane is surrounded by a horizon scrim that has a landscape and sky mapped onto it. Within the domain, the gap between the ground plane and scrim appears blue because it is the screen's background default color.
Model: Dang Nguyen

izens have built hundreds of buildings, roads, and houses from an available kit of parts or by inserting models of their own. However, despite its size, the city of AlphaWorld is finite. Beyond the last buildings the gridded ground plane pushes out toward the horizon. The view is pleasant – white-capped mountains under a clear sky. At the foot of the mountains the ground plane meets a lake that extends beyond our view to the right and left. Getting to the beach is a problem, though.

As we approached the mountains the ground plane kept extending. New chunks of grass grid appeared as our zone of resolution advanced with us. The edge of the plane – the beach – was always another hundred feet away. It turned out that there was no lake at all. The blue at the foot of the mountains was the gap between the ground plane and the cylindrical scrim. Flying above or below the ground plane revealed the model's artifice and the curve of the horizon.

## Movement and the Shape of Communities

It turns out that flying and teleportation are important to the shape of AlphaWorld. Although the novice starts by exploring the ground plane and buildings, a number of spaces actually hover above and are accessed by flying. Spaces exist below the ground plane as well but are not as prevalent. Nothing supports the hovering spaces, giving them a surreal, contrived quality.

A view from above AlphaWorld presents the viewer with a plan that resembles Los Angeles or some other urban sprawl. Houses, buildings and swimming pools litter the ground plane. Despite a grid of streets at the city center, roads are intermittent and disconnected – sometimes stopping after a few hundred feet. Often they lead nowhere, fragments isolated at the edge of the community.

And yet, despite this discontinuity, AlphaWorld has a structure. Beyond its core, the city extends in eight directions. From above, the plan resembles a star with eight rays diminishing as they project from the center. The rays extend in the four cardinal directions as well as northeast, northwest, southeast and southwest. Oddly, no roads project diagonally from the middle of the city. Indeed few diagonal roads exist at all. What would lead the citizens to build such a symmetry despite their otherwise haphazard, idiosyncratic construction? MUD construction was apparently left to the individual with little interference from the administrators. The absence of diagonal roads also indicates that the rays of construction weren't planned by the wizards.

Despite the absence of diagonal roads, the mystery is resolved by examining movement within the domain. A citizen can build anywhere that he finds an open, unclaimed piece of ground plane. AlphaWorld's core configuration reveals the grid used in laying out the original community. This area is dense with construction including residences and public buildings. It also contains the entry point of the community – where visitors log in.

Dynamic movement around the community takes time. If one is not inclined to roam the space, teleportation provides a quick alternative. Teleportation is also accurate. Users can enter an "address" and simply wind up at the destination with no guess work. This is accomplished by entering coordinates in the cardinal directions or distances in any of the four subsidiary directions.

Apparently, as the community outgrew its rectilinear core, it became more difficult for new builders to find empty plots for construction. Roaming around the grid of streets was laborious and unfruitful. Since space was plentiful at the edge of the core, builders would teleport there using any of the eight directions. Upon arriving they would wander around, find an available site and build.

Of course, a builder proud of her work would want to return periodically to enjoy or modify her project. Situating a structure at an arbitrary point would be hard to recall later. Consequently, a prudent builder would choose a site whose Cartesian coordinates were easy to remember – preferably one with the same x and y values or either x or y value being zero. Similarly, a simple distance in one of the secondary directions could pinpoint the construction site. The resulting pattern of AlphaWorld's development closely follows the options provided by teleportation (fig. 111).

Movement within a community, physical or otherwise, is critical to its form and reflects its administration. The shapes and locations of cities from ancient to modern times have been largely determined by their mode of transportation. Bruges and Amsterdam are characterized by the canals used for moving goods and people. Similarly, Houston and Los Angeles are inconceivable without the automobile. We have seen that LAMs of text MUDs are shaped by directional and categorical movement designed into their spaces. Like other dynamic, urban and on-line communities the configuration of AlphaWorld is based on its preferred mode of movement, teleportation.

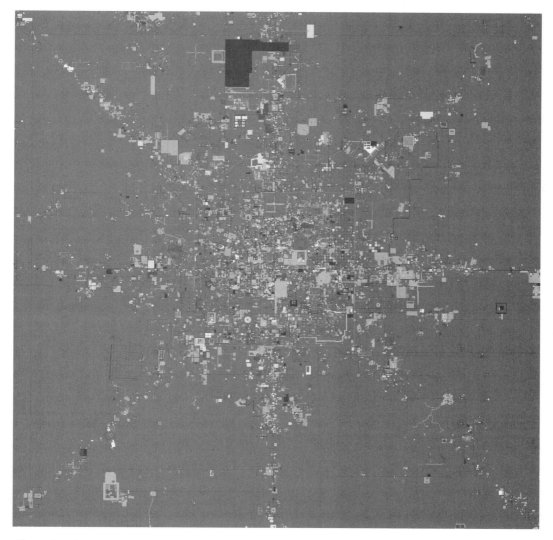

## Conclusion

The emergent patterns of development in text MUDs and WOOs often is the result of the chance-driven, iterative activity of their occupants. Since builders are not encumbered by gravity or weather, they project an architecture of desire. In the more participatory MUDs this construction is accretive and bottom-up. They are free of master plans and large-scaled infrastructure – other than those provided at the start-up. This resembles the development of traditional communi-

Fig. 111
Aerial view of AlphaWorld's main community. Radiating pattern of development and dense radius at the center are results of dynamic and categorical motion – teleportation – in the domain.

ties built up over time. Although initially the design may appear haphazard – a few buildings strewn on the land – over the years patterns emerge based on their use and local conditions. Cities built in medieval Europe bear the mark of slow, incremental growth in their dense fabric and branching roadways. The incremental growth of BayMOO likewise presents a bifurcating, organic structure. Even the development of AlphaWorld on its infinite grassy plane is guided by hidden principles of community growth and movement perhaps unanticipated by its creators.

In the next chapter we will see how the illusions of cyberspace can overlap with actual spaces and people. This is a theme we will pursue throughout the rest of this book.

# Merging Physical
# and Mediated Realities

Let us now consider whether the essence or very nature of a thing, and each individual thing, are the same or different...”

Aristotle. *The metaphysics,* Book VI, 1031b.

*This chapter describes the bridging of cognitive and perceived space through mediation. It presents collaboratories and work environments that incorporate physical and cyberspaces and will discuss the human and social issues that attend them.*

*So far we have seen abstract, on-line communities as independent of their physical counterparts. But what if the fantasy were taken away? What if the theme park became themeless? How would MUDs work if people used their real names, the roles they played – themselves? What if the spaces of the MUD reflected conditions of their physical counterparts? What bridges would link our electronic, cognitive space to our perceived world?*

*While the prospects of mixing illusion and physical space seem troubling, in fact we already use our technology this way. We accept that our telephone partner appears to be next to us. Teleconferencing similarly brings others into our range regardless of their location. Even without technology, our processes of perception and cognition are so complex that separating illusion from reality is itself daunting (figs. 112,113,114).*

*However, the* third place[1] *of multi-user domains merges the two. These spaces and avatars often float free of physical location and identity. Few MUD users know the true identities of their fellow citizens. While this is unnecessary for those who accept a clear division between the fantasy of the MUD and real life, the linkage between the user, his avatar and society is subtle and a potential resource for the creation of new kinds of mediated communities.*

*This third place, rather than solely being a moratorium space, could become a place of engagement where users gather to exchange ideas. In his proposal for a simulation of the physical world, Gelernter describes how those who use it would be better informed citizens of the world. Although Gelernter's proposal is not a multi-user domain as we have described it, it is spatial and shared by many as a common resource, like Wladek Fuch's VCNet. By bringing the information of the real world into cyberspace, the real world may be better managed by such an enlightened populace.*

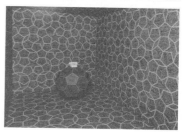

Figs. 112, 113, 114
In the installation "Interfaz" Spanish artist Manuel Saiz juxtaposed physical reality with two images of virtual space, a CAD model and a live video. The CAD model of a fictional space was used to create an actual room, complete with the flaws of a computer-generated image. Once the room was built, two monitors stood outside it (shown at top), one presenting a live, video image of the interior and the other showing the generating CAD model (lower images).

1. Here I refer to Ray Oldenberg's concept of an informal social place.

## Political Implications

Linking the real world to cyberspace has rich possibilities. Many newsgroups, chat rooms and multi-user domains are categorized according to interests including arts, entertainment, scientific research, and women's rights among others. These social domains are demographic gathering points. As opposed to politics based on physical territory – such as cities and states – these societies are de-territorialized.

Without physical boundaries, a domain can host citizens connecting from other countries. Already the politics of cyberspace have begun to affect "real" politics. Attempts by the German government to bring suit against Compuserve for trafficking sexually explicit material shows how terrestrial politics are challenged by those of cyberspace. Given trends in technology and global politics we can imagine that Internet sites specific to interests could become distributed homelands regardless of where their citizens live. These become the secular equivalents of other places of mind – Valhalla, Hades, Paradise – shared by many yet inhabited by none.

But the crucial difference is that, unlike their predecessors, these environments are manifest to the senses. Some domains are also information resources, forming an abstract agora for a distributed global population. These domains are actually a curious mix of memory palace and agora, for despite their ephemerality, they contain fixed objects and mnemonic structures. Not surprisingly, computer **memory** is the very substance of their being. As we have seen, aspects of MUDs often parallel the perceived qualities of our world. We use it both as site and subject of our public lives.

## Collaboratories: On-line Work Environments

The past ten years have seen the development of domains that do away with the playful themes of MUDs to focus on the productive interaction of their participants. Pavel Curtis, former researcher at Xerox PARC and founder of LambdaMOO, also created a MUD called JupiterMOO. This MUD was the shared site of an international group of astronomers and astrophysicists. Operating in a common space independent of physical location and time of day, researchers could converse, sharing information and observations. Technical reports and graphic files were posted within the domain as well, as part of the MUD's information resources. [2]

These workplaces without walls are called collaboratories, a term coined by William Wulf in 1989. They are characterized by their ubiquity and mediation through computer networks letting researchers in various fields – physics, astronomy,

2. Curtis, Pavel, and David Nichols. 1993. "MUDs grow up: Social virtual reality in the real world." Paper presented at Cyberconf 3 in Austin, Texas. Curtis has since founded PlaceWare, Inc., which develops software to support professional MUDs.

engineering – share resources, access to instrumentation and comraderie. For example, the Upper Atmospheric Research Collaboratory – UARC – whose server is located in Michigan, lets scientists share instruments in the study of "space weather," magnetic storms that disrupt transmission of power and communication. Such environmental monitoring is also the focus of the Collaboratory for Environmental and Molecular Sciences based at the Pacific Northwest National Laboratory in Richland, Washington.

Gary Olson, a cognitive scientist at the University of Michigan and creator of UARC, believes that the potential for collaboratories extends beyond research into the corporate world. Collaboratories are increasingly seen as media for the distributed work of multinational corporations. Automobile and furniture manufacturers as well as high-technology companies, he says, are highly interested in this. [3]

3. Ross-Flanagan, Nancy. 1998. "The virtues (and vices) of virtual colleagues." *MIT Technology Review.* March/April. pp. 54-59.

If the focus of many collaboratories was originally access to instrumentation and data, the inclusion of chat boxes and virtual rooms has turned them into on-line social environments. While not conventional MUDs, collaboratories share many of their attributes. Their intimacy and collegiality has a socially leveling effect – typical of MUDs – which lowers the barriers to dialog. A student logging into a collaboratory may have an otherwise unlikely conversation with a senior researcher.

This leveling of hierarchy and lowered barriers found in on-line environments is also useful in a corporate setting. Lisa Kimball, a director at Metasys in Washington, D.C., recalls a project for a client that was undergoing a merger with another company. In an effort to manage the stress of reorganization, the corporation retained Metasys, a provider of on-line corporate environments. Metasys created a multi-user domain in which various rooms housed discussion groups. Corporate employees and management would log in to converse, leave messages and vent their frustrations. They found that the moratorium of the domain facilitated discussions and that, in real life, the employees would pursue their on-line dialogs in the company hallways and offices. The overlap of the virtual onto the real helped the company through a time of emotional and organizational stress.

MUDs have found their way into the corporate environment. Chiat-Day, the advertising firm, created a graphic domain for its employees when it set up its operations in Manhattan in 1993. Designed by Art and Technology's Jeet Singh, it incorporated messaging and chat spaces, including a bar where employees could socialize whether or not they were concurrently on-site.

More recently Fore Systems, a developer of computer ATM networks, installed a graphic MUD to disseminate technical support to its non-technical staff. Using a client-based software from The Palace Inc., Fore created a 24-room intranet environment based in part on the physical layout of its campus. James Carlin, manager of Fore's marketing help desk, believes that information gathered during on-line dialog can be used to enhance their customer services. For instance, the ideas generated can be incorporated into reference files.

At this time only twenty percent of Fore's sales staff is physically present at its Pittsburgh headquarters. The company looks toward expanding this service into extranets so that its remote sales force can benefit as well. While graphic chat environments are rare on intranets, their use on the Internet is rising.[4]

## Reality Checks

The success of professional on-line communities and collaboratories depends on their users. The social leveling that lets a student casually converse with a researcher can be annoying for the researcher if the discussion is seen as an intrusion. What is an advantage for one may be a disadvantage for another.

Relationships between mediated workers and their on-site counterparts are also important. A study conducted by Eleana Rocco at the University of Michigan showed that groups that had face-to-face contact prior to on-line collaboration displayed more cooperation than those deprived of it. She had subjects play a computer game that required collaboration as well as competition. Groups that physically met for five to ten minutes prior to going on-line established a level of trust that the control group lacked. [5]

Gary Olson and his colleague Tom Finholt have closely monitored interaction in collaboratory domains. They have found that, though the topics of conversation are the same as they would be in real life, the quality of ideas is higher. Though they are not sure why this is, they note that spoken conversation is often comprised of short statements. Speakers often don't have time to develop ideas before the conversation moves on. The presence of text may compel correspondents to consider their thoughts before committing them to the screen. Apparently the increased flow of ideas is a chief advantage of these corporate and research domains. The medium seems to demand it.

While on-line environments offer much, they will never replace the innately physical aspects of social life. We have

4. Murphy, Kathleen. "Graphical chat makes move from games to intranets." *Internet World*, vol. 4, Issue 7, Feb. 23, 1998.

5. Ross-Flanagan, op. cit., pp.58-59.

Fig. 115
The sculpture "Transience" by artist Mark Palmer re-creates the ethereal quality of a CAD wire-frame model in steel. Here we have an inversion of conventional virtual reality. Instead of a computer model mimicking physical materials, the materials are used to represent the vectors of the computer model. Palmer believes that the sensuality VR lets us re-examine our habitual relationships with the world – it gives us the chance to experience a sensuality beyond the material world.

*seen in earlier chapters the complex role our bodies play during social interaction. Despite advances in human-computer interface design, we are accustomed to a quality of communication that no computer can yet convey. Though we may exchange information in a collaboratory, we can't shake hands or feel each other's presence.*

## Conclusion

*The preceding chapter has been a brief review of professional communities operating on computer networks. In these examples we have seen a link between actual people and their avatars, between electronic spaces and their actual counterparts (fig. 115). These different entities, real and emulated, combine to the advantage of their users.*

*In the next and final section of the book we will pursue this link between physical and cyberspaces. My aim in reconciling them is not to minimize their differences so much as to point out their collaborative strengths. Each, however distinct, extends us beyond ourselves to each other. Reconciling them may reveal new ways of sharing our common experience.*

# Bridging Spaces – Transcending Disciplines

"Fragmentation and synaesthesia have been two recurrent themes in Modernism. From Wagner's *Gesamptkustwerk*... to... the performance art of Laurie Anderson, artists have given expression to the 'invisible revolution' that is occurring as our senses reorientate to accommodate media that are instant, global and multi-sensory."

Cotton, R., and R. Oliver, 1993. *Understanding Hypermedia*. London: Phaidon Press Ltd. p. 21.

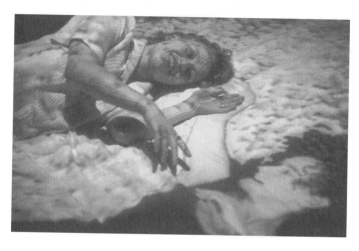

Fig. 116
Artist Paul Sermon has projected live videos of dancer Susan Kozel on a bed shared with audience/participants. The participants interact with the image despite the flattened abstraction.

*This chapter presents the work of artists and researchers that brings together material and electronic space. It discusses augmented reality, surveillance, and some of their social implications. We will see how aspects of symbolic, electronic space merge with those of conventional reality and how the traditional divisions between disciplines are transcended by digital technologies (fig. 116).*

*In the following pages we will see how cyberspaces have affected different fields. We will see how abstract arts manifest themselves tangibly and how those arts that once seemed concrete have become abstracted through simulation. While there is no denying that computation has affected our technical and professional environments, the effect on the humanities is startling. It's as though the confluence of symbolic and concrete spaces were a base condition – the foundation for a new discipline.[1]*

*Through this work we will see how space mediates the abstract and physical. I take these examples from the arts and humanities because these fields have at their heart a social function. To be effective, their work must communicate with the viewer, listener and reader. I hope to show how space and information combine to create unique, unprecedented experiences.*

1. Bødker, op. cit., p.44.
"As the use of artifacts is part of social activity, we design new conditions for collective activity, for example, new divisions of labor and other new ways of coordination, control, and communication."
Computer artifacts can change the conditions of our social-physical reality.

# Confluence and Transition

Gerhard Eckel faced a problem. A composer of modern classical music he was trained in twentieth century composition along
the lines of Karlheinz Stockhausen, Pierre Boulez and John
Cage. Cage's music had fascinated Eckel because, unlike
compositions that were determined a priori, Cage's were driven
by chance. Cage often prepared his music as instructions, giving the musician choices in its performance. The same piece
could sound quite different if played by another musician – or
even by the same musician on another day.

The problem was with the audience. Although the composer
and musician knew that chance-driven music could have a variety of presentations, the audience usually only heard one. How
could the audience tell that the piece was not just a recital of a
normally composed piece? How could they sense the contin-
gency of the composition?

Eckel took his cue from architecture. Unlike the narrative arts
of music and literature, architecture is ambient. A building or
city houses a multitude of choices and sequences – each
decided spontaneously by the user. Every movement results in
a unique narrative.

In the past few years Eckel has created several virtual environments at the GMD German National Center for Information
Technology in St. Augustin, Germany. Each is an architectural

Figs. 117, 118, 119, 120, 121, 122, 123
In a project entitled "Camera Musica," composer
Gerhard Eckel has created an architectural notation for music. The audience participates in the
creation of chance-driven music by navigating a
cyberspace. Approaching walls and objects
stimulates a musical response that forms part of
the overall "found" composition.

space acting as a system of musical notation (figs. 117-123). Because each is an interactive virtual reality, it is also a musical instrument. With the help of his colleagues Eckel has built a room bounded on all sides with projection screens. Images shown on the screen portray a building or set of rooms that comprises the musical composition.

A musician enters a space wearing a headset that lets him see the space in three dimensions. He also holds a controller with which he navigates the architecture by pointing. As he approaches walls and other objects a music synthesizer plays sounds specific to the object. Were one to move through the architecture in exactly the same way the resulting music would be identical. But since the musician has a choice of movement, the presentation is inevitably different. (Plates 37-39, 41-42.)

Marcos Novak, the forerunner of much current architectural interest in cyberspace, has similarly proposed a "navigable music." Rather than using physical architecture as his point of departure, he generates forms based on data in his computer. In "Navigable Music" these forms are crumpled planes forming landscapes of sound. By tracing a path across the surface with a 3D computer cursor, a synthesizer generates a series of sounds unique to each route. Whereas Eckel's product is recognizable as piano and orchestral music, Novak's is atonal — reinforcing the mechanical abstraction of the process.

Chance-driven processes in music remain controversial despite their long history. However, when computer and audience participation enter the scene, many preconceptions of music have to fall. In Eckel's compositions, for example, what is the composition — the product of the motion or the "frozen music" of the architecture? Is the architecture of virtual space the notation of the music or the instrument upon which it is played? In Novak's work, who is the composer? Perhaps in such cases, the artist is the one who starts the process that results in art. Novak may be the artist behind the process, for instance, but he is not the composer of the music. Novak's is a perfect example of how the distinctions between artistic disciplines blur and disappear in the face of digital technologies.

If music can freeze and later be thawed by chance, perhaps other dynamic, time-based arts may do the same. Take for example the recent work of Joachim Sauter and Dirk Lüsebrink of the German group Art+Com. In 1996 they responded to an architectural competition to design an archive for historic films in Berlin. Since the invention of cinematography Berlin has been the subject of many films — some brief clips, others full-length features. The competition brief solicited an architectural solution for organizing the films and providing a forum for viewing them. The sponsors assumed that the respondents would propose physical buildings...but not Art+Com.

In their design for the archive, Sauter and Lüsebrink describe an entirely virtual, on-line facility. All the historic films would be found there, categorized by the time and place they were created. The proposal, a sophisticated video done with computer graphics, entailed the construction of several CAD models documenting the vicinity of the Potsdamerplatz, the heart of the old city. One model was made for each decade of the century. Each was a matrix for locating a film segment. The brilliance of the scheme lay in how the films were represented.

Some films were made using a stationary camera. In others the camera moved, dollying or zooming to follow action or change of view. Let us say that a film was shot with a camera moving forward through Potsdamerplatz – the distance it traveled being twenty meters. Now imagine taking each cell of the film and placing it vertically, like dominoes, along the camera's path. This way each cell of the film would be linked with a particular camera location and view. Taken together, this horizontal stack of cells forms a film object situated in time and place. It is as solid – in its way – as any of the buildings or people it depicts (figs. 124-129).

This technique of creating film objects has precedents in the pioneering work of Ron MacNeil at MIT's MediaLab. As with Art+Com's proposal, his objects also stacked images as a way of archiving material. It also lent itself to analysis since cutting laterally through the object would reveal a cell of the film. Cutting longitudinally would produce a time smear – a slice

Figs. 124, 125, 126, 127, 128, 129
This set of images by Joachim Sauter and Dirk Lüsebrink of Art+Com shows how a film object is used. It exists as a form placed in the context of where the film was shot. Viewers approach the object from the end and move through it. As they proceed the object reveals its constituent cells, showing the film at the rate of movement. The sides of the object show the edges of the cells as a time smear.

through the film's time-space – like a motion blur in a photograph. Another proposal by British artist Rory Hamilton shows similar objects representing interactive films with branching, alternate plots (fig. 130). The crucial innovation of the Art+Com proposal was its time-space linkage to the film's subject matter.

Their proposal is haunting. Hovering ghostlike in the simulation of Potsdamerplatz are several oddly shaped forms – some curved like snakes, others succinct arcs. As one approaches a box from the end, he sees the first frame of the film object. Entering it he sees the successive cells at his rate of movement. If the visitor is moving at the same speed as the camera that took the film, the action observed appears normal.

If the viewer moves forward in time, say ten years, older film objects disappear from the model as new ones come into view. The irony, of course, is that these historical objects never existed. Yet they exist cognitively in the way that MediaMOO's ballroom hovers over the MediaLab. Perhaps they pose an updated model of the memory palace, one abstract and ethereal, yet anchored to the specifics of material space and time (fig. 131).

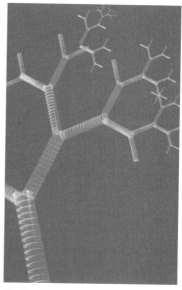

Fig. 130
This film object by British artist Rory Hamilton presents a method for organizing interactive films. The branching structure results from decision points within the plot structure. Audience participants can view the same film without having the same experience. They can actually navigate the plot by testing outcomes and re-tracing back to decision points to explore alternatives.

Fig. 131
Design proposal by Art+Com for a film archive for Berlin. Note gray, curved and rectilinear film objects hovering in the octagon of the new Potsdamer-platz. Joachim Sauter believes that processes such as those underlying the film objects can be lead to a repertoir of new forms. These forms may be manifested in actuality or in cyberspace.

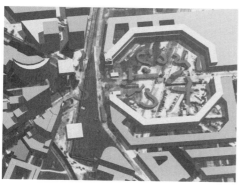

The proposal suggests that new films be continuously added to the archive. The archive, ideally situated in a cyberspace Web site, would contain professional as well as amateur films alike. Feature films and tourist videos would have the same status provided only that they accurately portray Berlin at a specific point in time. We will return to the modeling of surveillance again shortly.

## Using Algorithms in the Creation Process

Making abstract arts like film and music tangible is part of a larger problem. How do we render anything, concept or idea, tangible? This is a question of creativity in general. The work of artists and designers illustrates links between technology and humanity. But creativity, as we have seen in the work of Novak, may be independent of human agency. When the computer renders on the screen nearly any information it can process, artists involved with them must acknowledge their shared authorship.

Computers follow the instructions of their programs, processing data in ways defined by the programmer. A given data set, program and user will yield one solution. The same data set with another program – or algorithm – will yield a different product. Designers like Novak, Constantin Terzides and Knut Graf (figs. 132, 133, 134) have used computer algorithms to generate architectural and spatial designs using computers.

An algorithm is a step-by-step process leading to a solution. It is a logical equivalent to procedures we use to generate many artifacts. Given instructions with the appropriate materials, we could build a house, a car, possibly an artwork. The algorithm for production is distinct from its product, yet generatively related. Artists like Robert Morris and Sol Lewitt have long known this. It is an intrinsic part of socially collaborative disciplines like design, engineering and architecture. In fact, we could argue that the relationship between instructions and product is as natural as life itself – that computer algorithms are a pale shadow of material processes underlying the organic world.

This leads to some interesting considerations. If, for example, we take an algorithm to be equivalent to a DNA strand – the embodiment of genetic information – we can take advantage of processes that drive genetics and Darwinian selection. Let us say that we have two algorithms – lists of instructions. Each instruction is discrete, having its own place in the algorithm. Also, each algorithm is unique. Given the same data set to process, each would produce a different result.

Now, by exchanging individual instructions between the lists, we effectively mate the two. Depending on what we exchange, we get a different result – progeny of the two parent algorithms. Each child of this algorithmic union would produce a unique result in processing the original data set. Given parallels between biological and data-driven genetics, we can evaluate their results for fitness. Genetic algorithms (GAs) that create "fit" products survive while unsuccessful ones die out. The method by which the selection occurs may also be done algorithmically so that the final product is the one that yields the "fittest" results. It's possible also to do breeding by brute force, say the way a botanist may selectively breed tulips to achieve a perfect specimen.

Pioneered by John Holland at the University of Michigan, genetic algorithms have been used for years in computer sciences and engineering. They have been successful in everything from perfecting software to designing jet engines. GAs have formed the basis for the growing field of Artificial Life – which studies "life" within computers in the form of viruses, worms and potentially productive agents. More recently, artists like Darrel Anderson and William Latham have applied genetic processes to the creation of organic artworks. These works, rendered in

Figs. 132, 133, 134
German information architect Knut Graf has created "Bluebonnetspace," a cyberspace populated with objects generated algorithmically from the harmonic content of a voice sample saying the word "bluebonnet" three times. By changing parameters of the algorithms, he achieved different products. Then he placed the results in relationship to one another, forming the sculptural content of the space.

high-resolution graphics look disturbingly similar to plants and bodily organs found in nature. While their depth of resolution makes them almost palpable, they are often beautiful, static specimens hanging in cyberspace. But spatial qualities are not all that an organism displays. It also has behaviors.

The work of artist Karl Sims combines the organic generation of form with characteristics that, taken as a whole, become behaviors. Behavioral traits are passed from one generation to the next within the machine, the way features or colors may be passed along. If a creature is made up of discrete objects, each object may behave a certain way with respect to the rest. Say one object responds to its neighbor's tug by rotating, and the next responds to rotation by lifting. Combined, the three of them would appear to move in concert. Strangely, perhaps, but somehow organically.

Sims has bred many of these organisms at Genetic Arts, Inc. using the computer to evaluate and select aesthetically and dynamically "fit" creatures. In simulated environments constrained by gravity or water, these creations crawl, swim or fly depending on their "nature." Some even develop unpredictable behaviors, propelling themselves by falling and flipping to their destinations in cyberspace (figs. 135, 136, 137).

Just as genetic algorithms have succeeded in engineering and art, they are now finding their way into architecture. In certain buildings like auditoriums, the acoustics of a space can be optimized on a computer by using iterative GAs. Eric Bicci, a young architectural designer, has applied GAs to this use. He has also used GAs to produce designs that might not be physical spaces at all – just beautiful, deep space simulations on the screen. Likewise, Jeffrey Krause, of Blacksquare in San Francisco, uses GAs to create complex geometries that, although architectural in quality, may equally be sculpture or graphic art.

Krause, in a presentation at the 1997 ACADIA conference in Cincinnati, Ohio, explained his inspiration for using the algorithms. [2] As a student at the University of Southern California and later at MIT's School of Architecture, he was frustrated with the laborious effort of generating designs for his studio courses. After days of drawing, his instructor would make suggestions that forced him to reconsider, redesign and regenerate the project. The design cycle could take several days. Wouldn't it be great, he thought, if I could generate all possible options for the design and simply select the best? In the years since he has developed techniques for breeding entire schemes by using genetic agents that travel the design's cyberspace, breeding with and modifying whatever lies in their path (fig. 138).

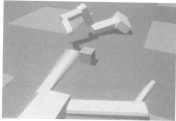

Figs. 135, 136, 137
Artist and computer programmer Karl Sims has produced creatures by using genetic algorithms not only to determine their shapes, but their behaviors as well. Shown above are two creatures competing for a small cube lying between them. Movement of the creatures is also determined by GAs. Some crawl, some swim. Others move by mechanisms not found in nature.

2. Krause, Jeffrey. 1997. "Agent Generated Architecture." In *ACADIA '97: Representation & Design. Proceedings of the 16th annual conference of the Association for Computer-Aided Design in Architecture.* eds. Jordan, P., B. Mehnert, A. Harfmann. pp. 63-69.

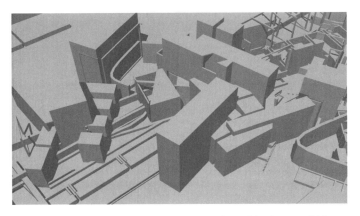

Fig. 138
Architectural composition by architect Jeffrey Krause of Blacksquare. The design was created using genetic algorithms that allowed him to "breed" the solution over several generations.

*Craig Caldwell, a computer scientist in New Mexico, and I have developed software on the brute force model of genetic algorithms. Using it, one can create a first generation of several designs and, through dialog with the computer, select favorites for successive breeding. The process is similar to that used by artists, but the product is intended also to be a social environment (fig. 139). While some results might be used as proposals for physical buildings, others might exist solely in the ether of cyberspace to host multi-user domains or collaboratories. Ideally, these GAs could become collaborative tools whereby a cyberspace community democratically evolves its environment. Combined with behavioral strategies employed by artists like Sims, these environments could be dynamic, mobile and ever evolving. They could change in response to deliberate choices of the community or from demographic information provided by the MUD system. Indeed, avatars are already being genetically bred for these environments. Why not the spaces themselves?*

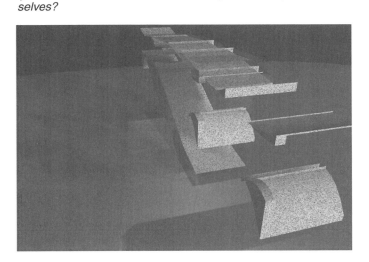

Fig. 139
Cyberspace social environment by author created using a genetic algorithm developed with Craig Caldwell. Automating such design/generation processes may be a useful method for developing on-line information environments. Animation of such processes can render live, fluid responses to the user.

*Envisioning Cyberspace*

# Embodiment in Electronic Media

Jamy Sheridan, an artist and professor at the University of Michigan School of Art, has also used GAs in his work. In performances combining projections of computer images and the human body he has created work that crosses the boundaries between the physical and virtual. Using software created with musician/programmer John Dunn, Sheridan has generated a series of animated computer images based on a traditional carpet pattern called the Tree of Life. Appropriately, portions of the symmetrical pattern are based on the genetic configuration of organisms. The patterns move and evolve, displace one another or dissolve into liquid dots flowing serenely across the screen.

But it's Sheridan's choice of screen that is most compelling. Several installations are flat on the floor with the projector mounted on the ceiling. The screen is actually a layer of white sand some two or three inches thick. The sand is uneven, filled with mounds and dips left by preceding audiences. The carpet of light is shown on this undulating surface – looking like fabric laid on the floor (plates 40, 41).

The work is incomplete without the body, however. Stepping onto the sand, participants enter an arena. Dots of light and fragments of the carpet's pattern wash over the body on the way to the sand. The carpet wraps the body in light. As the patterns flow, the sand appears to move, pulling the viewer along. Spilling a handful of sand momentarily connects the body to the sand with a veil of colored light. In the dark, it's as though all were dissolved, ebbing and flowing with the carpet's patterns.

The dematerialization of the body in Sheridan's work recalls our earlier discussion of mediated identity and presence in electronic environments. His work is not alone in this respect. A particularly compelling example is "Bodymaps: Artifacts of Touch" by Canadian artist Thecla Schiphorst. Many components of the installation are similar to Sheridan's. It too is an audience-participation piece using a horizontal surface for projection. While Sheridan's work projected onto the body, Schiphorst's projects the body itself.

Once again, the selection of the screen is important. Schiphorst's surface is a deceptively simple sheet of white velvet laid over a tabletop. The table stands alone in the room. Hidden sensors imbedded in substrate layers of the velvet sense pressure and heat. Passing one's hand lightly over its surface sends signals to a computer, activating a concealed projector above. Depending on which sensors are affected, a variety of brief video segments is shown onto the velvet screen below.

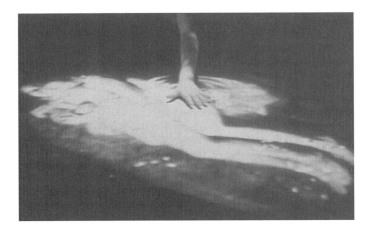

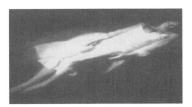

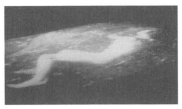

*The images are of the artist immersed in water, her eyes closed, her body moving as if in a dream (figs. 140, 141, 142). The movement is in slow motion, the images fading in and out of view. The videos are viewed on the basis of the gesture that evoked them – a slow, gentle wave of the hand may be rendered in the languid motion of the image, for instance. At times the body, filmed in white liquid – perhaps milk – disappears only to emerge from the white velvet a moment later.*

*Touch inspires the image – image inspires the touch. The sensuality of the velvet surface and the aquatic movement of the body make engagement with the piece a charged experience. The sense of bodily presence is augmented by the response of the system and the viewer's complicity (plate 48).*

German artist Monika Fleischmann and architect Wolfgang Strauss have produced several works using projection to dematerialize the body. In one, "Rigid Waves," the viewer engages a large screen that appears to shatter repeatedly into smaller pieces. The viewer begins with one large image but as the screen breaks up

each fragment contains a smaller image of himself – as though his identity were spread over an increasing number of avatars. The question of identity in electronic media pervades Fleischmann and Strauss' work, both in their installations and in their designs for cybereal environments.

In another collaboration, "Liquid Views," a horizontal computer screen is placed in a darkened room (fig. 143). On it is an image of water, a pool perhaps, with pebbles on the bottom. The viewer also makes out her reflection on the water's surface. The screen is touch-sensitive. Should the viewer touch her reflection, it breaks up as though she had touched the surface of a pool. Waves ripple to the edge of the screen, distorting the pebbles below. Adjacent wall-mounted screens display the same image, surrounding the viewer with the shifting self-image, distorted by her gesture.

Quebec artist Char Davies takes the theme of water, body and self in a different direction with "Osmose." This is a virtual environment to be explored with a head-mounted display. Vertical movement is achieved by inhaling and exhaling. This interface is drawn from Davies' experience as a scuba diver where using the air in one's lungs affects buoyancy.

The world Davies portrays is a rich, dream-like space populated with presences and metaphors. Some are recognizable – a tree, a clearing or rocks in a stream – others we can only infer. Osmose is a layered space with many levels (figs. 144-147). It appears to be based on a natural environment, yet examination reveals greater abstraction the farther down one goes. At its lowest levels, where metaphorically one expects soil and tree

Figs. 144, 145, 146, 147
Shown below are scenes from Char Davies' "Osmose." The virtual environment has a scale of abstraction that takes immersant visitors from the most natural, concrete images to the most symbolic. The strata of Osmose descend to the the rudimentary level of text shown in the bottom image, the extreme of abstraction.

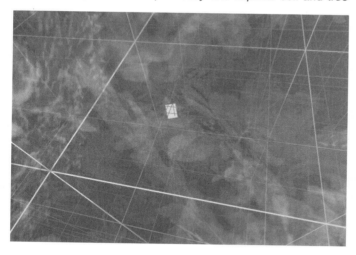

roots, we find instead planes of text based on Davies' writings and of those who inspired her. All the images above this level draw on their power. The abstract gives rise to the concrete.

Davies' piece is an internalized self-portrait. Visitors who don the headset find themselves in a highly personal, if uninhabited, world. Her texts, the buoyant motion, the dreamlike quality of the experience all contribute to its paradoxically cosmic intimacy. In other works discussed to this point we have seen the body as object and screen. Abstract though they may be, avatars are still object-like representations of the user. How different is this cyberspace where the body disappears entirely while Davies' presence remains. Even the viewer's breathing is co-opted into representing the author. The body has been dematerialized, abstracted and invested in the poetry of Osmose. While computation can render the abstract tangible – as in the work of Eckel and Art+Com – it can also abstract and ablate the concrete. Davies' artistic dematerialization of the body into ambience takes this process to an extreme.

Fig. 148
Image of Mark Pesce's on-line globe of the Earth. Satellite information was mapped onto a sphere and updated every hour. Viewers effectively could see their planet from a God's-eye view.

## World Views

We deal with dematerialization every day in our media and the electronic surveillance of our environment. Gelernter's Mirror World proposal is the ultimate extension of surveillance, a database equivalent of the Earth where every movement, change of light, and human activity is recorded for future reference. As an artifact, the mirror world is tied to the physical world by representation as well as surveillance, thus providing its users with an accessible model of the world.

Mark Pesce, a co-creator of the Virtual Reality Modeling Language, VRML, has approximated this in a sublimely effective experiment. Using VRML – a program invented for sharing three-dimensional environments over the Internet – he created a simple sphere. By tapping into the signals of weather satellites distributed around the globe, he was able to quilt together a surface for the sphere. The sphere became a model of the world's weather patterns updated every hour. Its viewers could see in it a live portrait of their planet (fig. 148).

Knowbotic Research similarly used remote sensing to create artworks in their native Germany. Sensors monitoring climatic conditions in Antarctica relayed data via satellites to the Internet. By processing this assembled data, the artists created an installation in a German gallery where sound and light conveyed the conditions of the polar environment. While Pesce's project normalizes the planet's weather, mapping it onto a globe, Knowbotic Research particularizes it – throwing the viewer into an abstracted simulation of a distant, alien place.

We see in these experiments the shadow of work done at the U.S. space agency, NASA. Messages sent back from a satellite orbiting Venus were used to create a three-dimensional model of the planet's surface. Once the model was assembled it could be navigated much like a CAD model. Viewers could virtually fly across the Venusian terrain, dipping into its valleys and soaring over its peaks.

Being able to visualize images of a planet – our own included – gives us a god-like capability. The information has been rendered in a compelling way, the models presented interactively. In Pesce's globe and NASA's Venus survey we see the planets with a disembodied eye. Sight has a privileged status in cyberspace. Vision is power.

## Two Models of Surveillance

But for many, monitoring climatic conditions on Earth is not the same as surveillance. Taking the image of an inanimate object is quite different from taking one of a person – particularly if he is unaware or unwilling to participate. And perhaps "taking" is the best way to describe it. The surveilled party "loses" privacy, and the camera gives nothing in return. Instead the image is transmitted, unrequited, to unknown destinations and viewers. We have met this condition earlier in our discussion of the television newscaster. But here it is different. The person surveilled is often unaware of being watched and is not compensated for his role in the surveillance. The observer steals the body image.

Steve Mann, in his research at MIT's MediaLab, has addressed surveillance with a number of projects and holds several patents on his designs for wearable computers. Since the 1970s he has worn a headset with cameras and microphone attached to computers at his waist or concealed in his clothing. A battery pack lets him move relatively unencumbered.

Mann has used his wearable computer – an invention called WearComp – in the on-going surveillance of his environment. His head-mounted camera keeps track of everything and everyone he meets (fig. 149). The information is then selectively posted on a Web site for access by anyone. He believes that in a future when such devices are inexpensive and ubiquitous any one of us could eavesdrop on another. This would be somewhat like George Wharton III's avatar bar where a user could casually select another avatar to peek in on what it sees.

Mann's premise is political. Currently only the powerful can covertly observe others. Mann's proposal distributes this capability to anyone that can afford it. In making the devices cheap, the power of surveillance is decentralized. Using the Internet

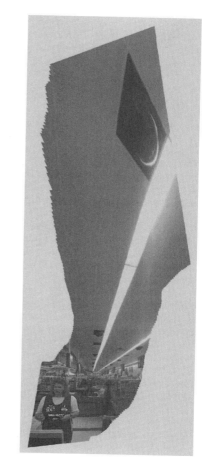

Fig. 149
Artist/engineer Steve Mann has used his inventions, WearComp and WearCam, to conduct a counter-surveillance of his environment. With his head-mounted camera and strapped-on computer he scans commercial spaces, automatically merging the images to form impromptu dioramas. Shown above is a store with a ceiling-mounted surveillance camera at the top of the image.

as a mode of delivery further democratizes the power. But in the end, of course, even the observer is observed.

This might be the unhappy implication of Gelernter's Mirror World – where everyone is each other's Big Brother. While the Mirror World hypothesis also aimed at distributing cognition through a collective model, its focus was on technical feasibility and the utopian aim of an enlightened democracy. However, Mann's work presents the unsettling human consequences of such surveillance. How would such a cyberspace be maintained? Satellites? Hidden cameras and microphones? Mann's proposal also diverges from Mirror World because the subject is not mapped onto an "objective" model. What the viewer sees on Mann's Web site is not like Pesce's globe – disembodied and abstract – but instead a trace of Mann's personal gaze. His very body movements are documented along with what he has seen. As in Davies' Osmose, viewers of Mann's site momentarily take his body as avatar.

The body and image of self are quite different in Mann's and Gelernter's models of surveillance. Gelernter's seeks to be objective, while Mann's shows the difficulty of being so. Yet the Mirror World hypothesis contains elements that – despite their technical orientation – draw on our innate capabilities of visualization, cognition and perception. In earlier portions of this book I have outlined those issues to show how computing ties into these skills. A mirror world is a cognitive shadow of the actual world. Unlike our cognitive space which is internal, this model is shared through computer networks, providing a basis for shared, democratic cognition.

The advantage of the computer model over Mann's video stream is its flexibility. Its supporting information may be represented in a number of ways. Without such intermediation, a video feed of a city would only look like a crowd of buildings. With a digital, 3D model laid over the view, we can see the buildings categorized by rent roll, use and construction rather than solely by location alone. Such a model, linked to the physical reality, could have several uses. Not only can the viewer observe a condition from a variety of standpoints, but he can make decisions that affect it – in turn, changing the model. This cybernetic cycle shows that the linked model of a mirror world could be an important planning and operational tool – a synthesis of physical and cyberspaces.

## Augmenting Reality

Steven Feiner and Blair MacIntyre at Columbia University are among the researchers who have explored such a synthesis. A form of what is called augmented reality, it entails the creation of a CAD model, computer graphic or data window that may be

associated with a physical object. This association is made possible through a transparent headset that lets users see through the display to the space beyond. Users see both the image and their environment unlike conventional virtual reality that blocks out the surroundings. As the user turns his head, objects move with his view, independent of the surroundings. Other objects in the display remain in place, apparently tied to the physical space. The electronic space of these objects is mapped directly onto the physical space. The two spaces co-exist in the mind of the viewer.

In order to manage this system Feiner, MacIntyre and their colleagues had to develop software that would track head motion and map graphics to its position. They intentionally kept the graphics simple in order to minimize the time for image regeneration. This gives the system a quick response time, enhancing the simulation. Although their earlier work was limited to the laboratory, they have since gone out of doors. In conjunction with Anthony Webster, a professor at Columbia University's Graduate School of Architecture, they have devised a wearable computer that augments the reality of the Manhattan campus.

While originally their work was hampered by the limited range of the tracking system, their Touring Machine – a pun on the device proposed by Alan Turing – uses the satellite data of the Global Positioning System, G.P.S., to situate the user's display. In their demonstration of the Touring Machine, the researchers attached virtual labels to the buildings of the university (figs. 150, 151). The approximate location of the labels was not distracting since accuracy of location was not crucial.[3]

In previous indoor projects Feiner and MacIntyre had better tracking capability and were able to simulate precisely the location of machine parts within a mechanism. In another study with Webster, Ted Krueger and Edward Keller, they mapped the structural system underlying the walls of their laboratory (fig. 152). Since a new kind of GPS they are about to use can give a centimeter-level accuracy, they hope to generate an augmented reality for Columbia, letting users "see" the subterranean tunnels underlying the campus.

Figs. 150, 151
The images at the left show an overlay of live images of the Columbia University campus and computer data linked to the buildings displayed. As the user moves about the campus, the labels remain spatially linked to the buildings. The cyberspace of the campus and its physical presence are merged into an augmented reality for the user. Such an overlap could be useful in creating information spaces that are linked to locations in the physical world. Images were photographed through the see-through head-mounted display.

Fig. 152
Augmented reality brings together physical and cyberspaces. Shown above is a computer model of a column's steel reinforcing merged with a view of the same column through a transparent visor. Shown also is a display of information related to the reinforcing. This study was done by Steven Feiner, Blair MacIntyre and Anthony Webster at Columbia University.

3. Feiner, S., B. MacIntyre, T. Höllerer, A. Webster. 1997. "A touring machine: Prototyping 3D mobile augmented reality systems for exploring the urban environment," in proceedings of International Symposium on Wearable Computing '97. Cambridge, Mass. Oct. 13-14, 1997. pp.74-81.

*Mann's surveillance system combined with such augmented realities could revolutionize our perception of the world. Both models are decentralized, incorporating ambient computing worn on the body. Users share their diverse points of view as well as a collective model linked to the physical world.*

## Conclusion

*In this chapter we have seen work done by artists and researchers in envisioning and creating cyberspaces – particularly those that merge physical and symbolic spaces. We have seen in their work how computation is used both to manifest the abstract and dematerialize the concrete – crossing the boundaries between perception and cognition. As computation becomes increasingly common to all disciplines we may see a merging of fields and, possibly, the development of new disciplines to meet the demands of cyberspace.*

*In the face of such change, there will be an evolving impact on society and culture. We have seen in monitoring and surveillance the human implications of merging physical and cyberspaces. This is a theme we will address directly in the next chapter.*

# Cybrids:
# Hybrids of Physical and Cyberspaces

"Developments in technology give professionals the power to produce larger and broader effects at the same time that they become more clearly aware of the remote consequences of their prescriptions."

"Tryin' to make it real...compared to what?"

Simon, Herbert. 1996. *The sciences of the artificial.* Cambridge, Mass.: MIT Press. p.150.

Les McCann, jazz musician

Fig. 153
Detail of a design for a proposed library that is a hybrid of physical and cyberspaces. Student project by Ranah Hammash.

*In this final chapter we will pursue cyberspace's manifestations in architecture and the physical world. The example of architecture shows how cyberspaces may affect our use of physical, social space and the resources of our material world. Though the focus will be on architecture, the reader may imagine many other disciplines to be affected similarly. The chapter will introduce the concept of "cybrids," hybrids that partake of physical and mediated space in the construction of our environment (fig. 153). It will also include a hypothetical scenario to show the implications of cybrids for culture and nature alike.*

## Integrating Two Types of Space

*Historically our information environment has been mostly physical. With the notable exception of memory palaces we have created permanent records with stone, papyrus, parchment and paper. We have housed these records – our externalized mem-*

ory – in books, files, art and buildings. Indeed many of our edifices are devoted not only to the comfort of their occupants, but also to the support of specific information environments. Libraries, schools, banks, office buildings and museums all support unique information structures rendered physical in their layout and construction.

However, as we are all too aware, information infrastructures are becoming increasingly transparent, transmuted into electronic signals and screen displays. William Mitchell, dean of MIT's School of Architecture, rightly observes that buildings will be directly affected by this technology. Cyberspace technology will also have a profound impact on our presence and engagement in the world.

If we accept similarities between perceived and cognitive spaces, we can question the need for physical realization. Taking the example of banks' automated teller machines, we can quickly see that a distributed presence mitigates against large central facilities. Some of banks' services have been outplaced – others may exist in no place at all.

To some degree, a project's requirements can be met with combinations of physical and emulated space. The mix of the two affects the scope of construction necessary to complete the project. Conceivably the material structure of a building may be displaced by the conceptual structure of an information system. This is particularly true of buildings that house information-rich activities. Libraries, art galleries, classrooms and laboratories already have equivalents in cyberspace as collaboratories, MUDs and Web sites. Even in a factory, which seems intrinsically physical, portions of the building are devoted to information work – offices, conference rooms, filing and administrative areas. The evanescence of such spaces could affect even the most earthbound of buildings.

Conversely, there may be good reasons to render cyberspaces physically. While it may seem odd that a building would reflect cyberspace, buildings often reflect the underlying organization of their occupants' information structure. Building design programs usually derive from this organization. The overlaps between physical and symbolic spaces could also have productive uses. Indeed, they already exist in surveillance systems and building management networks. Future buildings may capitalize on this overlap, letting the synergies between the physical and cyberspaces better serve their users.

## Fitness

Unlike their dynamic, cultural context, physical buildings themselves are inert. Over the life of a building the disparity between its context and form leads to misfits. This is not a fault of design strategy – buildings simply can't respond to change of their own volition. Misfits may involve size, configuration or even location as in cases where owners have moved their operations elsewhere.

Aesthetics, typology and other concerns are important in the design of buildings. However, viewing their design through the lens of function allows us to evaluate spatial solutions on verifiable bases of economy and efficiency. The compelling efficiency of cyberspace solutions may soon affect decisions on physical construction.

## The Use and Advantages of Cybrids

Despite their differences, physical and cyberspaces operate on similar anthropic principles. The reciprocity between these spaces can lead to objects that straddle both modes of being. These constructs, here called "cybrids," [1] employ each mode of space to its best advantage. They use on-line technologies to substitute simulations for physical space. Cybrids could have important effects on the creation of on-line communities and the design of our physical world. They offer new alternatives that can reduce the impact of development on our natural and urban environments.

1. **Cybrid**
An environment or artifact that incorporates both physical and cyberspaces. The relationship between these two types of space may be distinct, overlapping or congruent with one another.

### Economy

Cost effectiveness is one of cybrids' chief virtues. If aspects of a building can be served through cybrid technology, there could be substantial savings in a project. If the building's floor plan is reduced – and the reduction may vary greatly depending on the building type – a building's energy consumption and maintenance costs would likewise be reduced. These form a good part of the operating costs of a building.

Also, the building's utility becomes globalized, accessible to anyone who has the technology. The building not only serves the local community but remote "occupants" as well. This suggests a significant benefit in overall costs. The client's costs are reduced while – simultaneously – world benefits are increased. This surprising effect reveals the subtle influences this technology may have on the global economy.

The maintenance and installation of the computer support for such a virtual structure can be costly. However, the construction and maintenance costs of a comparable physical building would be much greater. Design, implementation and maintenance of a networked environment is often considerably less than comparably effective physical solutions. The cybrid's support costs would depend on the degree to which the building's program has been affected by the technology. I will pursue the issues affecting the economics of cybrids later in this chapter.

## Mediation and Options for Users

Building users may also gain from having their environment mediated by cybrids. If the building is globally accessible, the building is globally present. The architecture potentially becomes an instrument of persuasion – a form of promotion for the client. Architecture, which has a tradition of representing the client's values, now might become part of an owner's active, promotional arsenal.

## Access

If the building is accessible electronically there will be simultaneously an increased use of the facility plus a reduced need to be physically present at that building. This is borne out in recent developments in telecommuting. Increasingly, the employee no longer has to drive in to work. It is possible for an employee to be at work – sharing a symbolic workplace with colleagues – and not have to physically be there.

Obviously, these workers aren't as immediate as employees actually at the job. Employees at the office meet at water coolers, overhear remarks, sneeze and take up space. It's all part of their investment in their working environment. Mediated work is no substitute for actually being at a workplace. But cybrids offer clear advantages over other telecommuting options.

## Flexibility

Cyberspace is very quick to respond to change. Entire sections of MUDs can appear overnight and disappear just as quickly. We have seen previously that creating space in a MUD is not nearly as complicated as that of physical spaces. Compared with the effort of modifying a physical building, changing a MUD is nearly instantaneous, revocable and cost-free. The mediated portions of cybrids would be analogous to MUDs, offering emulated spatial and social environments.

The needs of a cybrid's users can be met on an on-going basis as opposed to constraining, one-time, physical solutions offered by conventional buildings. Yet, not all aspects of a cybrid can be managed in this way. There are portions of the building which must be physical. These include restrooms, mechanical rooms and – at the very least – the computer room itself! Still, a number of areas of a building could be substituted with electronic equivalents. For example, if the filing cabinets were to become an electronic database, there would be a floor area savings of 5 to 10 percent in each office.

## Representing Cyberspace

But what kinds of space would take their place? Cyberspace should not merely mimic spaces that might otherwise have been built. This would deny the fluid, symbolic nature of cyberspace. Instead designers should aim for emulations that provide the definition of physicality while surpassing it in amenity and flexibility. Design must not be limited to the reproduction of physical space – cyberspace offers freedoms not found in our world.

For example, databased simulations let cyberspaces constantly reconfigure themselves for functional or aesthetic reasons. While buildings have doors, furniture, and windows that move when necessary, cyberspaces may reconfigure at any scale or rate of speed. Potentially, designers of such spaces will create an ambient choreography that renders the real-time changes appealing and meaningful.

Information may render cyberspaces that have no physical parallel. For instance, if we look at a physical object closely, we get a larger more detailed image. In spite of scale, the spatial expression is the same. However, examining a cybereal object may disclose data on its past, its owner, or the code that went into its creation. This is an obvious extrapolation from the icons we see in the desktop metaphor of Macintosh or Windows. Metaphors lead us to the issue of representation.

An icon may represent a spreadsheet, which in turn may represent a physical object. Each representation has its own merit. Cyberspaces may be rendered in various ways according to their use. For instance, if the user wishes to view associated spaces, she may use another representation, say a flowchart or plan, to see them. The information feeding the three-dimensional representation is essentially the same as for the plan, although each is used differently. Cyberspace is an information display and 3D environments are only one of its manifestations.

## Relating Physical and Cyberspaces of a Cybrid

The relationship between the physical and cyberspaces can be distinct, congruent or overlapping. Possible strategies can be explained with the Venn diagrams shown on this page (fig. 154). There are many examples of Distinct Physical and Cyberspaces. The logical structure of a computer network rarely has anything to do with the layout of its host building. The spatial relationship between them isn't critical since the focus of use is on data management rather than the support of a navigable information space.

### Relationships between Physical and Cyberspaces

Distinct
Physical and Cyberspaces

Congruent Spaces

Overlapping Spaces

Fig. 154
The Venn diagrams shown above present different relationships between physical and cyberspace environments. The diagrams, while conceptual, illustrate current strategies employed in local area networks (distinct), security systems (congruent) and teleconferencing (overlapping).

Monitoring and surveillance demonstrate congruency *between the two modes of space. In some cases a building is represented in a database and linked to supporting cameras and sensors. The one-to-one relationship of the cyberspace map to the building can be used to control the building's service systems. However, congruency fixes the cyberspace into a map of its physical counterpart. Defined so rigidly, the on-line architecture can't benefit from cyberspace's inherent fluidity.*

The third *overlapping relationship is currently seen in analog and digital forms. Many teleconferencing and telepresence systems serve specific spaces in buildings. The space is perceived as a camera image and is usually not navigable by the viewer unless the camera is operated through remote control.*

*Digital examples include MUDs where their wizards have used existing buildings as models for the core configuration of their domain. This usually results in overlapping spaces since – as we have seen – the MUD community actively builds the bulk of the MUD's structure. The congruency between the MUD space and a physical space is often limited to the initial construction with the subsequent construction floating free of reference.*

*Despite this overlap, the "live" relationship between a MUD and its referent spaces is fairly rare. With the exception of users who happen to occupy the physical version of a cyberspace at the time they are playing the MUD, there seem to be few examples of interaction between spaces. Pavel Curtis' JupiterMOO project, done at Xerox PARC, came close to doing this, but other examples are hard to find.* [2]

*In most cases the MUD version of a building or city is an unlinked simulacrum, a stage set that merely resembles actuality. With the advent of Virtual Reality Modeling Language (VRML), RealVideo and other technologies a true dialog between on-line social environments and physical reality is possible. For example, a MUD player may come upon a room which has a link to a physical counterpart. A camera in the physical space can send an image to its cyberspace twin, rendering it visible to the MUD player. This linkage could conceivably be two-way, effecting an overlap between the physical and the cyberspaces.*

*Such interaction is a subject of research on augmented reality at Xerox PARC, Columbia University and elsewhere. In the last chapter we saw the powers of augmented reality – the visual overlay of 3D simulations onto physical objects. The overlap between physical objects and information in distributed computing potentially offers us an environment of "sentient" objects. At the 1996 ACM conference in Boston, William Buxton suggested that household appliances could communicate with one another – a Disneyesque scenario where alarm clocks chat*

2. To some degree, collaboratories like those created at the University of Michigan by Olson and Finholt overlap physical spaces – like remote arctic observatories – with a general information environment, including chat windows.

*Envisioning Cyberspace*

with toasters. The information required to manage this could also be mapped in a three-dimensional display as a cyberspace. Movement of physical objects would be reflected in the simulation. Certain configurations may have meaning in the way groupings of pieces do in a game of chess. The deliberate, ritual orientation of objects may inspire a technological metaphysics with mysteries of its own.

## Case Study – Designing Cybrids

To illustrate the design issues surrounding cybrids, I will discuss work done in a graduate design studio I conducted at the University of Michigan School of Architecture and Urban Planning. In the spring of 1997 my students worked on a project that related cyberspace to the space of physical architecture. The project addressed effects of information technology on the design of buildings, comprising a semester divided into research and design phases. The research phase was a concurrent study of physical and on-line environments. It included an investigation of several MUDs and analyses of four building types: a library, museum, classroom building, and an auditorium. In the study physical buildings were represented as data while the MUDs were represented as logical adjacency models to show the reciprocity of physical and cyberspaces.

After the analysis of the physical and cyberspaces, the students documented spatial anomalies of the MUDs and functional misfits of the real buildings. We have seen earlier how the medium of cyberspace can have surprising inconsistencies. The students quickly realized that objects and spaces in MUDs operated by laws of coding rather than those of reality. They saw this as a potential tool in developing their cybrid designs.

## Design Approaches for Cybrids

In their analyses of the existing buildings, students inferred the building's program – working backwards from plans and sections. They then took the existing building program and incorporated what they had learned from their MUD experiences.

There are many techniques for doing this. These include deciding which information-oriented spaces can be reinterpreted as cyberspaces, thereby reducing the overall scale of the physical building. Resulting designs would become chimeras of physical and cyberspaces, overlapping where appropriate and necessary.

Several students used information technology to influence the forms of their cybrids. One student, Mark Mitchell, used the passage of light through his site to determine the configuration of his art museum. The resulting form, though based on the

**Cybrids: Hybrids of Physical and Cyberspaces**

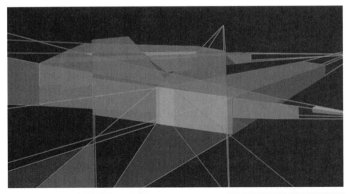

Figs. 155, 156
These images show a design proposal for an art museum by Mark Mitchell. The lower image shows the configuration of the physical building while the upper shows the museum's attendant cyberspace. The design of one space informed the other. The two overlap to form a cybrid of perceived and cognitive spaces.

*local geometry of the site, is surprisingly different from the surrounding architecture. Here the connections between the physical space and the cyberspace are visual alignments (figs. 155, 156). Museum-goers approaching the building would have clues to its cyberspace configuration. Conversely, on-line visitors could infer the building from what they saw in the museum's cyberspace.*

*Another student, Christopher Kretovic, scanned historical photographs of the site and reduced their collages digitally to determine his museum's structure and layout. Here the solution was less based on the current, physical context, instead reducing the design to an object half-buried in the site. Kretovic's design, like Mitchell's, proposed a co-dependency of physical and cyberspaces. In both projects, the overall spatial strategy was clear, yet the linkage between the physical and symbolic spaces was not resolved.*

*How users of connected physical and cyberspaces interact remains a difficult question. The interface between them could be made with screen displays, ambient computing and augmented reality – possibly a virtual reality projected onto its* physical equivalent. However, users of these interfaces will confront different problems. Screen displays disrupt the contiguity of the two spaces by "containing" the cyberspace environment. Distributed computing has a similar problem. We are not aware of a deep, 3D cyberspace unless it is presented to our senses. Smart objects may sense this space, but the space itself is not present to us in a meaningful sense. Finally an augmented reality requires often encumbering equipment. Actually, VR is often an individual experience, mediated through a personal headset or datagloves. Contained audio-visual environments (CAVEs) offer rooms that can be occupied by more than one person. But, like in VR, their users are isolated from their surroundings. The problem of the interface between "contiguous" physical and cyberspaces remains a promising subject for research.

## Metaphors and Evolving Structures

Linking the geometries of physical and cyberspaces seemed at the outset to be a reasonable choice for my students. But other avenues also proved fruitful. Several students bridged the two spaces using an orienting metaphor. In her design for a rare books library, Ranah Hammash described the building as a book with its cyberspace represented as pages released into the sunlight. Though the physical books were hidden from light, the cyberspace pages of the rare books would be available for all to see on the Internet – undermining the very notion of rarity in books. This evocative metaphor poetically orients users within the cybrid.

Metaphors unite the fabric of the physical building with that of the conceptual space. The purposes of cyberspace are dictated by more than just the access to data. As these spaces develop socially they will create cultures of their own. Narrative frameworks, like myth and metaphors, offer ways of organizing and correlating these modes of space. They let the user anticipate the cyberspace from evidence provided by the physical building. Conversely, the on-line user may intuit the presence of the building from its manifestation in cyberspace. The two spatial conditions are related; the narrative and spatial media provide the conceptual framework that unites them.

Of course, a metaphor can be a burden if belabored or poorly chosen. Cyberspaces offer experiences unprecedented in physical reality – their effectiveness may be limited by their concrete reference. Metaphors must be flexible enough to avoid this problem. Designers can avoid some difficulties by assuming the cyberspace to undergo constant changes governed by principles of design, growth or motion. Referring to processes avoids the constraints of conventional metaphor by remaining abstract yet meaningful.

For example, many cyberspaces designed in the study were dynamic, conveying the impermanence and subjectivity of the medium. The students examined principles underlying the physical architecture and then let the principles inform the cyberspace. This geometric, conceptual reference to the physical would only be the organizational skeleton of the cyberspace. Fixed-room configuration would only occur if the cyberspace overlapped a physical equivalent for needs of communication or surveillance.

With these principles it would be possible to have a number of evolving solutions. The cyberspace could configure itself coherently to the needs of the user. Once those users have left the space it could change for others. The designers felt that cyberspace might constantly evolve – possibly using genetic algorithms responsive to user preferences – while the physical architecture anchors the process with its material presence.

## Spatial Continuity

The designs stressed the continuity of the spatial medium from the analytical phase to the final stages of design. As they developed their building programs the designers determined which components of the physical building could be affected by the technology. Once this decision was made, however, they were responsible for integrating the cyberspace conceptually into the spatial matrix of the scheme.

In most cases the physical and cyberspaces overlapped in specific areas and the cyberspace developed from there according to underlying geometries of the physical scheme. I encouraged the students to derive principles from the site in order to develop their physical response to the problem. The building's relationship to the site was analogous to the cyberspace's relationship to the building. This showed the students how principles underlying the physical could be employed at higher levels of abstraction. This method is familiar to most architects and is common in architectural education, although the design of cyberspace is a recent development.

In several cases the students based their cyberspaces on the principles underlying their physical solution. Ranah Hammash's solution for a rare-books library used the freeform geometry of her physical building to extend and orient the cyberspaces beyond it (figs. 157, 158, 159). Watinee Thantranon's design for a law library was almost entirely a cyberspace with specific reference to the Gothic architecture of the law library at the University of Michigan (figs. 160, 161, 162). Christopher Kretovic's gallery vaults extended virtually into the ground plane to create a rough cylinder for a cyberspace extension.

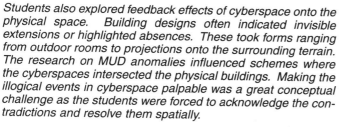

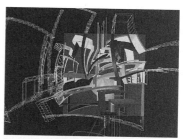

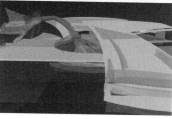

Figs. 157, 158, 159
This design proposal for a law library by Ranah Hammash eliminated all non-rare books and posted their contents on the Internet. This greatly reduced the area of the resulting building. Clockwise from the left is a plan detail, conceptual diagram and exterior view of the facility.

*Students also explored feedback effects of cyberspace onto the physical space. Building designs often indicated invisible extensions or highlighted absences. These took forms ranging from outdoor rooms to projections onto the surrounding terrain. The research on MUD anomalies influenced schemes where the cyberspaces intersected the physical buildings. Making the illogical events in cyberspace palpable was a great conceptual challenge as the students were forced to acknowledge the contradictions and resolve them spatially.*

*Although the cyberspaces referred to the architecture of the physical buildings, these spaces often did not take the shape of conventional rooms. Students took advantage of the disembodied nature of the space by stressing information display over containment. An example would be shards of information – like glass prisms – that became spatial when viewed closely. The effect would be like peering through a lens into the space beyond.*

*The students put a lot of emphasis on the design of the cybrids' social spaces. The embrasure of the users set the stage for social interaction. Whether or not these enclosures took conventional form was up to the designer. It was more important to provide a defined place for gathering and interaction.*

**Cybrids: Hybrids of Physical and Cyberspaces**

Figs. 160, 161, 162
These images show a cybrid library proposed by Watinee Thantranon. It is an extension of an existing law library at the University of Michigan. Nearly all portions of the design were to be electronic spaces rather than physical modifications to the existing structure. The image above shows the cyberspace in use, changing configuration according to the users' needs. The image on the top-left was part of an organizational study of the cyberspace.

The image at left is a view of the library as perceived by a user in cyberspace. At the far left is the library's lounge. A spherical auditorium is shown at the top of the image. The stacks are represented by the floating text. The cubes and splayed geometries are overlaps with physical staff offices and library reading hall respectively.

## Scenario: Deploying a Cybrid

*Imagine that a client approaches an architect to develop a cybrid. For our purposes, assume it will be the client's place of business, one that has informational as well as physical needs. This could be an office building, a school, a library or any number of building types.*

*After initial meetings and correspondence, the architect contacts his consultants and engineers. Some may be local but others are in remote places or time zones. The team agrees to meet regularly on neutral turf for progress updates. To facilitate this the architect creates a site on the World Wide Web that allows many modes of interaction. Text, graphics, spread-*

*sheets, 3D computer models, databases, materials libraries, sound files, animation are all supported by this multimedia site.*

*Most importantly, the site is a multi-user domain that lets the team meet continuously either through avatars or via live video feeds from their workplaces. Participants in different time zones contribute asynchronously by leaving messages, entering comments in a thread of published dialog or video clips much in the way that Usenet newsgroups operate.*

*The Web site is an information space, rendered three-dimensionally by the architect. By modeling satellite data he reconstructs the terrain of the physical site within the cyberspace. All pertinent information is included in this recreation: vegetation, power lines, water and sewer utilities, power, gas and media connections. Nearby buildings and streets are also part of this space. The architect may include sun angles, wind directions, celestial alignments, symbolic features – any number of elements that could influence the design.*

*Significantly, he creates a platform on this model that symbolizes the meeting space within the project's multi-user domain. When consultants, architect and client gather, they do so in the presence of the site's simulation in cyberspace. During the design phase the team collaborates in this space, referring to graphics, text and 3D displays in evolving the scheme.*

## Design

*One design strategy involves a kind of game that encourages imagination and cooperation on the part of team members. In a series of quick rule-driven exercises the team produces a number of optional solutions that are manifested in alternate incarnations of the site. [3,4] The computer evaluates each schematic solution for fitness according to predetermined constraints such as cost, energy consumption, acoustics,[5] air flow, daylighting – even feng shui.*

*Another approach uses computer agents assigned to building components that interact with one another, fighting for resources – fresh air, daylight, heat – until they reach a stable, optimal state.[6] Other tools include genetic algorithms that the team can breed for a variety of solutions, optimizing the project's functional or aesthetic parameters.[7] In assisting the team, the computer does not have the final word, it only provides options or makes suggestions through its agents. Ultimately, the team and client together determine which solutions to pursue.*

*Meanwhile the architect and client determine which functions need to be rendered physically and which might take form in*

3. McCall, R., and E. Johnson. 1996. "Argumentative agents as catalysts of collaboration in design," in *Design Computation: Collaboration, reasoning, pedagogy.* McIntosh, P., and F. Ozel, eds. Proceedings of ACADIA 1996 Conference, Tucson, Arizona. pp.153-162.

4. Knapp, R. W., and R. McCall. 1996. "Phidias II: In support of collaborative design," in *Design Computation: Collaboration, reasoning, pedagogy.* McIntosh, P.,. and F. Ozel, eds. Proceedings of ACADIA 1996 Conference, Tucson, Arizona. pp.147-152.

5. Mahalingam, Ganapathy. 1997. "Representing architectural design using virtual computers." in *Representation and Design.* Jordan, P., B. Mehnert, A. Harfmann, eds. Proceedings of ACADIA 1997 Conference, Cincinnati, Ohio. pp.51-61.

6. Pohl, Kym. 1996. "KOALA: An object-oriented architectural design system." Master's thesis, California Polytechnic State University, San Luis Obispo. unpubl.

7. Krause, op. cit., pp.63-72.

cyberspace. They may, for example, manifest the business's intranet and virtual private networks, facilitating intra-office communication and alliances with remote companies and agencies. Some functions may be partially replaced by cyberspaces, particularly information storage like files and libraries.[8]

Some of these functions are portrayed in cyberspace as ambient environments – others simply as graphic displays or placeholders for future use. Many are contiguous with, even overlapping, the cyberspace model of the proposed building. A few hover beyond the site's simulation while others are nested within one another, available by entering them or summoning them categorically into view.

The cyberspace of the design team is also a tool for the client. He may check in to see progress, attend meetings. With some preparation the cyberspace can host fund-raising activities, promoting the project with the interactive model and multi-user interface. Gatherings at different scales may be arranged live "on-site" or the event may continue throughout the preconstruction phase of the project under the auspices of an automated forensic agent that handles questions or relays messages. All the while, the design team works without interruption since the promotional activity is invisible to them.

## Construction and Deployment

Once the design is set and the physical portions of the cybrid are established, a directed, automated search is conducted for specialties involved in the construction. Contractors and subcontractors visit the physical and cybereal sites to meet with the architect and client. Those proposing alternates to the design change the cyberspace model to show the projected results. The computer evaluates these proposals for fitness just as it did with the original design team's work.

At the same time, contractors for the client's information technology systems submit proposals to extend the cyberspace component of the cybrid. Electronic Data Interchange, intra- and extranets, virtual private networks and Internet commerce are formatted within the domain of the cybrid. Cyberspaces for managing databases serve specific areas of the cyberspace and actual building. Multimedia spaces overlay physical meeting spaces and conference rooms.

Once all parties agree, development of the cyberspaces extends the original work of the architect as construction of the physical building begins. Meetings still happen in the cyberspace, sometimes overlapping discussions held on site. The two parallel spaces connect with sound and image, each informing the other during the meeting.

8. Anders, Peter. 1997. "Cybrids: Integrating cognitive and physical space in architecture," in *Representation and Design*. Jordan, P., B. Mehnert, A. Harfmann eds. Proceedings of ACADIA 1997 Conference, Cincinnati, Ohio. pp.17-34.

*Envisioning Cyberspace*

As the physical construction continues, the architect, contractor and consultants update the cybereal model of the building. This keeps it up to date and ultimately provides an accurate account of what was finally built.

The client, meanwhile, has already begun to use the cybrid. The cyberspace of the project is in place far in advance of the physical construction. Remote prospective employees are interviewed on-line. Databases are tailored for their final uses, plans for fixtures and furnishings are mapped into the cybrid's electronic model. Since the technical support for the cyberspace may theoretically be located anywhere, some business can already be conducted through the network months before the physical plant is completed.

Monitoring devices, sensors and servo-mechanisms are installed as the building proceeds. As sections are completed, the devices go on-line to their cyberspace equivalents. Feeding the cyberspace with updated information, they make it a valuable tool for the management of the physical environment. Communications, building systems' maintenance and operation, fire prevention and security all benefit from the mutual support of the cybrid's components. Computer agents determine which portions of the building require cooling and control the dampers in the ventilation system.[9] Selective camera/display connections between the physical and cyberspaces lets remote visitors converse with the occupants of the building. A contractor sent to modify a portion of the electrical system sees through the ceiling using a head-mounted augmented reality display that merges electronic and material spaces.[10]

## Operation

Upon completion of the project the cyberspace of the cybrid – no longer used by the design team – expands into a larger multi-user domain. This MUD may have different uses and levels of privacy depending on the client's operation. It can serve as an intermediary workplace for telecommuting employees and sales contractors. Or it might become a public Internet storefront for the business. It may even become a place of production, capitalizing on its computer/media aspects. Any organization that processes information would benefit directly.

The cyberspace portion of the cybrid is present to the rest of the world. It is ubiquitous while the building is local. As a result the cybrid is a tool for the promotion of the organization – the way Web sites are currently used for advertising. It contains not only the configuration of the physical building, but also the non-physical components of the business – literature, advertising, communications. These manifest themselves in different ways, regenerating themselves uniquely for each visitor.

9. Recent research at Xerox PARC proposes the use of forensic agents in mechanical systems that "bid" for service to parts of a building. The higher bidding agents will receive power, heat, cooling according to need. This market model for building operation can reduce energy costs by up to 20 percent.

10. Feiner et al., op. cit., pp. 74-81.

In ensuing years, the physical plant undergoes change. Plans derived from the cyberspace assist in additions and modifications to the structure. With each change the cyberspace is updated – always keeping pace with or preceding construction. The cyberspace undergoes change as well. Users influence its configuration, the functions of its information structure change. Only some of these are manifested in the physical structure, most being distinct and untethered. The cybrid's database constantly evolves, changing by the moment in response to its occupants and users.

## Afterlife

Finally, the building is no longer required. The owner's operation has been relocated or needs a new building for expansion. The cyberspace component of the cybrid can be reused at the new location or become the source of data for sale of the material structure. Or it can provide demolition plans for the building's removal. Further, with its database model of as-built conditions, it can provide information for the reclamation of materials for recycling. In the end, all that remains of the cybrid is the ghost, the cyberspace that attended the construction, life and death of the building.

And yet it is a lively ghost. So long as some computer maintains the database and multi-user domain, the cyberspace remains active. In this form, it may still be the client's business space, regardless of where the company has relocated. Or it might be an historic archive of the building it once supported. It might even take on a life independent of the physical operation. For instance, a long-defunct nightclub could still host parties long after its physical demise. Just as buildings take on new owners, so too might cyberspaces be converted to new uses.

# Social and Environmental Impact of Cybrids

Nearly all the components of this scenario are either already in use or possible with today's technology. Despite the familiarity, the creation of cybrids poses surprising challenges. It's dangerous to overgeneralize the outcome of a cybrid strategy. Each case would need to be assessed individually. For instance, the consequences of such a strategy for an urban office building would be quite different from those of a suburban library. Still it's useful to point out the issues affected. Who benefits? Who suffers? At what scales are the consequences felt? Do the benefits to the owner, for instance, outweigh the burden borne by the community?

While it's tempting to imagine totting up the pluses and minuses of cybrid strategies, such information is scarce. This is partially because cybrids are too new for us to have accurate data.

*Also, the impact of such strategies is hard to foresee. Take the example of typical computer networks in a company. What was intended originally as an accounting system now supports intra-office communication, even advertising and sales on the Internet. People tend to use technology in ways not originally intended by its inventors. William Gibson, creator of the concept of cyberspace, says that the street finds its own uses for technology.*

*Even so, the question of impact is too tempting to ignore. While we can't assign dollar values, it is at least worthwhile listing what the issues are – or what we guess them to be. Benefits at one scale may prove elusive at another. For instance, the reduction in air pollution resulting from telecommuting to cybrids would be a direct benefit to the community. However, the proprietor of the cybrid may only benefit indirectly – the environmental issue having a lower priority among those influencing his decision to build a cybrid. For such reasons I will describe the effects of cybridization on three scales: the proprietor, the local community, the world. Cybrids will have critical implications – positive and negative – in each arena.*

## Cybrid Operators

*The earlier scenario proposes the cybrid largely from the standpoint of the owner. It shows how preferring this strategy over conventional development affects the project's generation and life cycle. A primary benefit to the owner is choice since not all solutions – spatial or otherwise – need to be built. In the early stages the owner and architect determine the physical and symbolic components of the cybrid. Ultimately it is the owner's choice as to how much of the facility is physical. A number of factors influence this decision – available resources, tax advantages, business strategy. Reduced taxes may result from a smaller building – or if a good portion of the cybrid is a product of fixture expenses rather than construction.*

*The smaller building resulting from the cybrid approach reduces the initial capitalization of the project. There will be the added expense of the supporting computer network. However, it's highly unlikely that these incremental costs will be of the same order of magnitude as the construction and maintenance of comparable physical space, particularly if we consider future modifications or reorganization. Still, we have to bear in mind the obsolescence of computer-related equipment as part of the on-going maintenance costs of the cybrid. Even if these costs go down with the increasing capacity of the technology, they cannot be ignored.*

*Another benefit of the strategy is that the operation of the cybrid begins earlier than a conventional building project. Since the* cyberspace component of the project is likely to function far in advance of its physical counterpart, it may already be a site for doing business. If the client were concerned about generating revenue from his investment, the cyberspace is likely to pay back sooner than the physical plant.

Not only are costs of construction reduced but those of maintenance and up-keep as well. This is effected by the reduced area of building as well as the on-going automated monitoring of building systems. Conceivably, such an active vigilance over the building could affect other costs as well, including reduced insurance premiums and building security expenses.

The primary advantages to the proprietor are not in cost savings engendered by "cheap" cyberspace. For, in using a cybrid strategy, the entire operation changes. **The real benefit to the owner is a wise allocation of resources, time and effort to transform his operations, extending and accelerating them in ways not previously possible.**

On-line commerce, extranets, collaboratories and ever-changing business alliances demand flexibility and choice. Even close to home, an employer's flexibility in time and place may help him get better qualified employees, wherever they may be. What flex-time is to a commuter, flex-space is to the telecommuter.

But what are the costs to the proprietor of the cybrid? First off, the cyberspace component of the cybrid is not physical space. As we have seen throughout this book, there are as many differences between material and emulated spaces as there are similarities. Identity, propriety and territory in cyberspace are subjects of intense scrutiny for this reason. We can expect that interaction in cyberspaces will be attended by ambiguity and uncertainty for the foreseeable future. Cybrids blur the distinctions between the physical and symbolic, the real and fantastic. Designers of cyberspaces must take care that the metaphor of physicality doesn't mislead them – or their clients.

The abstraction of the workplace may have a negative effect on its culture. There may be a reduced mutual commitment between an employer and a telecommuting employee if the employee worked on site previously. Whether this results in less job security for the employee is debatable since telecommuting workers require less overhead than those physically on site. Also, it is difficult to predict how telecommuting will be qualitatively improved with cybrid implementation. Once again, each application of the strategy depends on the nature of the client, the purpose served by the cybrid and the culture of the organization.

## The Community

Likewise the effect cybrids may have on the local community is also contingent on its client and the degree of implementation. The negative effects of cybridization might be offset by bringing new business into town via the Internet, for instance. However, the net effect on the community is harder to assess than for the limited entity of the business.

By reducing the size of the physical plant, the client affects long-term revenues of the host community. Smaller buildings reduce the need for construction and affect the associated market for materials and labor. In the course of operation, the cybrid's maintenance and operation costs are also less than those for a conventional building. This reduces the need for support services supplied by the host community. Since many properties are assessed for taxation on the basis of their size, the tax revenue generated by a cybrid would likely be less than otherwise possible. Also, since the proprietor of a cybrid will be more likely to employ telecommuters, many of his employees will not pay the same local taxes as their resident counterparts.

Service businesses attending and benefiting from commuter traffic will also suffer. If telecommuting and outsourcing are an important part of the cybrid proprietor's business, the local telephone company may be the only local business to gain. Toll booths, parking lots, coffee shops, newspaper stands, delicatessens, shops, restaurants and theaters would all feel some effect from the reduced traffic. Indeed, without having accurate numbers to evaluate, of the three – proprietor, local community and world – the local community would be hit hardest by cybridization.

And yet even here there are advantages. Cybrids are a high technology answer to many environmental, urban problems. Clearly, reduced commuter traffic – even of mass transportation – curbs the pollution of the environment. The health of the community would no longer be a cost of doing business. Also new service businesses would be created to serve the needs of the telecommuter.

Net gains and losses due to cybridization and telecommuting are hard to assess because many parts of communities are affected differently. We are confronted with apples-to-oranges comparisons. How can we compare loss in commuter-generated revenues to increased efficiency in doing business?

Stability of local economies might be a longer-term benefit of cybridization. Cybrids are not limited to new projects alone. Cybrid extensions may be a business' alternative to leaving a community to find more space. Also, since starting a business with a cybrid may require less time and capital, local business development corporations may sponsor cybrids as a way to generate new economic growth.

A final point regarding telecommuting addresses the scope of the community. Are we only talking about the community local to the physical plant of the cybrid? Or the aggregate community of all the workers who contribute to the business? So far we have focused only on the former. Yet if it's the latter, the benefits of the cybrid strategy are much clearer. The telecommuter who works at home still has to eat, shop and support his own operation. The business lost to the city to which he would have commuted is now gained by his home community.

Before leaving our discussion on the community, we must consider one last troubling issue. Who is participating in this process? Clearly those literate and aware of the technology. Cybrid operators and Internet commuters are obviously beneficiaries. The benefits of cybridization on local communities is debatable – as we have seen. However, there are signs of polarization between the technology haves and have-nots. The advantages of cybridization to a poor inner-city child are much less than to a computer-trained job applicant.

And the stratification doesn't end with computer literacy. Electronic and computer networked businesses acquire a culture of their own – the ways of operating in it are sufficiently abstract to require training beyond operating a machine. As a result, fewer job opportunities are open to the uninitiated. This, apart from social, economic or ethnic issues, drives yet another wedge dividing our communities. William Mitchell, dean of MIT's School of Architecture, has worked with colleagues and community groups to mitigate against this effect in the Boston area. It remains a challenge to our education system and local governments to close this gap.

## The World

While this cloud looms over the advance of global technologies, its edges gleam with potential. The same technology makes possible friendships and alliances without regard to time or place. It makes the needs of those far away as real as those that attend us locally. And if we are aware of each other's needs, we are tacitly responsible to them. This may not be the force that changes the world – any technology is subject to abuse – but its benefits cannot be ignored.

On a pragmatic level, cybrid's availability on world-wide networks is a global amenity. Given current examples of collaboratories that share equipment and remote observation stations, cybrids offer a new way to distribute facilities. A school that might otherwise not be able to afford tools for research can tap into a university cybrid developed expressly for that purpose. A hospital lacking advisory staff or data facilities might access them through a cybrid based at a regional medical center. A small business might be able to take on a larger international clientele by linking up with a global company through its cybrid extensions. The combined potential for international alliances and shared resources is another clear, if unquantifiable, advantage of the cybrid strategy.

What the long-term effects of this might be is hard to say. Cybrids are, after all, a special case of cyberspace, one that stresses the continuity of the spatial medium. In this scenario we have seen how the cybrid condition affects different scales of society. Yet these observations are necessarily conditional. Cybrids already manifest themselves in local area networks as well as sited multi-user domains. Where they may evolve to next depends on social/economic forces and the imaginations of their developers.

## Cybrids – Abstract and Concrete

The technological artifacts of cyberspace range in degrees from the materially concrete to the most abstract. At the abstract end of our scale, the shifting, ever-changing representation of data manifests itself to our senses if not our cognition. At that end of the scale technology speaks more to itself than to its users. Designers working at this level of abstraction run the risk of alienating users unless the work is anchored in common experience or metaphor. This is not insurmountable – **the fine arts offer many examples of such grounding without loss of quality.**

Cybrids hover between the extremes of our scale. They draw on our spatial abilities to create information environments, although they may appear unprecedented in form and use. In our architectural example, the cybrid overlapped a building, anchoring the cyberspace to the material world. Even so, portions of the cybrid's cyberspace were not spatial in any conventional sense.

The most abstract example of a cybrid would be a conventional local area network whose content is independent of the physical building. Near it on the scale of abstraction would be a database of constantly updated information from a building's support systems. Slightly more concrete would be one that includes a visual representation of the building that may or may not be linked to the monitoring data. Some text MUDs and collaboratories already operate this way. The Chatting Zone's model of Ipswich, Ireland, for instance, has no on-going connection to the physical community. Yet, Jay's Place is meticulously realistic in its depiction of a real midwestern town.

More concrete models would include functional connections between the building and its cyberspace shadow. This is a matter of turning the monitoring of the building into a two-way cybernetic connection. Mechanical and electrical systems would be controlled through the cybereal portion of the cybrid.

Adding people to the cybrid returns it to the concrete world of shared experience. Although not physical, the symbolic space of the cybrid is now linked operationally and socially to the physical building and its inhabitants. There may be fictional components of the cyberspace – places and entities. But grounding the cybrid, unifying its actual and symbolic spaces, brings the cybrid as close to concrete as possible. This continuity of spatial media, bridging our perceived and cognitive worlds, will affect the way we relate to the world. As we create the new tangibility of cyberspace we invent new ways to relate to one another, personally and socially.

## Mythic Space

The architectural process I offer to illustrate cybrids is only one example among many. Most of the arts and technologies presented in this book show a similar integration of physical and symbolic space. This is the understandable result of creative processes. **It is innate to human thought and not limited to individual disciplines.**

Our arts and sciences trade on our ability to commute between cognitive and perceived spaces. We express internal states through the humanities and internalize our world in the pursuit of knowledge. Of all animals, we alone travel on the scale of abstraction, abstracting and materializing our world.

All our endeavors begin with the most abstract imaginings. As they evolve they take various incarnations in words, sketches, calculations, and models. These are intermediate forms, projecting their physical embodiment into our space of cognition. We contemplate and critique them, turning them over in our minds. Ensuing notes and drawings pursue new directions, traveling down our scale toward materiality.

We may believe that these mediating artifacts are distinct from the final product but this is not so. Even the product is subject to our reflection. Artifacts never really leave this intermediacy. They are themselves the media for thought. So long as we use them, they persist both in the world of our senses and that of our imagination.

Cybrids and cyberspace extend a long human tradition of mythic objects and spaces. Our memorabilia and historical places are important not only for their material presence but also for *the memories and events that they evoke. Our myths and traditions only enrich these sites in our minds. The fictional ballroom hovering over the MediaLab is not so far removed from the places and things that haunt our material world. In our minds King Kong still clings to the spire of the Empire State Building and the oracle still sits at Delphi.*

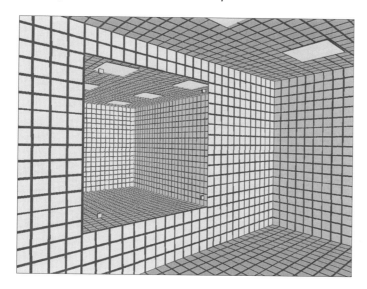

Fig. 163
Shown at left is a scene from Peter Maloney's "Work in Progress," a virtual environment that is based on the ancient technique of memory palaces. An audience is led through the space in real-time by the artist who uses the objects in the room to generate a narrative description of this parallel world.

*Cybrids: Hybrids of Physical and Cyberspaces*

## Artifacts | Spaces | Motion

### Abstract

Fig. 164

| | Artifacts Non-Electronic | Artifacts **Electronic** | Spaces Non-Electronic | Spaces **Electronic** | | Motion Non-Electronic | Motion **Electronic** |
|---|---|---|---|---|---|---|---|
| **> Cognition — Cognitive Presence** | Symbolic Thought / Speculative Thought / Referential Thought | **Direct Brain Stimulation** | Symbolic Thought / Memory Palaces / Referential Thought / Body Zones & Territory | **Direct Brain Stimulation** | **Cognitive Categoric Motion** — *Static:* Translate; *Discrete:* Project/Remember; *Episodic:* Manipulate Mental Model (also Dynamic) | | **Direct Brain Stimulation** |
| **Perceivable Representation — Symbolic Presence** | Symbols / Diagrams / Painting / Arch. Design / Site Plan / Portrait / Photo | **Text Interface** / **2D GUI** / **Spatial GUI** / **Unlinked Digit. Simulation** / **Linked Digital Simulation** / **TV/Video Image** | Textually Depicted Space / Graphically Depicted Space / Photographic Space | **Text Interface** / **BBS** / **Chat Rooms** / **Text MUDs** / **2D GUI** / **Spatial GUI** / **Graphic MUDs** / **Video Games** / **CAD Images** / **TV/Video** / **Cybrids** | **Perceived Categoric Motion** — *Static:* Interpreting Image; *Discrete:* Browsing Library, Unsorted Slides; *Episodic:* Pages of Book, Film Strip | | *Static:* **Text to Graphic Mode**, **Viewing CAD model**; *Discrete:* **Surfing Web**, **Teleporting in MUDs**, **Change TV Channels**; *Episodic:* **Walking in Text MUDs**, **Search Games** |
| **Physical Presence — Tools for Symbolic Work** | Type-writer / Paint Brush / Camera | **Computer** / **Telepresence/Surveillance** / **Distributed Computing** / **Smart Objects** / **Transistor** / **Toaster** | Cybrids / Physical Model / Architecture | **Augmented Reality** / **Telepresence/Surveillance** | **Perceived Dynamism** — Film | | **Video Games** / **Video** |
| **Physical Presence — Material Artifacts** | Lawn-mower / Hopewell Mounds | | Urban Environment / Clearing in Forest | | **Physical Dynamism** — Bodily Movement / Non-Human Physical Motion | | **Electro/ Mechanical Movement** |

### Concrete

*Perception <*

216     *Envisioning Cyberspace*

# Conclusion

The words "real" and "virtual" are the rock and hard-place of any discussion on cyberspace. Because the words are freighted with cultural associations they quickly turn dialogs into confrontations. While "real" connotes truth, "virtual" conveys subjectivity at best. These terms do not account for subtleties of meaning, physiological response, symbolic usage, or the differences between social actualities and internal states. All of these are "real" and "virtual" to varying degrees.

To avoid these hazards, I have presented cyberspace – and space itself – as a tool for cognition and perception, the two forms of thought largely comprising our mental activity. In the course of this book I have used a scale to discuss the concrete and abstract attributes of artifacts, spaces and movement. The extremes of these scales are rarely attained, as most phenomena hover between states of being and meaning. We understand them through perception and cognition.

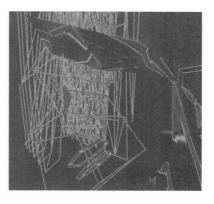

At left, I again present these scales of abstraction to show their relationship to one another. Note that many of the p h e n o m e n a described are part of our cultural and social landscape. They form our social environment – our

Figs. 165, 166
These images by artist Thomas Corby were created by taking live data from the Internet by using an autonomous agent and mapping it as immersive spaces. Sensors placed in the actual installations fed in ambient sounds and images allowing a mix of actual and virtual data objects.

shared "reality" – regardless of how abstract they may seem. The artifacts of cyberspace can be as immediate and pertinent as material presence itself (figs. 165, 166). Relegating them to the status of "virtual" dangerously underestimates them by ignoring their potential.

Space is the medium by which we understand our world, ourselves and each other. And cyberspace is its electronic extension. The development of an anthropic cyberspace should be based on our use of space to think and relate to each other.

Cyberspace will continue to grow parallel to its technology. Transmission speeds and increased bandwidth will allow greater opportunities for designed experience. Modeling the interaction and design on our innate use of space is a first step in converting information to knowledge and extending ourselves to others. Space is the language we all share.

# Bibliography

Albert, M. K., and D. D. Hoffman.1995. "Genericity in spatial vision," in *Geometric representations of perceptual phenomena*. Papers in honor of Taro Indo on his 70th birthday. Mawah, N. J.: Lawrence Erlbaum Associates. pp.95-111.

Altman, Irwin. 1981. *The environment and social behavior*. New York: Irvington Publishers Inc.

Anders, Peter. 1997. "Cybrids: Integrating cognitive and physical space in architecture," in *Representation and design*. Jordan, P., B. Mehnert, and A. Harfmann, eds. Proceedings of ACADIA 1997 Conference, Cleveland, Ohio. pp.17-34.

Anders, Peter. 1996. "Envisioning cyberspace: The design of on-line communities," in *Design computation: Collaboration, reasoning, pedagogy*. McIntosh, P. and F, Ozel, eds. Proceedings of ACADIA 1996 Conference, Tucson, Arizona. pp.55-67.

Ardrey, R. 1966. *The territorial imperative*. New York: Atheneum.

Arnheim, Rudolph. 1974. *Art and visual perception: A psychology of the creative eye*. Berkeley, Calif.: University of California Press.

Astheimer, P., and C. Knöpfle. 1996. "3D morphing and its application to virtual reality," in *Virtual environments and scientific visualization '96*: Proceedings of Eurographics workshops in Prague, Czech Republic, 1996, and Monte Carlo, 1996. M. Göbel, ed. Vienna: Springer Verlag. pp.85-93.

Aumont, Jacques, 1994. "The image," in *Geometric representations of perceptual phenomena*. Papers in honor of Taro Indo on his 70th birthday. Mawah, N. J.: Lawrence Erlbaum Associates. pp. 20-33.


Badler, Norman I., Carey B. Phillips, and Bonnie L. Weber. 1993. *Simulating humans: Computer graphics, animation and control*. New York: Oxford University Press.

Balageur, J. F., and E. Gobetti. 1993. "Virtual Reality Builder II: On the topic of 3D interaction," in *Virtual worlds and multimedia*. Magnenat Thalmann, N. and D. Thalmann, eds. New York: Wiley Press. pp. 99-110.

Barry, Ann Marie Seward. 1997. *Visual intelligence: Perception, image and manipulation in visual communication*. Albany, N. Y.: State University Press of New York.

Bellman, Kirstie. 1997. "Playing in the MUD: Turning virtual reality into real education and training," in *Virtual reality, training's future?: Perspectives on virtual reality and related technologies*. Seidel, Robert J., and Paul R. Chatelier, eds. New York: Plenum Press. pp. 9-17.

Benedikt, Michael. 1994. *Cyberspace: First Steps*. Cambridge, Mass.: MIT Press.

Berger, John. 1973. *Ways of seeing*. London: British Broadcasting Corporation.

Bettelheim, Bruno. 1977. *The uses of enchantment: The meaning and importance of fairy tales*. New York: Vintage Books.

Bødker, Sussane. 1990. *A human activity approach to user interface design*. Hillsdale, N. J.: Lawrence Erlbaum Associates.

Breiteneder, C. J., S. J. Gibbs, and C. Arapis. 1996. "TELEPORT: An augmented reality teleconferencing environment," in *Virtual environments and scientific visualization '95*. Proceedings of Eurographics workshops in Prague, Czech Republic, 1996, and Monte Carlo, 1996. M. Göbel, ed. Vienna: Springer Verlag. pp. 41-49.

Broughton, John. 1989. "Machine dreams: Computers in the fantasies of young adults," in *The individual, communication and society: Essays in memory of Gregory Bateson*. Rieber, R., ed. New York: Cambridge University Press.

Bruckman, Amy, and Mitchel Resnick. 1995. "The MediaMOO project: Constructionism and professional community." *Convergence* 1(1).

Burdea, Grigore C. 1996. *Force and touch feedback for virtual reality*. New York: John Wiley and Sons.

Buxton, W. 1994. "Human skills in interface design," in *Interacting with virtual environments*. McDonald, L., and J. Vince, eds. New York: Wiley Press. pp. 1-11.

Buxton, W. 1990. "The 'natural' language of interaction: A perspective on nonverbal dialogs," in *The art of human-computer interface design*. Laurel, B., ed. Reading, Mass.: Addison-Wesley.


Casti, John L., 1997. *Would-be worlds: How simulation is changing the frontiers of science*. New York: John Wiley and Sons, Inc.

Cirlot, J. E., 1995. *A dictionary of symbols*. New York: Barnes and Noble Books.

Clark, Herbert H., and Susan Brennan. 1990. "Grounding in communication," in *Socially shared cognition*. Resnick, L.B., J. Levine, and S.D. Behrend, eds. American Psychological Association.

Cooper, L.A. 1975. "Mental rotation of random two-dimensional shapes." *Cognitive Psychology*, 7, pp. 20-43.

Crompton Smith, Gillian. 1994. 'The art of interaction," in *Interacting with virtual environments*. McDonald, L., and J. Vince, eds. New York: Wiley Press. pp. 75-78.

Curtis, Pavel. 1992. "MUDding: Social phenomena in text-based virtual realities," in proceedings of 1992 Conference on Directions and Implications of Advanced Computing. Berkeley, Calif., May 1992. XeroxParc technical report CSL-92-4. Available by anonymous ftp: parcftp.parc.xerox.com in directory /pub/MOO/papers/ in files DIA92.

Curtis, Pavel, and David Nichols. 1993. "MUDs grow up: Social virtual reality in the real world" (Austin, TX) 1993. Available by anonymous ftp: parcftp.parc.xerox.com in directory /pub/MOO/papers/ in file MUDsGrowUp.

Cutt, Paul. 1991. "The sense of touch in virtual reality," in *Beyond the vision: The technology, research and business of virtual reality*. Proceedings of virtual reality 1991 the second annual conference on virtual reality, artificial reality and cyberspace. September 23-25, 1991. Westport Conn.: Meckler Media. pp.43-44.

**D**avis, Martha. 1982, *Interaction rhythms*. New York: Human Science Press.

Davison, A., P. Otto, and D. Lan-Kee. 1994. "Visual programming," in *Interacting with virtual environments*. McDonald, L., and J. Vince, eds. New York: Wiley Press. pp. 27-42.

Dery, Mark. 1996. *Escape velocity: Cyberculture at the end of the century*. New York: Grove Press.

Dowding, Timothy. 1991. "A self-contained interactive skill trainer," in *Beyond the vision: The technology, research and business of virtual reality*. Proceedings of virtual reality 1991 the second annual conference on virtual reality, artificial reality and cyberspace. September 23-25, 1991. Westport, Conn.: Meckler Media. pp. 44-50.

Downes-Martin, S., M. Long, and J. Alexander. 1992. "Virtual reality as a tool for cross-cultural communication: An example from military team training," in *Visual data interpretation*. 10-11 Feb. 1992. San Jose, Calif./ Joanna R. Alexander, chair and director; sponsored by SPIE, The International Society for Optical Engineering, ISNT The Society for Imaging Science and Technology. Bellingham, Wash.: SPIE. pp. 28-38.

**F**ast, Julius. 1971. *Body Language*. New York: Pocket Books.

Fisher, Scott S. 1990. "Virtual interface environments," in *The art of human-computer interface design*. Laurel, B., ed. Reading, Mass.: Addison-Wesley. pp. 423-438.

**G**elernter, David. 1991. *Mirror worlds: Or the day software puts the universe in a shoebox: how it will happen and what it will mean*. New York: Oxford University Press.

Gentner, D., and M. Imai. 1992. "Is the future always ahead?: Evidence for system-mappings in understanding space-time metaphors," in proceedings of 14th Annual Conference of the Cognitive Science Society, July 29-August 1, 1992. pp. 510-515.

Gibson, James J. 1982. *Reasons for realism: Selected essays of James J. Gibson*. Reed, E., and R. Jones, eds. Hillsdale, N. J.: Lawrence Erlbaum Associates.

Goffman, Erving. 1967. *Interaction ritual*. Chicago: Aldine Publishing.

Goffman, Erving. 1959. *The presentation of self in everyday life*. Garden City, N.Y.: Doubleday and Company.

Goldberg, David E. 1989. *Genetic Algorithms: In search, optimization and machine learning*. Reading, Mass.: Addison Wesley Publishing Company.

Grandin, Temple. 1995. *Thinking in pictures and other reports from my life with autism*. New York: Vintage Books.

Grantham, Charles E. 1991. "Visual thinking in organizational analysis," in *Beyond the vision: The technology, research and business of virtual reality*. Proceedings of virtual reality 1991 the second annual conference on virtual reality, artificial reality and cyberspace. September 23-25, 1991 Westport Conn.: Meckler Media. pp. 70-76.

**H**all, Edward T. 1966. *The hidden dimension*. Garden City, N.Y.: Doubleday and Company.

Hall, Edward T. 1959. *The silent language*. Garden City, N.Y.: Doubleday and Company.

Harris, Paul. 1977. "The child's representation of space," in *The child's representation of reality*. Butterworth, G., ed. New York: Plenum Press.

Hart, John. 1993. On recording virtual environments," in IEEE Symposium on Research Frontiers in Virtual Reality, 1993. Proceedings of the IEEE 1993 Symposium on Research Frontiers in Virtual Reality, San Jose, Calif. October 23-26, 1993. Sponsored by IEEE Computer Society Technical Committee on Computer Graphics in cooperation with ACM and SIGGRAPH. Los

Alamitos, Calif.: IEEE Computer Society Press. pp. 80-84.

Hayles, N. Katherine. 1996. "Boundary disputes: Homeostasis, reflexivity and foundations of cybernetics," in *Virtual realities and their discontents*. Markley, Robert, ed. Baltimore: Johns Hopkins University Press. pp. 11-38.

Heim, Michael. 1995. "The design of virtual reality," in *Cyberspace, cyberbodies, cyberpunk: Cultures of technological embodiment*. Featherstone, Michael, and Roger Burrows, eds. London: Sage Publications. pp. 65-78.

Heim, Michael. 1993. *The metaphysics of virtual reality*. Oxford: Oxford University Press.

Heinze, H. J., S. Luck, T. Münte, A. Gös, and S. Hillyard. 1994. "Attention to adjacent and separate positions in space: An electro-physiological analysis," in *Perception and Psychophysics* 1994, 56(1). pp. 42-52.

Henley, Nancy. 1997. *Body politics: Power, sex and non-verbal communication*. Englewood Cliffs, N. J.: Prentice Hall.

Hilts, Philip J. 1995. *Memory's ghost: The strange tale of Mr. M.* New York: Simon and Schuster.

Holland, John. 1995. *Hidden order: How adaptation builds complexity*. Reading, Mass.: Addison Wesley Publishing Company.

Johnson-Laird, P.N. 1981. "Mental models in cognitive science," in *Perspectives on cognitive science*. Norman, D. A., ed. Hillsdale, N.J.: Lawrence Erlbaum Associates.

Kay, Alan. 1990. "User interface: A personal view," in *The art of human-computer interface design*. Laurel, B., ed. Reading, Mass.: Addison-Wesley. pp.191-208.

Kay, Alan. 1984. "Computer software," in *Scientific American*, September, 52-59.

Koriat, Asher. 1994. "Object-based apparent motion," in *Perception and Psychophysics*. 1994, 56(5), pp. 392-404.

Krueger, M. W. 1991. *Artificial reality*. 2d ed. Reading, Mass.: Addison-Wesley.

Krueger, M. W. 1990. "Videoplace and the interface of the future," in *The art of human-computer interface design*. Laurel, B., ed. Reading, Mass.: Addison-Wesley.

Kurtenbach, G., and Eric A. Hulteen. 1990. "Gestures in human-computer communication," in *The art of human-computer interface design*. Laurel, B., ed. Reading, Mass.: Addison-Wesley.

Kwok, Man-Ho, and Joanne O'Brian. 1991. *The elements of feng shui*. New York: Barnes and Noble Books.

Lakoff, George, and Mark Johnson. 1981. "The metaphorical structure of the human conceptual system," in *Perspectives on cognitive science*. Norman, D. A., ed. Hillsdale, N.J.: Lawrence Erlbaum Associates.

Lakoff, George, and Mark Johnson. 1980. *Metaphors we live by*. Chicago: University of Chicago Press.

Landsberg, Alison. 1995. "Prosthetic memory: Total Recall and Blade Runner," in *Cyberspace, cyberbodies, cyberpunk: Cultures of technological embodiment*. Featherstone, Michael, and Roger Burrows, eds. London: Sage Publications. pp. 175-189.

Lansdown, John. 1994. "Visualizing design ideas," in *Interacting with virtual environments*. McDonald, L., and J. Vince, eds. New York: Wiley Press. pp. 61-74.

Laurel, Brenda. 1991. *Computers as theater*. Reading, Mass.: Addison-Wesley.

Laurel, Brenda. 1990. "Interface agents: Metaphors with character." in *The art of human-computer interface design*. Laurel, B., ed. Reading, Mass.: Addison-Wesley.

Laurel, Brenda. 1986. "Interface as mimesis," in *User centered system design*. Norman, D. A., and S. W. Draper, eds. Hillsdale, N.J.: Lawrence Erlbaum Associates. pp. 67-85.

Laurendeau, Monique, and Adrien Pinard. 1970. *The development of the concept of space in the child*. New York: International Universities Press.

Long, M., J. Alexander, S. Downes-Martin, J. Morrison, W. Katz, and E. Short. 1992. "Virtual environment debriefing room for naval fighter pilots: Phase I," in *Visual data interpretation*, 10-11 Feb. 1992, San Jose, Calif./ Joanna R. Alexander, chair and director; sponsored by SPIE, The International Society for Optical Engineering, ISNT The Society for Imaging Science and Technology. Bellingham, Wash.: SPIE. pp.49-60.

Loomis, J. 1993. "Understanding synthetic experience must begin with the analysis of ordinary perceptual experience," in *IEEE Symposium on Research Frontiers in Virtual Reality*. 1993. Proceedings of the IEEE 1993 Symposium on Research Frontiers in Virtual Reality, San Jose, Calif. October 23-26, 1993. Sponsored by IEEE Computer Society Technical Committee on Computer Graphics in cooperation with ACM Ind SIGGRAPH. Los Alamitos, Calif.: IEEE Computer Society Press. pp. 54-58.

Luria, A.R. 1987. *The mind of a mnemonist*. Cambridge, Mass.: Harvard University Press.

Lupton, Deborah. 1995. "The embodied computer/user," in *Cyberspace, cyberbodies, cyberpunk: Cultures of technological embodiment*. Featherstone, Michael, and Roger Burrows, eds. London: Sage Publications. pp. 97-112.

MacLeod, D., I. A. Willen, J. Douglas. 1995. "Is there a visual space?" in *Geometric representations of perceptual phenomena*. Papers in honor of Taro Indo on his 70th birthday. Mawah, N. J.: Lawrence Erlbaum Associates. pp.47-61.

Markley, Robert. 1996. "Boundaries: Mathematics, alienation and the metaphysics of cyberspace," in *Virtual realities and their discontents*. Markley, Robert, ed. Baltimore: Johns Hopkins University Press.

Maunsell, John H.R. "The brain's visual world: Representation of visual targets in cerebral cortex," in *Science*, 3 November, 1995. pp. 764-756.

McCluskey, James. 1991. "Educational applications of virtual reality: Medium or Myth?," in *Beyond the vision: The technology, research and business of virtual reality*. Proceedings of Virtual reality 1991 the second annual conference on virtual reality, artificial reality and cyberspace. September 23-25, 1991. Westport Conn.: Meckler Media. pp. 148-153.

McLuhan, Marshall. 1964. *Understanding media*. New York: McGraw-Hill.

Millar, Susanna. 1994. *Understanding and representing space: Theory and evidence from studies with blind and sighted children*. New York: Oxford University Press.

Minsky, Marvin. 1981. "K-lines: A theory of memory," in *Perspectives on cognitive science*. Norman, D. A., ed. Hillsdale, N.J.: Lawrence Erlbaum Associates.

Mitchell, William. 1995. *City of bits*. Cambridge, Mass.: The MIT Press.

Mok, Clement. 1996. *Designing business*. San Jose, Calif.: Adobe Press.

Moravec, Hans. 1988. *Mind children: The future of human intelligence*. Cambridge, Mass.: Harvard University Press.

Mozer, M. C., R. Zemel, and M. Behrmann. 1992. "Discovering and using perceptual grouping principles in visual information processing," in proceedings of 14th Annual Conference of the Cognitive Science Society, July 29-August 1, 1992. pp. 283-288.

Naimark, Michael. 1990. "Realness and interactivity," in *The art of human-computer interface design*. Laurel, B., ed. Reading, Mass.: Addison-Wesley. pp. 455-460.

Negroponte, Nicholas. 1990. "Hospital corners," in *The art of human-computer interface design*. Laurel, B., ed. Reading, Mass.: Addison-Wesley. pp. 347-354.

Nelson, Theodor H., 1991. "How many D's in reality?" in *Beyond the vision: The technology, research and business of virtual reality*. Proceedings of virtual reality 1991 the second annual conference on virtual reality, artificial reality and cyberspace. September 23-25, 1991. Westport Conn.: Meckler Media. pp. 154-174.

Nelson, Theodor H. 1990. "The right way to think about software design," in *The art of human-computer interface design*. Laurel,.B., ed. Reading, Mass.: Addison-Wesley.

Newell, Allen. 1981. "Physical symbol systems," in *Perspectives on cognitive science*. Norman, D. A., ed. Hillsdale, N.J.: Lawrence Erlbaum Associates.

Newman, Oscar. 1973. *Defensible space*. New York: Macmillan Publishing Company.

Norman, Donald A. 1993. *Things that make us smart*. Reading, Mass.: Addison-Wesley.

Norman, Donald A. 1991. "Cognitive artifacts," in *Designing interaction: Psychology at the human-computer interface*. Carroll, J. M., ed. New York: Cambridge University Press. pp. 17-38.

Norman, Donald A. 1990. "Why interfaces don't work," in *The art of human-computer interface design*. Laurel. B., ed. Reading, Mass.: Addison-Wesley. pp. 209-220.

Norman, Donald A. 1988. *The psychology of everyday things*. New York: Basic Books.

Norman, Donald A. 1981. "Twelve issues for cognitive science," in *Perspectives on cognitive science*. Norman, D. A., ed. Hillsdale, N.J.: Lawrence Erlbaum Associates.

Norman, Donald A. 1981. "What is cognitive science?" in *Perspectives on cognitive science*. Norman, D. A., ed. Hillsdale, N.J.: Lawrence Erlbaum Associates.

O'Connor, N., and B. Hermelin. 1973. "The spatial or temporal organization of short term memory," in *Quarterly Journal of Experimental Psychology*, 25, pp. 335-343.

Owen, David. 1986. "Naive theories of computation," in *User centered system design: New perspectives on human-computer interaction*. Norman, D. A., and S. Draper, eds. Hillsdale, N.J.: Lawrence Erlbaum Associates.

Paivio, A. 1975. "Perceptual comparisons through the mind's eye," in *Memory and Cognition*, 3, pp 635-647.

Papert, Seymour. 1980. *Mindstorms: children, computers and powerful ideas.* New York: Basic Books.

Pausch, R., M. A. Shackleford, and D. Proffitt. 1993. "A user study comparing head-mounted and stationary displays," in *IEEE Symposium on Research Frontiers in Virtual Reality.* Proceedings of the IEEE 1993 Symposium on Research Frontiers in Virtual Reality, San Jose, Calif. October 23-26, 1993. Sponsored by IEEE Computer Society Technical Committee on Computer Graphics in cooperation with ACM and SIGGRAPH. Los Alamitos, Calif.: IEEE Computer Society Press.

Penn, A., N. Dalton, L. Decker, C. Mottram, and M. Nigri. 1997. "Intelligent architecture: Desktop VR for complex strategic design in architecture and planning," in *Virtual reality, training's future?: Perspectives on virtual reality and related technologies.* Seidel, Robert J., and Paul R. Chatelier, eds. New York: Plenum Press. pp. 121-132.

Penzias, Arno, 1989. *Ideas and information.* New York: Simon Schuster Inc. pp. 41-45.

Pérez-Goméz, Alberto. 1990. *Architecture and the crisis of modern science.* Cambridge, Mass.: MIT Press.

Piaget, Jean. 1985. *The equilibration of cognitive structures.* Chicago: University of Chicago Press.

Piaget, Jean. 1980. *Adaptation and intelligence: Organic selection and phenocopy.* Chicago: University of Chicago Press.

Piaget, Jean. 1960. *The child's conception of physical causality.* Paterson, NJ: Littlefield, Adams & Co.

Piaget, J., B. Inhelder, and A. Szeminska. 1960. *The childs conception of geometry.* New York: Basic Books.

Poster, Mark. 1995. "Postmodern virtualities," in *Cyberspace, cyberbodies, cyberpunk: Cultures of technological embodiment.* Featherstone, Michael, and Roger Burrows, eds. London: Sage Publications. pp. 79-96.

Pylyshyn, Z.W. 1973. "What the mind's eye tells the mind's brain: A critique of mental imagery," in *Psychological Bulletin*, 80, pp 1-24.

Rawlins, Gregory J. E., 1997. *Slaves of the machine: The quickening of computer technology.* Cambridge, Mass.: MIT Press.

Regan, Clar      Some effects of using virtual reality technology," in *Virtual reality, training's future?: Perspectives on virtual reality and rela      ologies.* Seidel, Robert J., and Paul R. Chatelier, eds. New York: Plenum Press. pp. 77-83.

Resnick,     Thinking like a tree – and other forms of ecological thinking." Unpublished

Rheingol      d. 1990. "What's the big deal about cyberspace?" in *The art of human-computer interface design.* Laurel, B., ed.
Reading      Addison-Wesley.

Robins      1995. "Cyberspace and the world we live in," in *Cyberspace, cyberbodies, cyberpunk: Cultures of technological embo      eatherstone, Michael, and Roger Burrows, eds. London: Sage Publications. pp. 135-155.

Robi      l. 1994. "Biomedical virtual environments," in *Interacting with virtual environments.* McDonald, L., and J. Vince, eds.
Nev      ey Press. pp. 79-92.

Ro      L., and D. Adelstein. 1993. "Perceptual decomposition of virtual haptic surfaces," in *IEEE Symposium on Research
Fi      Virtual Reality.* 1993. Proceedings of the IEEE 1993 Symposium on Research Frontiers in Virtual Reality, San Jose,
C      ber 23-26, 1993. Sponsored by IEEE Computer Society Technical Committee on Computer Graphics in cooperation with
      SIGGRAPH. Los Alamitos, Calif.: IEEE Computer Society Press. pp.46-53.

      anagan, Nancy. 1998. "The virtues and vices of virtual colleagues," in MIT's *Technology Review*, Mar/Apr. pp. 52-59.

      itt, Gerhard. 1993. "Virtual reality in architecture," in *Virtual worlds and multimedia.* Magnenat Thalmann, N., and D. Thalmann,
      New York: Wiley Press. pp. 85-96.

      fto, E., R. Bareiss, and M. Birnbaum. 1992. "A memory architecture for case-based argumentation," in proceedings of 14th
      nual Conference of the Cognitive Science Society, July 29-August 1, 1992. pp. 307-311.

      imon, H. A. 1981. *The sciences of the artificial.* 2nd ed. Cambridge, Mass.: MIT Press.

Smith, Bradford. 1991. "The use of animation to analyze and present information about complex systems," in *Beyond the vision: The technology, research and business of virtual reality.* Proceedings of virtual reality 1991 the second annual conference on virtual reality, artificial reality and cyberspace. September 23-25, 1991. Westport Conn.: Meckler Media. pp.190-199.

Smolan, Rick, and Jennifer Erwitt. 1996. *24 hours in Cyberspace: Paintings on the walls of the digital cave.* New York: QUE Macmillan Publishing.

Sobchack, Vivian. 1995. "Beating the meat/surviving the text, or how to get out of this century alive," in *Cyberspace, cyberbodies, cyberpunk: Cultures of technological embodiment.* Featherstone, Michael, and Roger Burrows, eds. London: Sage Publications. pp. 204-214.

Spence, Jonathan D. 1985. *The memory palace of Matteo Ricci.* London: Faber.

Spencer, C., M. Blades, and K. Morsely. 1995. "The child in the physical environment," in *Geometric representations of perceptual phenomena.* Papers in honor of Taro Indo on his 70th birthday. Mawah, N. J. Lawrence Erlbaum Associates.

Spoehr, Kathryn T. 1994. "Enhancing the acquisition of conceptual structures through hypermedia," in *Classroom Lessons.* McGilly, K., ed. Cambridge, Mass.: The MIT Press.

Subotsky, Eugene V. 1996. *The child as a Cartesian thinker.* East Sussex, U.K.: Psychology Press.

Sugarman, Susan. 1987. *Piaget's construction of the child's reality.* New York: Cambridge University Press.

Sutherland, Ivan. 1963. "Sketchpad: A man-machine graphical communication system." Proceedings of the spring joint computer conference: 329-346.


Thagard, P., D. Gochfeld, and S. Hardy. 1992. "Visual Analogical Mapping," in proceedings of 14th Annual Conference of the Cognitive Science Society, July 29-August 1, 1992. pp. 522-528.

Todd, S., and W. Latham. 1994, "Interacting with artificial life," in *Interacting with virtual environments.* McDonald, L., and J. Vince, eds. New York: Wiley Press. pp. 271-285.

Toffler, Alvin. 1980. *The third wave.* New York: Bantam Books.

Tomas, David. 1995. "Feedback and cybernetics: Reimaging the body in the age of the cyborg," in *Cyberspace, cyberbodies, cyberpunk: Cultures of technological embodiment.* Featherstone, Michael, and Roger Burrows, eds. London: Sage Publications. pp. 21-44.

Tuan, Yi-fu. 1974. *Topophilia: A study of environmental perception, attitudes, and values.* New York: Columbia University Press.

Tufte, Edward R. 1990. *Envisioning information.* Cheshire, Conn.: Graphics Press.

Tufte, Edward R. 1983. *The visual display of quantitative information.* Cheshire, Conn.: Graphics Press.

Turkle, Sherry. 1996. *Life on the screen.* New York: Simon and Shuster.

Turkle, Sherry. 1984. *The second self: Computers and the human spirit.* New York: Simon and Shuster.


Uttal, William R. 1988. *On seeing forms.* Hillsdale, N. J.: Lawrence Erlbaum Associates.

Uttal, W., N. Davis, and C. Welke. 1994. "Stereoscopic perception with brief exposures," in *Perception and Psychophysics*, 56(5), pp. 599-604.


Vinge, Vernor. 1981. "True Names," in *Binary Star No. 5*, Frenkel, James R, ed. New York: Dell Publishing.

Vurpillot, Eliane. 1976. *The visual world of the child.* New York: International Universities Press.


Walker, John. 1990. "Through the looking glass," in *The art of human-computer interface design.* Laurel, B., ed. Reading, Mass.: Addison-Wesley.

Walter, Eugene V. 1988. *Placeways: A theory of the human environment.* Chapel Hill, N. C., and London: University of North Carolina Press.

Wathen-Dunn, Weiant. 1964. *Models for the perception of speech and visual form.* Cambridge, Mass: MIT Press.

Watts, Alan. 1989. *The way of Zen.* New York: Vintage Books.

Whorf, Benjamin Lee. 1956. *Language, thought, and reality.* New York: The Technology Press and John Wiley and Sons.

Wilson, Rober Rawdon. 1995. "Cyber(body)parts: Prosthetic consciousness," in *Cyberspace, cyberbodies, cyberpunk: Cultures of technological embodiment.* Featherstone, Michael, and Roger Burrows, eds. London: Sage Publications. pp. 239-259.

Wurman, Richard Saul. 1996. *Information architects.* Zurich: Graphis Press Corp.


Zeki, S. 1992. "The visual image in the mind and brain," in *Scientific American*, September, pp. 69-76.

Zeltzer, D., Jordan, M. 1994. "Virtual actors in virtual environments," in *Interacting with virtual environments.* McDonald, L., and J. Vince, eds. New York: Wiley Press. pp. 229-252.

# Index

Note: The n after a page number refers to a note; the f after a page number refers to a figure; plate refers to color plate number.